795

WITHDRAWN

The
New
Borzoi
Book
of
Ballets

by Rosalyn Krokover

Alfred A. Knopf

NEW YORK

1956

The

New

Borzoi

Book

of

Ballets

L.C. catalog card number: 56–5791
© Rosalyn Krokover, 1956

THIS IS A BORZOI BOOK
PUBLISHED BY ALFRED A. KNOPF, INC.

FIRST EDITION

The present book replaces THE BORZOI BOOK OF BALLETS
by Grace Robert originally published in 1946 by
Alfred A. Knopf, Inc. and no longer in print.

To Harold

Acknowledgments

Without the co-operation and kindness of many people in the ballet world this book would still be in the process of being written. To Genevieve Oswald, dance librarian of the New York Public Library, I give thanks for help in using the library's extensive clipping and card files, as well as bound volumes of programs. John Martin, dance critic of the *New York Times,* kindly allowed me to browse through his own collection of programs and pictures. To Catharine Miller and Gladys Chamberlain of the 58th Street Music Library I am indebted for the many fine books they supplied me for reference work.

I am also deeply indebted to John Onysko, of the Ballet Theatre office for allowing me unlimited time and liberty to survey old program books in search of the original casts and dates. (If every ballet company had as businesslike an office, life

Acknowledgments

would be much easier for those endeavoring to compile facts on ballet in America.) Sally and Martin Kamin, of the Kamin Dance Bookshop, New York, freely lent me books and pictures. Isadora Bennett and Richard Pleasant were most helpful in clarifying some early Ballet Theatre *premières*. Marjorie Barkentin supplied pictures and information for the Marquis de Cuevas Grand Ballet de Monte Carlo. Lillian Moore verified some of the early American *premières* of certain classics, and Igor Schwezoff cleared up some of the mystery-shrouded Original Ballet Russe dates by checking through his scrapbooks.

The illustrations in this book have come from many sources, notably Martin Feinstein and Michael Sweeley of the Hurok management; Lydia Joel and Don Duncan of *Dance Magazine;* Walter Alford; Arthur Todd; Wilbur Pippin; Alfred Valente; Fred Fehl; and Radford Bascombe. To them, and to all the others whose time I selfishly monopolized, my appreciative thanks.

The following authors and publishers must be thanked for permission to quote from their books: Serge Lifar, from *The History of Russian Ballet* (Roy Publishers, New York); Fernau Hall, from *World Dance* (A. A. Wyn, New York); and Serge Grigoriev, from *Diaghilev Ballet 1909–1929* (Constable, London).

Herbert Weinstock, my editor at Alfred A. Knopf, Inc., has done much more than edit. His pertinent suggestions and comments have more than once brought order out of despair, and his appreciable part in the organization of the material has considerably lightened my burden.   R. K.

Contents

x

xi

Illustrations

---

xiii

Lucia Chase in the roles they created for Ballet Theatre; set and costumes by Marcel Vertès.

Photograph by Maurice Seymour

5. A. BOURRÉE FANTASQUE: Tanaquil LeClercq, Todd Bolender, and other members of the New York City Ballet.

Photograph by Fred Fehl

B. THE CAGE (New York City Ballet).

Photograph by George Platt Lynes

6. COPPÉLIA
A. Ballet Russe de Monte Carlo production (scenery and costumes by Pierre Roy), Alexandra Danilova as Swanilda.
B. Frederic Franklin (Franz) and Alexandra Danilova (Swanilda).

Photograph by Fred Fehl

7. DAPHNIS AND CHLOE: Sadler's Wells Ballet adaptation by Frederick Ashton; Michael Somes as Daphnis; scenery and costumes by John Craxton.

Photograph by Roger Wood, from the Dance Collection of Arthur Todd

8. A. DIM LUSTRE: Hugh Laing and Nora Kaye (Ballet Theatre); scenery and costumes by Motley.

Photograph by Bob Golby

B. JUDGMENT OF PARIS: Antony Tudor, Hugh Laing, and Agnes de Mille in 1955 Ballet Theatre revival.

Photograph by Fred Fehl

9. FANCY FREE: five members of the original Ballet Theatre cast— Janet Reed, Muriel Bentley, Harold Lang, Jerome Robbins (with fist upraised), and John Kriza; scenery and costumes by Oliver Smith.

10. A. FILLING STATION: Janet Reed and other members of New York City Ballet; scenery and costumes by Paul Cadmus.
B. THE NUTCRACKER: Maria Tallchief, André Eglevsky, and other members of the New York City Ballet revival; scenery by Horace Armistead; costumes by Karinska.

Photographs by Fred Fehl

Illustrations

18. IVESIANA: Allegra Kent being passed from man to man in "Unanswered Question" movement (New York City Ballet).

    Photograph by Radford Bascombe

19. PETROUCHKA

    A. Alicia Markova, Nicholas Beriosov, and Leonide Massine (Ballet Russe de Monte Carlo, late 1930's).

    Photograph by Gilbert Adams

    B. Lucia Chase, Dimitri Romanoff, and Michael Kidd in Ballet Theatre production; scenery and costumes after Alexandre Benois.

20. A. PILLAR OF FIRE: original Ballet Theatre cast—Annabelle Lyon, Antony Tudor, Lucia Chase, Nora Kaye, and Hugh Laing; scenery and costumes by Jo Mielziner.
    B. A STREETCAR NAMED DESIRE: Christine Mayer, John Kriza, Nora Kaye, George Tomal, and Scott Douglas (Ballet Theatre); scenery by Peter Larkin; costumes by Saul Bolasni.

    Photograph by Fred Fehl

21. A. PRODIGAL SON: Francisco Moncion in the New York City Ballet production.
    B. GRADUATION BALL: Ruth Ann Koesun and David Lichine, choreographer of the ballet (Ballet Theatre).

    Photographs by Fred Fehl

22. RODEO

    A. Opening scene of Ballet Theatre production; scenery and costumes by Oliver Smith; Allyn McLerie (on ground) as the Cowgirl.
    B. Final scene; front, center, Allyn McLerie and John Kriza.

    Photographs by Roger Wood

23. ROMEO AND JULIET: scenes from the Delius-Tudor ballet (Ballet Theatre); sets and costumes by Eugene Berman; with Alicia Alonso and Hugh Laing.

    Photographs by Sedge Le Blang

24. SCHÉHÉRAZADE: scenery and costumes "after Léon Bakst" (René Blum's Ballets de Monte Carlo production, vintage 1932).

xvii

The

New

Borzoi

Book

of

Ballets

Looking at Ballet

 Ballet has been variously defined, in terms ranging from the purely descriptive to the metaphysical and the Platonic. Most definitions concern the organization of rhythmically moving human bodies in spatial patterns joined to a musical impulse. Those who have the classic ideal of ballet in mind would add a proviso to the effect that these human bodies are idealized bodies, tending toward ideal patterns—a sort of Platonic Ideal of movement and pattern. Nearly all definitions, however, omit one factor that sets ballet off from all other forms of dance: the specific vocabulary of movement involved. Generally speaking—all definitions, of course, are subject to modifications—ballet uses a vocabulary of movement built on traditional techniques developed over the centuries and involving five specific positions. These positions are theoretically as stylized

3

as the Manual of Arms. But an accretion of experimentation and usage as the years pass constantly makes changes in any "basic" vocabulary.

To many of us the concept of the Platonic Ideal most closely touches on the mysterious essence of ballet. The effort to master the technique of ballet is back-breaking, leg-numbing work that takes years of practice and discipline. Clad in tights and tunic, the perspiring dancer works for hours, day in and day out, year after year, at the *barre,* one-two, one-two, *plié, petit battement, degagé, rond de jambe.* But on stage the dancer is an idealized creature not of this earth who has cast off the restraints of the body. Perspiration and toil have been left at the *barre.* We see transfigured beings moving with untold grace, delicacy, and loveliness, the men cavaliers all, proud yet tender, the women ethereal and floating toward the skies. (This is the great difference between ballet, which idealizes the woman by placing her *en pointes*—on her toes—and accents her spiritual qualities, her lightness and fragility, and modern dance, which has the woman barefoot and often on the ground, accenting her role as the mother of us all. But that is another story.)

Ballet is an art, and as such follows esthetic laws. In any ballet one looks for organization—the shaping hand of the choreographer, who has created an esthetic unity from the raw materials of movement and music, the two basic elements. Within those two primary essentials—movement and music—the choreographer, like any creator, has infinite leeway. He may base his ballet on a plot or he may work in purely abstract lines. He may or may not use *décor* and costumes. He may think entirely in terms of ensemble movement or he may wish to use set pieces and solos. He may organize his patterns and steps according to orthodox principles or he may experiment along hitherto-unknown lines. No matter how he works, he is, or should be, aiming at an end result that will arouse an esthetic reaction in the beholder. His success depends upon his ideas and workmanship, his ability to integrate, his inventive capacity, and the feeling of individuality he conveys.

For a ballet is more than a string of connected movements.

Unless there are communication, meaning, a thread of emotional consistency, and continuity, the choreographer has failed in his purpose. Naturally his initial objectives must be considered. A choreographer who has tried to create a comic ballet must be judged differently from one who has tried to create one dealing with the four corners of the universe. This is, of course, an esthetic truism, though one often overlooked in our masterpiece-conscious age. In short, a ballet follows the general rules pertaining to all forms of art. It is as simple—and as frightfully difficult!—to come to grips with as a work of art in any form.

A special factor in ballet, as pertains to the observer, is empathy, a factor well known in sports. In the arts it is nowhere so strongly manifest as in ballet. Empathy is a sort of self-identification with something, whether sound, sight, or idea. When you see a fighter pound another on the jaw, you wince: you are identifying yourself with the recipient of the attack. When, snug in a concert hall seat, you listen to music, you tend to rise with a long melody, sink when it sinks.

At the ballet, where superbly trained and beautiful bodies are constantly in motion, you will be experiencing the empathic effect constantly, much as an onlooker at a baseball game experiences it (as many philosophers have suggested, there is a close affinity between art and games). Sport-goers and ballet-goers both respond, in their ways, to perfect timing, co-ordination, execution, and form. A handsomely executed *grand jeté* will make us take a deep breath and, figuratively, rise with the dancer. A ballerina *en pointes* arouses the empathic reaction: before she is *en pointes* she is a woman; on her toes she is an idealized woman who floats, not walks, and is a symbol of grace and purity. And we float with her. A man performing an *entrechat-huit* is an Icarus leaving earth behind in a superb demonstration of bodily control. And we leave earth with him.

Ballet can have as many manifestations as there are creators to work in the medium. Two broad divisions, for example, concern the plotless and the dramatic ballet. A choreographer like George Balanchine, the outstanding contemporary exponent of

5

the plotless ballet, has many times stated his belief that dancing to music is enough; you don't have to tell a story; there is enough esthetic satisfaction in organizing a group of dancers through a series of abstract movements (often tinged with an emotional mood despite the abstraction). The result is "pure" ballet: a Bach fugue as against a Strauss tone poem. Antony Tudor, on the other hand, perhaps the outstanding representative of the dramatic ballet, works best when he has a story on which to base his movements. He is anything but abstract; his dancers are generally human beings who suffer, love, exult. His choreographic movements and patterns are all designed to accent the emotions of his characters and their reaction to specific situations.

Perils abound in both procedures. The abstract ballet can be perfunctory, sterile, over-intellectual, unemotional. The dramatic ballet can be so overweighted with plot that dance values become secondary; it can fall back on sensationalism that has nothing to do with art. But in the hands of masters both types of ballet can inhabit Parnassus. For again the basic esthetic rules hold. The end result is what counts.

Such imponderables as style and quality naturally have a major bearing on the end result. Few terms are harder to define than these. Every choreographer, every dancer, every painter and musician—every creator and interpreter, in short —has his own style. It is an intangible. At a ballet, when we have the feeling of a creative choreographer handling materials with a complete knowledge of his craft, with power of communication, with logic and personality (and is not personality the most important thing in art?), with subtlety and the ability to make you feel that he has solved his problems, you can be assured that the ballet has quality.

Style is easier to define in an interpreter. A dancer must have quality of movement. It goes without saying that the dancer must have a well-grounded technique. Without technique, one is lost; it is useless to have ideas if they cannot be expressed. But, important as technique is—and don't let anybody tell you it is not the basic requisite for any dancer—it becomes an

6

esthetic affront if it is not used for artistic ends. Every last bit of technique should be made to express quality of movement.

Quality of movement is that magic which transforms Odette from a human being into a swan; which makes Giselle a peasant girl in one act and a disembodied spirit in the next. Quality of movement separates the mere dancers from the artists. Many are called, few are chosen; many can dance, few are artists.

Even fewer are so-called universal artists. Who alive is responsive to all schools, all philosophies, all art? Thus it does not necessarily follow that a dancer capable of making a tremendous impression in a Tudor ballet can also convince the observer that Odette is a swan and not a human being. In the same way, a great Liszt pianist may not have the temperament to make a convincing emotional experience out of Mozart or Beethoven. A performer's mental and physical limitations are seldom overcome. Dancers are born with their share of physical shortcomings. A dancer may have the strength and perseverance to acquire a secure and even dazzling technique, more than enough to handle the most difficult roles with ease. But because of the way the arms are set into the shoulders, or because of the length of the neck, or for any one of a number of physical reasons about which nothing can be done, it will be impossible for that particular dancer to develop a lyric line—a line that starts from the extended toe in an arabesque, floats through the torso to the extended arms, and prolongs itself into infinity for an eternity. It is that quality, among others, that a great classic dancer must have; it gives the added dimension needed for any of the important classic roles.

Such quality is part of technique, but at the same time far transcends technique. We all enjoy the fireworks of the Black Swan *pas de deux,* but whoever walks away from *Swan Lake* with only those fireworks in his recollection might just as well have gone to a circus. Either the performance as a whole was very bad indeed or he has missed the essential point of the ballet —the reason *why* the thirty-two *fouettés* occur at precisely that point in the third act. Those *fouettés* are not a stunt; they are the emotional climax reached as a result of specific occurrences in the plot. After all, one doesn't sit through the Brahms Violin Concerto waiting for the cadenza. The music has a definite plan, of which the cadenza is but one part, perhaps the least essential part.

It must be emphasized that ballet is not the easiest art to assimilate, nor is there any reason why it should be. It is a complicated synthesis of several arts, each with its own peculiar problems. I do not wish to imply that it is only for connoisseurs. Choreographers have not created their works for a specialized portion of the population; they aim their expression at every man, and ballet is no more for connoisseurs only than is opera or symphony. You can enjoy the Brahms Fourth without knowing in detail the mysteries of sonata form, and you can enjoy *Pillar of Fire* without knowing the difference between a *jeté* and an *arabesque*. Yet you can understand neither work if you approach it without previous collateral experience in the respective arts. Between liking a work and understanding it lies a chasm. The intelligent observer owes it to himself to acquire at least a minimum knowledge of an art in which he is interested. In art, as in life, you can get out only as much as you put in.

One should go to a ballet performance fortified with some knowledge of the substance of the ballets being performed. The individual, isolated steps and their nomenclature are relatively unimportant. Much more to the point is a realization of what the choreographer is trying to achieve, of the mood of his work, the symbolism (if any) employed, the deployment of the forces on the stage, and the clarity of total design.

Sometimes it is necessary to adjust one's habits of viewing. We become conditioned to a certain approach to the dance, and have a habit of forgetting that other approaches may be equally valid. Style in ballet varies from country to country, though nearly everywhere in the world it has evolved from a combination of Russian, Italian, and French elements. The Russians favor an open style of dancing characterized by spacious lines and movements. Their ballet is in the grand tradition—flamboyant, extroverted, rich. There is something almost imperial in their approach to the dance. The classic Italian school is more delicate, expresses itself in a more delicate framework. The English and the Danes have possibly been more influenced by the Italian school than by the Russian. The French school is a little fussier than the Russian or Italian; it has a rococo feeling. As for the Americans, they have accepted freely from many sources. Possibly the American style of ballet dancing is closest to the Russian. This is explained in part by the fact that in the thirties (the most important formative years of the ballet renaissance in this country) many of the schools were dominated by Russian or Russian-trained teachers.

But what finally evolved has its own character. American ballet dancers tend more toward rhythmic abandon than do those of other countries. Their work is sharper, more objective, less reliant on emotionalism and the grand manner. Critics complain that the American dancer lacks lyricism and heart, which may be true to a certain extent, but is not an ironclad proposition. Certainly a school of dance that has produced an Alicia Alonso, a Nora Kaye, and a Maria Tallchief need not be ashamed of itself.

Whether or not America has produced a school of choreography is a hard question to answer. This country is represented in the repertoire by ballets like Jerome Robbins's *Interplay* and Eugene Loring's *Billy the Kid,* ballets that could not conceivably have been created anywhere else in the world. The subject matter of these works has nothing to do with their Americanism. *Interplay,* as a matter of fact, is plotless. In the past there have been ballets on American subjects which were in no way representative of America. Leonide Massine's *Union Pacific* and *Saratoga* are two examples; their entire concept and technique were alien to the American *ethos. Interplay,* on the other hand, is American, and is immediately felt to be by American audiences and recognized as such by foreign ones. In many touches it departs from the continental tradition, especially in its free rhythms and unself-conscious use of jazz elements. As yet, however, the number of American ballets is too small to let us form a conclusive opinion.

9

The New Borzoi Book of Ballets

Tradition has been mentioned above. Ballet's strong tradition stems from pioneers like the eighteenth-century Noverre. At the same time, paradoxically, while ballet may be the most tradition-bound of all arts, specific ballet traditions are no longer than the memory of a particular group of people. For until recently no universal workable system of notation was in use, nor was the motion picture camera in general use, and all ballets were truly writ in water. We all know, anyway, that tradition changes from generation to generation and that the traditions of one age often appear dated to the next. As the older dancers and choreographers become inactive, they pass their lore on to younger people, and younger people have never hesitated to make whatever changes suit them. When we see ballets composed as little as one generation ago, it is highly doubtful that we are seeing a faithful re-creation of the original work. Memories falter. Even if the original choreographer happens to be around—and his memory may be no better than the next man's unless he is fortunate enough to re-stage a ballet with the original principals—we can be nearly sure that we are seeing only an approximation. His ideas too will have changed over the years. Some choreographers revise their ballets from season to season, even from performance to performance.

And ballets undergo changes as they enter the repertoires of various companies. Dancers have always changed steps to suit their own particular strengths. Ordinarily it is expected that a ballerina will modify a role, in certain particulars, to suit herself. Assume that, some years ago, a choreographer created a ballet with a specific ballerina in mind. This ballerina may have had tremendous elevation, and so the choreographer designed a role based on steps to show off that particular attribute. Then, after some time, the ballet dropped from the repertoire. Later it was resurrected and restaged without the services of the original ballerina. Instead we have a ballerina whose elevation is mediocre, but whose turns are dazzling. The role will now be dominated by turns, and nobody will object except some old-timers, who will parade their knowledge.

Ballerinas may even modify a role from performance to per-

10

formance much as an opera-singer not in especially good voice will arrange for a high C to be transposed down. A ballerina may, at curtain time, not feel up to the demands of thirty-two *fouettés*. The performance will not fall to pieces if she replaces them, as sometimes happens. On a subsequent evening she again will be in form, and back come the *fouettés*.

One thing presumably never changed is the music, though at some performances one sits in horror at what is happening to the poor composers. Ballet orchestras have never, in our day at any rate, rivalled the major permanent symphonic ensembles; nor could they under the circumstances to which ballet today is geared. A pick-up orchestra and a minimum of rehearsals are the rule, and few are the conductors who can do more than merely maintain a steady beat, meanwhile holding their breath lest the horns bobble or the violins make a false entry.

In recent times the trend has been away from commissioned scores. It was not always so. In the two Diaghilev decades, virtually every important composer—Stravinsky, Prokofiev, Ravel, Falla, Debussy, and Roussel, to mention only a few—composed music for the Ballets Russes. A decline in original ballet music set in after Diaghilev's death. Since then there have been notable exceptions—the Stravinsky-Balanchine *Orpheus* springs immediately to mind, and many of the Sadler's Wells ballets have used music commissioned from British composers—but for the most part choreographers today, especially in America, work from the body of the established orchestral repertoire. Bach, Mozart, Beethoven, Berlioz, Liszt, and goodness knows how many others have had their music used for choreographic purposes. An economic factor is, of course, involved. With the costs of commissioning, copying, and rehearsing a new score what they have become, there is little choice left but to use works in the public domain.

The late thirties witnessed critical agitation about this procedure; today it is taken for granted. It does seem to be true that choreographers treat so-called "classical music" with more respect than they showed it in the thirties, when the symphonic ballets of Massine were twisting knots into such scores as Beethoven's Seventh Symphony and Brahms's Fourth. Balanchine today, on the other hand, will use such severely abstract scores as Bach's Concerto for Two Violins and Mozart's *Sinfonia Concertante* for violin and viola for abstract ballets in which Bach and Mozart are not interpreted, but supplemented. Balanchine, himself a trained musician, would probably recoil from the thought of using an "absolute" score for a story ballet.

Tudor, none of whose ballets is abstract, has only once created a ballet to a commissioned score. He has used Arnold Schoenberg's *Verklärte Nacht* for his *Pillar of Fire*, Strauss's *Burleske* for his *Dim Lustre*, Chausson's *Poème* for his *Lilac Garden*. Each of these ballets is a masterpiece. Quite conceivably, Tudor could use a Beethoven symphony or even a Schubert quartet for one of his dramatic ballets and avoid the bizarre treatment that previous choreographers gave the standard musical repertoire. Which makes one wonder if any music is really unfit for use by a choreographer of taste, sympathy, and understanding. The ideal, of course, is to have a composer write a new score for a new ballet, but less and less of that is happening today in the three best-known American-based companies.

Of those three, the oldest is the Ballet Russe de Monte Carlo, a company that represents "traditional" Russian ballet. It can trace its lineage back to the Diaghilev Ballets Russes, but its tradition is rather diluted and tarnished today. The Ballet Russe de Monte Carlo is not the artistic factor it used to be; it has lost its personality, and represents neither the force of traditional Russian ballet nor the best of the new elements in contemporary ballet.

Ballet Theatre, formed in 1940, is still a considerable force. Perhaps it started out in too big and ambitious a fashion, for it could not adhere to its original program, and for several years was operating in almost a perfunctory manner. Recent seasons, however, have indicated a return to strength; its basic principles were too strong for the group to disappear. As originally conceived, Ballet Theatre represented a belief that ballet should incorporate the best of all schools. There was a traditional wing, an American wing, and an English wing. In the early years the company had a tremendous galaxy of great dancers and gifted choreographers—probably the most stunning group since the great days of the Diaghilev ballet. The company had decided character, and was responsible for some of the most brilliant *premières* and performances of our generation. Its repertoire was well balanced, and it had Tudor on hand to prepare his own ballets. It also was the first to recognize the talents of Jerome Robbins and Michael Kidd. In all, Ballet Theatre has been a tremendous stimulus to the American ballet scene.

The New York City Ballet, which came into being as such in 1948, really was born when Balanchine and Lincoln Kirstein formed the School of American Ballet in 1934. This company represents *avant-garde* tendencies. Until recent seasons its repertoire contained only contemporary ballets, most of them in the neo-classic style stemming from the Russian school, and most of *them* created by Balanchine. The company hardly has a rounded repertoire in the sense that Ballet Theatre has one. One season, not long ago, the New York City Ballet presented twenty-nine productions: nineteen by Balanchine, six by Robbins, and one each by Boris, Ashton, Dollar, and Christensen. Thus the company is largely a reflection of one person; and as Balanchine is a cosmopolitan without specific national tendencies, the company is too. (These remarks are not to be construed as condemnation; they are description.)

As the world's outstanding exponent of neo-classic choreography, Balanchine has created a large number of works that have attracted international attention, and he has built his company into a remarkably secure organization. This security, however, pertains to his own style of choreography. A Balanchine-trained dancer does not easily adapt herself to other companies, and the reverse is also true. Most Balanchine-trained dancers feature precise motions and a strongly academic technique rather than the grand gesture and the lyric line. His approach, despite his Imperial School training, is very twentieth-century.

13

Naturally Balanchine has had an influence on the younger generation. But, in view of the repertoires of the various companies in the last few years, the future of the young choreographer in America does not appear very bright. Surprisingly few creative dance talents are being developed; and it cannot be that this country truly lacks young creative figures in ballet. Things have arrived at a point where a choreographer as young as Jerome Robbins can virtually be regarded as an old master —and with no younger potential masters in sight. Take the repertoire of the New York City Ballet. Robbins is well represented by six or seven ballets, none of them very new. Todd Bolender has created only one work for the New York City Ballet since the *Miraculous Mandarin* of 1951; that work is *Souvenirs,* which received its *première* in the fall of 1955. Ruthanna Boris is represented only by *Cakewalk* (1950). William Dollar's ballet in this company's repertoire is *The Duel,* originally choreographed in 1949. Lew Christensen's total with the company is three ballets.

Ballet Theatre offers even fewer chances for the young choreographer. Herbert Ross is the only newcomer; the repertoire is built largely on Tudor, de Mille, Loring, Robbins, and classic ballets. The Ballet Russe de Monte Carlo has a negligible record of accomplishment as regards the young choreographer.

It might be argued that some young creative talent has been tried and found wanting by each of these companies. Which, of course, is true, but is basically specious as an argument. Todd Bolender, Ruthanna Boris, William Dollar, Lew Christensen, Michael Kidd (who has turned to Hollywood and Broadway), and others have proved their talent. They simply are not producing. And no new talent can be seen on the horizon. Could the answer be that the directors of the companies today do not have the imagination and initiative to recognize and develop choreographic talent? This does not augur well for the future.

A fourth American company should be mentioned, even though it has not been functioning in this country. That is the Marquis de Cuevas Grand Ballet de Monte Carlo. The Cuevas

Ballet stems from the International Ballet, which had one unsuccessful season at the International Theatre, New York, in 1944. Following this costly lesson, the Marquis became artistic director for Colonel W. de Basil's Original Ballet Russe during the 1946–7 season. Later he organized the Grand Ballet Russe de Monte Carlo, under the patronage of the Prince of Monaco. The choreographers and dancers of the International Ballet formed the nucleus of the new company.

What makes the Grand Ballet de Monte Carlo an American group is the little-known fact that it operates under an American charter from Albany, New York. Its personnel, too, is dominated by Americans. At the point of writing, Marjorie Tallchief (sister of the New York City Ballet's Maria Tallchief) and her husband, George Skibine (a naturalized American) are among the principal dancers. George Zoritch, also American by choice, is on the roster. John Taras, born and trained in this country, is the ballet master, and has contributed several ballets to the company's repertoire. Rosella Hightower, who rose through the ranks of Ballet Theatre, was for many seasons the company's ballerina. She left to rejoin Ballet Theatre in 1955.

A short New York season in 1950 gave American audiences a chance to assess the development of the Cuevas group. It presented some standard ballets from the classical Russian and the Diaghilev repertoires; it had works by Balanchine, Taras, Ana Ricarda, and Skibine; and one of its most attractive novelties was Nijinska's *Les Biches,* to music by Poulenc. The company, though dominated by Americans, had a continental flavor, with a tight organization and a feeling of intimacy. The *corps* was fairly well trained; the solo dancing on a generally strong level. It was not a flashy company (in 1950, at any rate), nor could it be rated as a great one, even discounting its difference in approach and standards. But it presented ballet with honesty, and one would like to see it several more times before arriving at any final decision.

Of all the visiting companies, the Sadler's Wells Ballet has attracted most attention. Through this organization America has had the opportunity of beholding the great full-length

Tchaikovsky ballets, *Sleeping Beauty* and *Swan Lake,* as well as other full-length ballets like *Sylvia* and *Cinderella.* The company has a skillful choreographer in Ashton, though many feel that the modern wing of Sadler's Wells is its weakest. Sadler's Wells is a superbly trained organization that has restored to ballet some of its rightful pomp. Its costumes are gorgeous, its sets elaborate; and the company presents a ballet without skimping. The painstaking care with which Sadler's Wells presents every ballet in its repertoire guarantees a consistent standard of performance. The Sadler's Wells Theatre Ballet, a junior company, has also toured America. It is a sprightly group that lacks the professionalism of the parent company.

Other foreign organizations have toured America throughout the years. We also have seen small native groups starting on a modest scale. Some have disappeared; some are in the process of growth. The impact of the Broadway theater and of television is another strong factor in the American ballet renaissance.

What with native and touring companies, and representatives from European ballet groups who have appeared in this country as guest artists, America has had the chance to see the great dancers of the world, those within the Iron Curtain excepted. Not too many of us have memories that extend back to 1916, when the Diaghilev company appeared here. But many of us have seen most of the dancers active in America since 1933, when Colonel W. de Basil and the Ballet Russe de Monte Carlo gloried in three "baby ballerinas."

Those "baby ballerinas" were Irina Baronova, Tatiana Riabouchinska, and Tamara Toumanova. Baronova, beautiful and fair, with high Slavic cheekbones and a perfect figure, was probably the most versatile of the three. Many of us thought her the most interesting as a dancer. Like the great sopranos of the Golden Age of singing, she could handle a variety of roles, from the balletic equivalents of Wagner through Donizetti. Her Princess Aurora was unsurpassable, and so was her effervescent Lisette in *La Fille mal gardée.* She had elegance and grandeur, and yet a peculiar earthy quality. Toumanova, referred to by many as the "black pearl," was dark and sultry, and had a magnificently controlled technique, though she lacked the spontaneity of some other great dancers. She excelled in the "grand ballerina" roles—Aurora, the Swan Queen —but showed her versatility in *The Three-Cornered Hat* and *Cotillon.* Riabouchinska, like the other two, had an all-encompassing technique. She was more delicate, however, and could summon up an ethereal quality. Few have danced so beautifully the Prelude in *Les Sylphides.* Of this great trio, only Toumanova is before the public today. Baronova lives in England and takes an occasional acting role. Riabouchinska, married to David Lichine, has not danced regularly with a major company for some years.

What a galaxy there was in the period up to America's entry into the war! The pert Alexandra Danilova, whose career extended back to the latter days of the Diaghilev company, was enchanting audiences in such of the lighter roles of the repertoire as Swanilda in *Coppélia* and the Glove Seller in *Gaîté Parisienne.* She also did the heavy roles, though her temperament made her something very special in the soubrette side of the repertoire. Mia Slavenska, a hard-working, competent, all-around dancer, was seen in many roles, and was recently prima ballerina at the Metropolitan Opera House. Alicia Markova, the incomparable Swan Queen and Giselle, the light-as-air dancer who always seemed in secret Mona Lisa communion within herself, immediately achieved recognition here as a supreme artist.

The assorted Ballet Russe companies brought some remarkable male dancers to this country. Character dancers like Simon Semenoff, Leonide Massine, Yurek Lazowsky, and Marc Platoff offered unforgettable interpretations. Nobody yet has rivalled Semenoff's Charlatan in *Petrouchka* while in the title role of the same ballet Massine and Lazowsky set a standard that no male dancer has succeeded in duplicating. Roland Guerard, the first American male dancer of consequence in the thirties, was a handsome and accomplished partner and a brilliant technician whose dancing in the *Bluebird* Variation is still discussed with awe. In the late thirties a magnificent group of *danseurs nobles* was seen: George Skibine, George Zoritch, Paul Petroff, Igor Youskevitch, André Eglevsky, and Frederic Franklin. Youskevitch, one of the great classic dancers of our time, is subtle, graceful, completely masculine, and a magnificent technician. Eglevsky is noted for his elevation and *batterie*. His is a more exhibitionistic type of dance than Youskevitch's. Franklin, who can dance classic and character roles at will, is a debonair sight on the stage, and a superb showman with a wonderful sense of theater. The initial Ballet Theatre season in 1940 introduced Anton Dolin, a flashy dancer and model partner, especially for Markova. Dolin also had a gift for reconstructing the choreography of the classics. His *Pas de Quatre,* in the repertoire for many years, was a delightful throwback to the age of Taglioni.

Ballet Theatre was responsible for the emergence of many dancers new to us. In the early forties there were Karen Conrad, a bewitching dancer with remarkable elevation and technical clarity; the regal Nana Gollner; Nina Stroganova, a serious ballerina who was almost a throwback to Imperial Ballet days. Viola Essen was much talked about then. And from its *corps de ballet,* Ballet Theatre developed many stars—Nora Kaye, Alicia Alonso, Rosella Hightower, Michael Kidd, and Jerome Robbins among them. Of these fine dancers, Kaye developed into America's greatest dramatic ballerina, Alonso into a supreme classic stylist. Hugh Laing was given the opportunity to exploit his unique personality; he is an intense dramatic dancer, the male counterpart of Kaye, in whom flames slumber. Later, Janet Reed, pert and charming, came to the fore. So did John Kriza, a well-rounded dancer and man of the theater, at home in classic and modern styles.

The New York City Ballet has spawned at least one ballerina —Maria Tallchief, who came to the company by way of the Ballet Russe de Monte Carlo. Tallchief has an infallible technique and precise bodily command. Few living dancers have as much finish and authority. She is not a warm dancer; at least, she is not the emotive kind. But within her classic scope she is perfect. Tanaquil LeClercq of this company defies classification. She is an interesting dancer with unmistakable individuality, and she illuminates the stage when she steps on it. Her forte probably is outside the classic repertoire; choreographers could be busy for years devising roles for her.

From Sadler's Wells have come a brilliant trio—Margot Fonteyn, Beryl Grey, and Moira Shearer. Fonteyn, whose *port de bras* is probably the most perfect to be found anywhere, is the rare type of artist who seems to achieve identification with every role she takes. Her technique, never of a showy nature, is strong enough to enable her to do anything she wants to do, and she has so thought through her roles that every movement and gesture has a meaning. Grey, with her long extensions and tremendous sweep, is always an exciting dancer to watch, and as a technician she is stupendous. Shearer, who has not appeared here in recent seasons, is a finished stylist with a warm, feminine quality.

Indications are that several young dancers may be able to fill the gap when the Fonteyns, Alonsos, and Tallchiefs of today retire. Nadia Nerina, Svetlana Beriosova, and Elaine Fifield, all of Sadler's Wells, are potential ballerinas. (It might be mentioned here that the dance world recognizes a specific hierarchy for female dancers: members of the *corps de ballet, coryphées, soloistes, premières danseuses,* and *ballerinas.* There also was a higher classification in Russia—*prima ballerina assoluta.* Only two dancers in history—Pierina Legnani and Mathilde Kchessinska—have held that exalted title.) Lupe Serrano of Ballet Theatre and Jillana and Carolyn George of the New York City Ballet also convey in their dancing the qualities of individuality, discipline, and personality which are necessary to make a ballerina. Of the young men before the American public, Erik Bruhn of the Royal Danish Ballet, who has been a guest with Ballet Theatre, already is a *danseur noble* with a brilliant future. With proper guidance and training, Jacques d'Amboise of the New York City Ballet could develop into an unusual dancer.

And a word should be said in praise of the many dancers who

may not be of ballerina status, but who are accomplished, versatile, and the backbone of any company with which they are associated. In this group are excellent soloists like Patricia Wilde, Diana Adams, Ruth Ann Koesun, Barbara Lloyd, Yvonne Mounsey, and Melissa Hayden—dancers who are strong technicians, always dependable, ready to step into any number of roles.

Ballet activity in America has even extended to satisfying the ballet-goer's need for information about the art. From British and American publishers comes a steady flow of ballet books of all kinds: from elementary primers to "how-to" ballet books, criticism and exegesis, and esoteric studies. A more encouraging sign would be hard to find, for the fact that the American public is prepared to invest in ballet books is indicative of healthy interest and appreciation. And even if the time has not yet come when the dance has its equivalent of *Grove's Dictionary of Music and Musicians,* it does boast of a one-volume encyclopedia edited by Anatole Chujoy. This *Dance Encyclopedia* (A. S. Barnes and Company, New York, 1949) is a useful reference work despite some omissions and inaccuracies unavoidable in a pioneer work of this sort. It is a basic book for any library on the dance.

Many excellent books are available for those who desire to read up on aspects of ballet. Still indispensable is Cyril Beaumont's historic *Complete Book of Ballets* (G. P. Putnam's Sons, New York, 1938), in which reposes a vast collection of data about many ballets, some of them still in the repertoire, many long since departed. In 1952 the British Book Centre in New York made available for American distribution Beaumont's *Supplement to the Complete Book of Ballets* (Putnam & Co., Ltd., London). Several previously undescribed ballets by the nineteenth-century choreographers Auguste Bournonville and Charles Didelot are included in this supplement, as are some twentieth-century ballets produced through 1941. Beaumont also managed to collect some data on eleven Soviet ballets. Another fine book that deals with ballet plots and collateral information is George Balanchine's *Complete Stories of the*

Great Ballets (Doubleday & Company, Inc., New York, 1954). This book concentrates mostly on ballets that are being produced in America, and is especially valuable for the light Balanchine throws on some of his own ballets. The second part of the book contains information on history and appreciation, plus some pertinent advice to young dancers and their parents. *The Borzoi Book of Ballets,* by Grace Robert (Alfred A. Knopf, New York, 1946), predecessor of the present volume, has fully documented material on many ballets in the repertoire a decade ago.

The above books are stories of the ballets. Several excellent and not too complicated handbooks of ballet technique can be consulted with profit. Chief among these are *Fundamentals of the Classic Dance,* by Agrippina Vaganova, translated from the Russian by Anatole Chujoy (Kamin Dance Bookshop, New York, 1946), and *The Classic Ballet: Basic Technique and Terminology* (Alfred A. Knopf, New York, 1952). For the latter book, Lincoln Kirstein contributed a preface about the historical development of ballet, and Muriel Stuart wrote the greater part of the text. At times the explanations may be a little involved for the layman, but if you want to know the difference between a *pirouette en dehors* and a *petit temps lié,* this is one place to look. The detailed illustrations by Carlus Dyer are a big help. Vaganova's is an authoritative handbook on Russian technique. She was a ballerina in the Imperial Ballet and for many years after she left the stage in 1917 she was considered the greatest teacher of her generation in Russia.

A somewhat more simplified book is Kay Ambrose's illustrated *The Ballet-Student's Primer: A Concentrated Guide for Beginners of All Ages* (Alfred A. Knopf, New York, 1954). Two other excellent little books by Ambrose are *The Ballet-Lover's Companion* (Alfred A. Knopf, New York, 1949) and *The Ballet-Lover's Pocket Book* (Alfred A. Knopf, New York, 1945). Gail Grant's *Technical Manual and Dictionary of Classical Ballet* (Kamin Dance Bookshop, New York, 1950) is a short, but very comprehensive book in dictionary form, running from *adage* to *voyagé,* and is extremely handy for quick consultation on ballet terminology. It is the only book of its kind to make a comparative examination of Russian, Italian, and French techniques. Also short, to the point, and full of helpful suggestions for the beginner, is Arnold Haskell's *How to Enjoy Ballet* (William Morrow, New York, 1951).

Two books not on ballet proper, but good background reading for ballet, are Curt Sachs's *World History of the Dance* (W. W. Norton and Company, New York, 1937) and Paul Nettl's *The Story of Dance Music* (Philosophical Library, New York, 1947). Those with a scholarly bent of mind can, if they wish, read studies of great early dance innovators, such as *The Chevalier Noverre: Father of Modern Ballet,* by Deryck Lynham (Sylvan Press, London, 1950, distributed in America by the British Book Centre, New York). Noverre's *Letters on Dancing and Ballets* have been translated by Cyril Beaumont (Beaumont, London, 1930), and Mary Stuart Evans has translated an important work by the nineteenth-century master, Carlo Blasis, which glories in the name of *An Elementary Treatise Upon the Theory and Practice of the Art of Dancing* (Kamin Dance Bookshop, New York, 1944).

Many books are devoted to a particular period, or to a study of a particular organization. Naturally Diaghilev and his Ballets Russes have received a major share of attention. Serge Lifar's book, *Serge Diaghilev* (G. P. Putnam's Sons, New York, 1940), is a full-scale study of the great Russian impresario, though the reader should be warned that it is colored by Lifar's prejudices. Serge Grigoriev's *Diaghilev Ballet 1909–1929* (Constable, London, 1953) and Alexandre Benois's *Reminiscences of the Russian Ballet* (Putnam & Co., Ltd., London, 1941) contain an extraordinary amount of information about the original Ballets Russes. Benois is especially readable; he was a balletomane in St. Petersburg before the turn of the century, and he captures the flavor of the early period as well as that of the great years of Diaghilev. Grigoriev is more sober and factual, but he too has information and gossip not available elsewhere. Tamara Karsavina's *Theatre Street* (E. P. Dutton, New York, 1931), in addition to a long section on the first years of the Ballets Russes, takes us into the Imperial School at St. Petersburg and tells us of the day-by-day routine of the aspiring ballerina. Serge Lifar's *A History of Russian Ballet* (Roy Publishers, New York, 1955) contains a long section on Diaghilev's company and also a fairly comprehensive study of Russian ballet from the very beginnings. This book, however, is carelessly edited and contains numerous mistakes. It is the only book of its type available. The closest thing to it is a study of Russian ballet from its beginnings until 1881 by Cyril Beaumont entitled *A History of Ballet in Russia* (Beaumont, London, 1930). This book, like so many others on dance, is not available in the United States except through specialized bookshops.

Two standard books about the American scene are George Amberg's *Ballet in America* (Duell, Sloan and Pearce, New York, 1949) and Anatole Chujoy's *The New York City Ballet* (Alfred A. Knopf, New York, 1953). Both are thorough, sympathetic, and informative. Mary Clarke's *The Sadler's Wells Ballet* (The Macmillan Company, New York, 1955) is required reading, as much for its information on the organization and ideals of the company as for its analysis and discussion of its dancers and repertoire.

Everybody should make an attempt to read some of the reviews of one of ballet's earliest and greatest critics—Théophile Gautier. Cyril Beaumont has translated a group of Gautier reviews which appeared between 1837 and 1848; the title of the book is *The Romantic Ballet* (Beaumont, London, 1932). Lincoln Kirstein's *Blast at Ballet* (Kirstein, New York, 1938) is, in a way, criticism, and his well-taken points are still valid. Edwin Denby's *Looking at the Dance* (Pellegrini and Cudahy, New York, 1949) is a collection of Denby reviews which appeared in the New York *Herald Tribune* and several other periodicals. Denby's sensitive, impressionistic, rather precious criticisms could well add a new perspective to the layman's enjoyment of ballet.

Several British personalities have had perceptive things to say about ballet. Ninette de Valois, the guiding spirit of Sadler's Wells, wrote a very stimulating book named *Invitation to the*

Ballet (John Lane, London, 1937), which unfortunately has had no distribution in America. It should be reprinted, for it contains much information about ballet and ballet companies offered by no other publication. It is written in a literate manner, too. Richard Buckle's *The Adventure of a Ballet Critic* (Cresset, London, 1953; distributed in America by the British Book Centre, New York) is chatty, gossipy, and full of tales about this or that personality. Rayner Heppenstall's *Apology for Dancing* (Faber and Faber, London, 1936) is a serious book of essays with some unconventional ideas strongly expressed. Extremely ambitious, and recommended to the reader, is Fernau Hall's *World Dance* (A. A. Wyn, New York, n.d.), released in this country in 1954. It is probably the best one-volume history of the ballet (and other forms of dance), with a detailed examination of virtually every creative figure. Hall is opinionated and sometimes violent, but you do not have to accept all his conclusions: you cannot but be stimulated by his love for ballet, impressed by his knowledge, and interested by his opinions.

Ballet in America has never flourished as it flourishes today. A new and very responsive audience is being built. Every year sees more performances, more students in ballet schools, more general activity in the field. For the first time, too, the federal government is taking an interest. Through the intervention of the State Department, sparked by the work of the International Exchange Program of the American National Theatre and Academy (ANTA), several of our ballet companies have had chances to visit other parts of the world. No ballet company —nor, indeed, any other of this country's artistic institutions— has as yet received any direct form of federal subsidy, but at least a step has been taken to recognize their importance in the world's cultural exchange. If ever the government—whether on the federal, the state, or the local level—puts itself actively behind the arts, and is able to keep its interest divorced from politics, activity in America will be more than a renaissance. It may well be an explosion.

The Age of Anxiety

One bemused observer at the *première* of *The Age of Anxiety* called it "The Age of Psychiatry." What with its evident Freudian symbolism and its preoccupation with some neuroses of contemporary man, the ballet created a great deal of talk, pro and con. There was a good deal of "con," especially in England when the New York City Ballet took the work there. "Auden's poem achieved a fairly high degree of obscurity," complained the British critic, Fernau Hall, "but it was pellucid in comparison with Robbins's ballet. Robbins placed everything on a rarefied plane of abstraction, introducing Jungian archetypal myths such as the dream journey to find happiness and yet falling back on images of the utmost melodramatic crudity (e.g. having the dancers whip their other selves, presumably to suggest masochism)." But many other voices were raised to hail the ballet as a significant contribution to contemporary art. When dealing with an anxiety neurosis, these observers pointed out, a choreographer must of necessity use symbolism involving the psyche; and, after all, has not the jargon of the psychiatrist's couch invaded much of our lives in all spheres of activity?

Both Leonard Bernstein's musical score and Jerome Robbins's choreography were inspired by W. H. Auden's poem, *The Age of Anxiety,* published in 1946. Bernstein's score was not composed for the ballet: he composed it as his Symphony No. 2, and it was played by the Boston Symphony Orchestra in 1949. At that time Bernstein acknowledged his indebtedness to the Auden poem, calling both the poem and the symphony "the record of our difficult and problematical search for faith." Robbins, who created his ballet in 1950, also paid tribute to the poem, although he admitted taking certain liberties with it. "It is a ritual in which four people exercise their illusions in their search for security. It is an attempt to see what life is about." The New York City Center program booklet says much the same thing: "This ballet was inspired by Leonard Bernstein's Symphony No. 2 and the W. H. Auden poem on which it is based. The ballet follows the sectional development of the poem and music and concerns the attempts of people to rid themselves of anxiety."

The ballet is in six sections, given in the program as follows:

1. THE PROLOGUE: *Four strangers meet and become acquainted.*

2. THE SEVEN AGES: *They discuss the life of man from birth to death in a set of seven variations.*

3. THE SEVEN STAGES: *They embark on a dream journey to find happiness.*

4. THE DIRGE: *They mourn for the figure of the All-Powerful Father who would have protected them from the vagaries of men and nature.*

5. THE MASQUE: *They attempt to become or appear carefree.*

6. THE EPILOGUE.

The *première* took place at the New York City Center of Music and Drama on February 26, 1950. The leading roles were danced by Francisco Moncion, Tanaquil LeClercq, Todd Bolender, and Jerome Robbins. Also in the large cast were Yvonne Mounsey, Pat McBride, Beatrice Tompkins, Melissa

Hayden, Herbert Bliss, Dick Beard, Shaun O'Brien, and Edward Bigelow. Oliver Smith designed the scenery, Irene Sharaff the costumes. The piano solo in the symphony was played by Nicholas Kopeikine.

The scenery suggests a city scene. The four strangers meet; they are nervous, neurotic people, unsure of themselves. Their very inadequacies draw them together. This is the Prologue. In the Seven Ages section, a series of seven variations, the dancers depict man as a child, man as an adolescent, a young person in love, man faced with the problem of choosing a life's work, man as a member of society, man faced with social problems, and man at the end of his career. In the Seven Stages the four principals take a symbolic trip on their "dream journey to happiness." They are accompanied by their doubles. They do not find happiness, but wander about in a miasma of insecurity. The Dirge presents the All-Powerful Father who will solve all emotional problems. But in the end he fails too; he is nothing, really, but an empty shell, a figment that mankind invents because it is too weak to face reality. In the Masque the four principals attempt to become carefree. They dance with artificial gaiety to jazz rhythms. This too, however, is a pitiful escape, and they know it. One by one they stop; no use pretending. The Epilogue leaves all questions unanswered. The four people split up and go their separate way, strangers again. Not with a bang but a whimper.

Age of Anxiety scored a real *succès d'estime*. To some observers, though, it raised a few questions. Is modern civilization as empty and wretched as the ballet would suggest? Is our generation as insecure? Or—purely a hypothetical question—is the choreographer demonstrating his own insecurity in terms of a universal application? *Age of Anxiety* undoubtedly is a very chic ballet in its grisly way, and what Virgil Thomson used to call the intellectual audience dotes on it. These questions and reservations aside, *Age of Anxiety* is decidedly a reflection on a certain part of our society, and it has been done with considerable skill. But we can cheer up. The mental condition of the world is nowhere near the parlous state that *Age of Anxiety* suggests.

Apollon Musagète

Apollo, Leader of the Muses

The year is 1927. "I was asked," Stravinsky has written in his memoirs, "by the Washington Congressional Library to compose a ballet for a festival of contemporary music which was to include the production of several works especially written for the occasion. . . . This proposal suited me admirably, for, as I was more or less free just then, it enabled me to carry out an idea which had long tempted me, to compose a ballet founded on movements or episodes in Greek mythology plastically interpreted by dancing of the so-called classical school."

He chose as the theme of his new ballet score the figure of Apollo, "leader of the Muses," who would inspire the other Muses with his own art. He also reduced the nine Muses to three—Calliope, Polyhymnia, and Terpsichore. These three, he considered, were the most characteristic representatives of choreographic art. Calliope personified poetry and its rhythm. Polyhymnia, finger on lips, represented mime. Stravinsky quotes Cassiodorus in relation to Polyhymnia: "Those speaking fingers, that eloquent silence, those narratives in gesture, are said to have been invented by the Muse Polyhymnia, wishing to prove that man could express his will without resource to words." Terpsichore, to Stravinsky, personified dance, combining in herself the rhythm of poetry and the eloquence of gesture. It is she who among all the Muses takes the place of honor beside the *Musagète*.

The composer specifically set out to compose a "white ballet" in neo-classic style. The term, "white ballet," goes back to the days of Théophile Gautier and the second quarter of the nineteenth century. Marie Taglioni, the most popular ballerina at that time, invented a costume of white material which other ballerinas immediately adopted. In the white ballet, or *ballet blanc*, the emphasis is on pure dance. Stravinsky considers the *ballet blanc* to be dance in its highest manifestation, and he wanted to get a comparable quality into his music. This was his reasoning: "I found that the absence of many-colored effects and of all superfluities produced a wonderful freshness. This inspired me to write music of an analogous character."

He settled on a diatonic style as best suited for his purpose. That, in turn, determined the nature of the instrumental ensemble he employed. Because *ballet blanc* is clean and direct, and lacks contrast in color, and because the diatonic style of composition avoids chromatic coloration, Stravinsky decided to set aside the usual symphony orchestra, with its mixtures of strings, wood, brass, and percussion. He also discarded ensembles of wood and brass as being too colorful and sensuous. Instead he chose the unadorned string orchestra. The unadorned design of the classical dance, he felt, could not be better expressed than by a melodic flow in the sustained, singing quality of string tone.

In July, 1927, Stravinsky started the composition of *Apollon Musagète*. He finished it at the beginning of 1928. The ballet was first presented at the Library of Congress in Washington, D.C., on April 27, 1928, with choreography by Adolph Bolm,

29

as a commission from Elizabeth Sprague Coolidge. "As I was not there," Stravinsky has tactfully written in his autobiography, I cannot say anything about it." Bolm danced Apollo; Ruth Page was seen as Terpsichore, Berenice Holmes as Polyhymnia, and Elise Reiman as Calliope. The ballet created a heated argument, with critics vigorously disagreeing about its merits.

That first version is not before the public today. Diaghilev expressed interest in the score, and when Stravinsky agreed to let the Ballets Russes stage *Apollon Musagète,* young George Balanchine was assigned the choreography. Stravinsky, a hard man to please, was more than satisfied with Balanchine's work. On June 12, 1928, the composer conducted the first Paris performance of *Apollon Musagète* at the Théâtre Sarah Bernhardt. He has written about the event in his memoirs: "As a stage performance I got more satisfaction from this than from *Les Noces,* which was the latest thing Diaghilev had had from me. Balanchine, as ballet-master, had arranged the dances exactly as I had wished—that is to say, in accordance with the classical school. From that point of view it was a complete success, and it was the first attempt to revive academic dancing in a work actually composed for the purpose." Fokine's *Les Sylphides,* which goes back to 1908, is also a *ballet blanc,* but uses orchestrations of pieces by Chopin. Balanchine, says Stravinsky, "designed for the choreography of the *Apollon* groups, movements and lines of great dignity and plastic elegance as inspired by the beauty of classical forms. As a thorough musician—he had studied at the St. Petersburg Conservatory—he had no difficulty grasping the smallest details of my music, and his beautiful choreography cleverly expressed my meaning."

Stravinsky goes on to praise the dancers. He was less satisfied with the costumes and *décor,* about which he and Diaghilev did not see eye to eye. Stravinsky wanted it simple—white skirts, a severely conventionalized theatrical landscape; whereas Diaghilev, with the public in mind, wanted to have something spectacular. He engaged a painter named André Bauchant, who worked somewhat in the style of *le Douanier* Rousseau. The results were, as might be expected, colorful and interesting, but they in no way resembled anything Stravinsky had in mind.

The "graceful Nikitina"—Alice Nikitina—was Terpsichore in the Paris *première* (she alternated in the role with Alexandra Danilova); Lubov Tchernicheva was Polyhymnia; Felia Dubrovska was Calliope; and Serge Lifar danced the title role. Stravinsky conducted. The program described the ballet as "a piece without a plot."

A decided story line is nevertheless present, abstract as it is. The action is supposed to take place on the Aegean island of Delos. In the opening sequence, Leto gives birth to Apollo. Two nymphs bring him a stringed instrument and show him how to use it. They place his hands on the strings and guide him through their mysteries. In a following scene Apollo has become complete master of the instrument. As he plays it, three Muses appear. They dance and he joins them. He then presents to each an appropriate symbol—tablets to Calliope, a mask to Polyhymnia, a lyre to Terpsichore. He commands them to create. Calliope is the first to perform, dancing to a melody based on the classic Alexandrine meter. Apollo does not approve. Nor does he approve of Polyhymnia's dance. Her lips have moved—and Polyhymnia, the Muse of mime, should never need speech to express an idea. Terpsichore's dance, however, pleases Apollo. Then he himself dances, after which he has a duet with Terpsichore. The other two Muses join in. At the conclusion of the dance, Zeus, Apollo's father, calls for him. Apollo listens as the three Muses sit upon the ground. He walks behind them, lifts them to their feet, and blesses them. They form an intertwined quartet. Apollo finally takes leave and starts the climb to Olympus. The Muses follow him. Leto, Apollo's mother, watching his farewell to earth, beckons to him and then falls, overcome, into the arms of her maidens.

America first saw this version in a memorable all-Stravinsky evening at the Metropolitan Opera House, New York, on April 27, 1937, when the American Ballet presented the American *premières* of *Le Baiser de la fée* and *Jeu de cartes* as well. The cast consisted of Lew Christensen (Apollo), Daphne Vane (Calliope), Holly Howard (Polyhymnia), Elise Reiman (Terpsichore), Jane Burkhalter (Leto), and Kyra Blank and Rabana Hasburgh (Nymphs). Stravinsky conducted; scenery and costumes were by Stewart Chaney. Ballet Theatre later revived the work. The most recent revival took place at the City Center of Music and Drama, New York, on November 25, 1951. In the New York City Ballet Company's cast were Maria Tallchief (Terpsichore), Tanaquil LeClercq (Polyhymnia), Diana Adams (Calliope), and André Eglevsky (Apollo).

The New York City Ballet performances have been noteworthy for the brilliant work of the female principals, each of whom has been able to employ the Balanchine-Stravinsky idiom with dignity and the necessary plastic line. *Apollon Musagète* has, however, been less fortunate in its male dancers. The most recent trio of Apollos—Eglevsky, Igor Youskevitch, and Nicholas Magallanes—have not been very convincing. Eglevsky and Youskevitch, two romantic dancers, have seemed self-conscious and even somewhat apologetic as Apollo; they posed rather than danced, striking attitudes they fondly imagined to be godlike. The ballet, it might be mentioned, is not pure *ballet blanc* as seen in the New York City Ballet or Ballet Theatre productions; the girls wear white, short, soft clinging skirts, rather than the three-quarter length skirts of traditional *ballet blanc*. *Apollon Musagète* is a twentieth-century, neo-classic adaptation of the white ballet.

Le Baiser de la fée

The Fairy's Kiss

 Just as Stravinsky was finishing the music of *Apollo,* he was approached by Ida Rubinstein to compose a ballet for her repertoire. Rubinstein had danced with Diaghilev's Ballets Russes before branching out on her own. She had created the role of Zobeide in *Schéhérazade* in 1910 for the Diaghilev company, and had danced several other roles. In later years she organized her own company (she had plenty of money) and commissioned works from the best creators in circulation.

Alexandre Benois discussed the matter with Stravinsky in 1928; it was Benois's idea that he compose something inspired by the music of Tchaikovsky. "My well-known fondness for the composer," Stravinsky has written in his memoirs, ". . . induced me to accept the offer. It would give me an opportunity of paying my heartfelt homage to Tchaikovsky's wonderful talent. As I was

33

free to choose both the subject and scenario of the ballet, I began to search for them, in view of the characteristic trend of Tchaikovsky's music, in the literature of the nineteenth century. With that aim I turned to a great poet with a gentle, sensitive soul whose imaginative mind was wonderfully akin to that of the musician. I refer to Hans Christian Andersen, with whom in this respect Tchaikovsky had so much in common. . . . In turning over the pages of Andersen, with which I was fairly familiar, I came across a story which I had completely forgotten that struck me as being the very thing for the idea that I wanted to express. It was the very beautiful story known to us as *The Ice Maiden.* I chose that as my theme, and worked out the story on the following lines. A fairy imprints her magic kiss on a child at birth and parts it from its mother. Twenty years later, when the youth has attained the very zenith of his good fortune, she repeats the fatal kiss and carries him off in supreme happiness ever afterwards. As my object was to commemorate the work of Tchaikovsky, this subject seemed to me to be particularly appropriate as an allegory, the Muse having similarly branded Tchaikovsky with her fatal kiss, and the magic imprint has made itself felt in all the musical creations of this great artist."

Bronislava Nijinska was the choreographer, and the world *première* of *The Fairy's Kiss* took place on November 27, 1928, at the Paris Opéra. Ida Rubinstein, of course, danced the leading role, and Stravinsky conducted. An interested spectator was Diaghilev, who was wondering if his Ballets Russes was going to have a rival. On the basis of what he saw, Diaghilev decided that he did not have to worry too much. In a letter to Serge Lifar he had some malicious things to say about Rubinstein a few days before the *première* of *Baiser:* "The theater was packed, but a good many of the audience had been given free tickets by the management. . . . The evening was as dull as any provincial show." As for poor Ida, Diaghilev really flayed her: "Not even I could recognize her. She was bent, her red hair disheveled, wearing ballet shoes. . . . Nothing is left of her face except an enormous gaping mouth with close set teeth trying to grimace a smile. It was ghastly. . . . She is as old as the devil."

About *Le Baiser de la fée* Diaghilev wrote another letter to Lifar: "Just back from the theater with a terrible headache brought on by what I've seen and particularly by Stravinsky. . . . It is very hard to specify exactly what it is, more like a bad suite by Tchaikovsky than anything else, tearful and monstrous, apparently orchestrated 'in masterly fashion' by Stravinsky (I say 'apparently' because to my mind the harmony is dull and the execution quite dead). . . . It is impossible to describe what goes on on the stage. . . . Though the theater was full, it made one think of a drawing-room in which a highly respected guest had just made an unfortunate noise. Everybody pretended that there was nothing wrong, and Stravinsky got two curtain calls. His ballet is stillborn." But, then again, Diaghilev did not like women, especially women who threatened to become rivals; and he had it in for Stravinsky because the composer had left the Ballets Russes.

Diaghilev, however, was right about the ballet being stillborn. In its original version it dropped from the repertoire. Stravinsky himself did not care for Nijinska's choreography, which "left me cold," he said.

Sadler's Wells presented a version with choreography by Frederick Ashton on November 26, 1935, but the production seen in America is, with some modifications, the one that George Balanchine created for the American Ballet in 1937. The occasion was a Stravinsky festival at the Metropolitan Opera House, and the evening of April 27, 1937, saw the American *première* not only of *Le Baiser de la fée,* but also of *Apollon Musagète* and *Jeu de cartes.* Balanchine, of course, used Stravinsky's score, which is a suite built from Tchaikovsky melodies that the composer culled from various sources, employing some of their original melodic content, but transmuting them through his own creative alchemy. He dedicated the score "to the memory of Peter Tchaikovsky. . . . It was his Muse (like our Fairy heroine) whose fatal kiss, imprinted at birth, made itself felt in all the work of that great artist, and eventually led him to immortality. Thereby does our ballet (with a similar tale) become an allegory."

At the Metropolitan *première* the scenery and costumes were those of Alice Halicka. Leading roles were danced by Gisella Caccialanza (the Bride), Leda Anchutina (the Friend), Kathryn Mullowney (the Fairy), William Dollar (the Bridegroom), Annabelle Lyon (the Mother), and Rabana Hasburgh (the Shadow). Stravinsky conducted.

Le Baiser de la fée is entitled a "ballet-allegory" in four scenes. The first tableau is entitled Prologue—The Snowstorm. The curtain rises on a stage that is almost dark. Snow is falling. A woman seeks her way, holding a newborn child. The snow comes down more and more heavily—groups of dancers representing snowflakes block her attempts to escape—and she dies of cold. A beautiful fairy, the Ice Maiden, arrives, bends over the baby, kisses him, and disappears. A party of rescuers enters and finds the baby.

In the second tableau, twenty years have passed. The boy, grown into handsome maturity, is to marry a miller's daughter, and the townspeople are celebrating. The boy and the girl dance together, but he soon withdraws. A mysterious woman enters and reads his palm. He is both frightened and attracted; she is the Ice Maiden, though of course he does not know her identity. She leads him away. The third tableau takes place in the interior of the mill, where the Bride is getting ready for her marriage. She dances with her friends, gossips with them. Finally she is alone, waiting for her lover. He comes in; they do not see each other at first, but finally embrace. They dance a *pas de deux;* then she dances alone for him. The Ice Maiden briefly appears and vanishes, scaring the Bride (the boy does not see her). As a group of peasant girls enters, the lovers leave the stage. He returns for a dance and is followed by the Bride, who also dances. All leave except the Groom. A veiled figure enters. He thinks that it is his bride; but she has never looked so lovely, so mysterious, and so distant. In a trance he moves toward her. They dance together, and he finally lifts her veil. It is the Ice Maiden, and she leads him away.

The fourth tableau is an Epilogue. The Bride comes into the room searching for her lover. She cannot find him. Suddenly she sees a vision—the vision of her lover striving to ascend to a summit high in the sky, whence the Ice Maiden looks down on him.

Le Baiser de la fée created much initial excitement among American ballet *aficionados*. George Amberg found a "wonderfully sustained atmosphere of transcendental drama, enhanced by nostalgic charms reminiscent of the early romantic era." Lincoln Kirstein, in his *Blast at Ballet,* called *Baiser* "a touching evocation of the early period of the Romantic ballet of the 1830's. . . . Balanchine recalled the Maryinsky Theatre of his youth, only his choreography was not a reproduction of, but a sophisticated comment on the school of Petipa and Ivanov, turned towards an epoch in the dance fifty years before their time." The critics were enthusiastic. Edwin Denby's comment was representative: "Ballet at its grandest."

The work has never been a permanent part of the repertoire, though it is occasionally revived. The Ballet Russe de Monte Carlo presented *Baiser* on April 10, 1940, with the Halicka sets and costumes, at the Metropolitan Opera House. Alexandra Danilova, André Eglevsky, and Mia Slavenska danced the leading roles. Danilova as the Bride was enchanting. One of the most charming scenes in the ballet is the third tableau, where the Bride is preparing for her marriage. The music is scintillating, and the dancing has equal sparkle. Danilova, always an intensely human dancer, and always herself, made the Bride's role radiate tenderness and longing, and coquetry, too. The coquetry took place with her friends. When the Groom entered, she made it clear that she was a young girl in love; and, with Frederic Franklin as her lover, the scene was irresistible. *Baiser* was seen off and on for several years as performed by the Monte Carlo company.

On November 28, 1950, again with the Halicka sets and scenery, the New York City Ballet Company presented a revival at the City Center of Music and Drama in New York. Tanaquil LeClercq, Nicholas Magallanes, and Maria Tallchief were the principals. One reason why the ballet may not be in the active repertoire is its staging difficulties. Balanchine admits that the final tableau needs a very deep, high stage. This scene has never been satisfactorily worked out. At the early revivals, the Groom, trying to make his way to the Ice Maiden, looked like a fly caught in a particularly sticky spider web. Subsequent performances have provided a modification of this ludicrous sight, but no real solution has been found.

Ballet Imperial

 Although not a regular visitor to the stage, *Ballet Imperial* is one of George Balanchine's strongest works. That it has not achieved more popularity is surprising; far less effective ballets are constantly revived. And, one notes with some puzzlement, when *Ballet Imperial* is brought back for an odd performance here or there, it is always well received by audiences.

The "Imperial" part of the title suggests the Imperial Ballet of pre-war Russia. Balanchine designed the ballet, which he completed in 1941, as a tribute to Marius Petipa and Peter Ilyich Tchaikovsky. The ballet is set to Tchaikovsky's Piano Concerto in G, his second, a piece of music that seldom turns up in the concert hall (for the same perplexing reason that the ballet itself seldom turns up). The G major Concerto, though possibly more difficult, is not as flashy as the immensely popu-

39

lar Concerto in B flat minor, but it is more subtle, equally as melodious, and has some brilliantly conceived sections. Like many Tchaikovsky works, it engages in an uneasy flirtation with the classical sonata form and, academically speaking, has its failings. But the music is music of genius, and one can forget that sometimes it does not proceed by the rules.

As for the tribute to Marius Petipa, the famous Russian choreographer who was largely responsible for *Swan Lake* and *Sleeping Beauty,* Balanchine above all active choreographers has the right to act as master of ceremonies. For Balanchine grew up in the Imperial School of Ballet in St. Petersburg, and is imbued with the Petipa tradition. There always has been a strong classic strain in Balanchine, and throughout his career he has been able, in such works as *Ballet Imperial* and *Theme and Variations,* to re-create the classic Russian school of choreography as has no other contemporary.

Ballet Imperial is virtually plotless, though Balanchine, as so often elsewhere, introduces a love theme into the slow movement. For the most part, *Ballet Imperial* is pure and simple dance—classic Russian ballet, with plenty of opportunities for virtuosity, in a choreographic language peculiar to Balanchine. Like every creator, Balanchine has his fingerprints. He is very fond of certain groupings; he features many academic types of movement; his technical vocabulary is unmistakable; and he likes to use small groups in entwining patterns.

Ballet Imperial has three movements, one for each movement of the Tchaikovsky concerto. The first movement, *allegro brillante,* presents the intricate evolutions of eight couples, eight girls, and two soloists, one of them the ballerina, who enters and dances to a cadenza by the solo piano. Two male dancers later join the ensemble, and one of the high spots of the movement is a *pas de trois* by the ballerina and the men.

The second movement is *andante non troppo.* Here a slight story line is indicated. The substance of the movement is a lyrical encounter between the ballerina and her partner, both of whom dance against a small group of eight girls. The partner pleads his love to the ballerina. At first the course of his love is not smooth, but by the time the movement is over he is her cavalier.

The third movement, *allegro con fuoco,* is brilliant and objective, with many intricate patterns, and with the figures of the ballerina and her cavalier set against the busy action. All the regal splendor of the Imperial Russian Ballet is suggested here, though in a language far more complex than Petipa or anybody else in his period would have dared to attempt.

Ballet Imperial received its first performance by the American Ballet at the Hunter College Playhouse, New York, on May 27, 1941. The leading roles were danced by Marie-Jeanne, Gisella Caccialanza, and William Dollar. In the revival by the Ballet Russe de Monte Carlo at the City Center of Music and Drama, New York, on February 20, 1945, the leading roles were taken by Mary Ellen Moylan, Maria Tallchief, and Nicholas Magallanes. Scenery and costumes were by Mstislav Dobujinsky; they were a spectacular attempt to convey the flavor of the Imperial period. This was one of Moylan's best roles. She had exactly the regal quality required, and she has hardly ever equaled the brilliance she displayed here. From her entrance in the opening movement she took command of the stage; and at the end, when she was carried high on the shoulders of her partner, she was in all truth a queen. *Ballet Imperial* demands no less.

In 1950 Balanchine went to London to stage the work for Sadler's Wells. The *première* took place on April 5 at the Royal Opera House. New scenery and costumes were designed by Eugene Berman. Margot Fonteyn, Beryl Grey, and Michael Somes danced the leading roles.

Billy the Kid

There never was any doubt at all, from the moment of its Chicago *première* in 1938, that *Billy the Kid* would be a permanent repertoire item. A hit, a palpable hit. In those years, too, Americana was very much in the air. The big five of American music —Roy Harris, Aaron Copland, Walter Piston, William Schuman, and Samuel Barber—were going to be the nucleus of a school of composition that would raise America to unprecedented heights. Artists like Marsh and Groth were putting on canvas unmistakably down-to-earth American material. And when the American choreographer, Eugene Loring, handled a piece of American folklore like *Billy the Kid,* to a ballet libretto by the American Lincoln Kirstein, to a peculiarly American score by Aaron Copland—well, everybody just *knew* that a vital new philosophy of American dance was on the scene and would develop.

But it did not develop—not in the expected direction, anyway. That does not detract from *Billy,* which is the first important American ballet and remains a remarkably convincing work.

"Billy the Kid" was the name given to one William Bonney, a Western gunman who was born in Brooklyn. Much ink has been spilled over him. Some have called him a cruel, vicious killer, who shot his first man when he was twelve and continued killing cold-bloodedly until Pat Garrett caught up with him in 1880. Others have called him a crazy, mixed-up kid who really had a heart of gold (and twenty-one certified killings) underneath that baby face. Anyway, Billy the Kid has passed into the American *mythos.*

Loring took the sentimental view of Billy. His ballet is full of symbolism, and an opening episode tries to explain what made Billy act the way he did. Many critics have objected to some of the detail in *Billy the Kid,* calling sections false and psychologically unconvincing. Yet as a whole, the ballet—and there is no disagreement on this—manages to convey a picture and a feeling of the post-Civil War West, the frontier, the surge of the settlers, and the inexorable progress of the people.

Copland's fine score helps enormously. The composer liberally used authentic Western and cowboy melodies, putting them through the Copland wringer until they came out transmogrified. It is one of his most supple and evocative pieces of music, superbly scored, and its degree of realism perfectly matches Loring's realistic approach.

The ballet's one act is in several scenes. As the curtain goes up, a cowboy is seen. He is Pat Garrett, who symbolizes the pioneer spirit of the frontier. He is facing the West; and as he breaks the path, others follow. We see the stage begin to fill with people, all pushing forward with determination. Loring skillfully has used movements suggestive of men on horseback. With the mood established, there is a blackout. The next scene takes place in a bustling frontier town. Cowboys, ladies, and strollers march by. A young boy and his mother come forward. He is Billy. Two men get into an argument, guns are pulled, and a wild bullet hits Billy's mother. Billy stands horrified for a moment, then pulls out a knife and in a frenzy stabs the killer. The killer, a Mexican, is named Alias in the ballet, and he figures throughout as a Nemesis who crops up in various guises and finally helps kill the Kid.

A desert scene follows. Billy the Kid comes on, no longer a callow youngster, but a sinuous, dangerous-looking man. He practices his gunplay with lithe motions. Three men arrive to hunt him down. He crouches, hides, fires. The leader falls dead. The Kid executes a little dance of triumph. Another blackout. In the next scene Billy the Kid and Pat Garrett, the sheriff, are playing cards. Pat catches Billy cheating. They argue, and Pat angrily rides off, only to return with a posse. A gun battle between the forces of Garrett and Billy the Kid ensues, and Billy is captured. He is carried off to jail. A celebration follows, during which Billy's girl, a Mexican, searches for him. Blackout.

Billy the Kid is in jail, and Alias is his jailer. In an elaborate sequence, Billy manages to get the jailer's gun and shoots him dead. After a blackout we are again in the desert. Billy is being pursued. Alias, now turning up as an Indian guide, leads him to a hiding place. Dead tired, Billy falls asleep. In a dream he sees his girl. He dances with her (a *pas de deux* that could almost be right out of a classical ballet). He goes back to sleep. Pat Garrett enters, brought by Alias. Billy wakes, startled, grabs his gun. *"¿Quién es?"* he calls out. Hearing nothing, he is reassured and lights a cigarette. The light is all that Pat Garrett needs. One shot rings out, and Billy is dead. In a bit of symbolism, a group of mourning Mexican women enters and laments the passing of Billy.

The Epilogue is a continuation of the Prologue. Pat Garrett leads a group of pioneers Westward.

Loring choreographed the work for the appropriately named Ballet Caravan, and it received its *première* at the Chicago Civic Opera House on October 16, 1938. Loring himself danced the title role. Others in the cast were Marie-Jeanne as the Mother and Sweetheart, Lew Christensen as Pat Garrett, and

Todd Bolender as Alias. Jared French was responsible for the scenery and costumes. In the Ballet Theatre revival, at the Chicago Civic Opera House on December 8, 1940, Loring again danced Billy. Loring also was the dancer in the New York presentation at the Majestic Theatre the following February 13. Others in the cast were Alicia Alonso, Richard Reed, and David Nillo. Ballet Theatre has intermittently revived the ballet since then in a version directed by Michael Kidd, generally with John Kriza as Billy. Copland's score, incidentally, was played on two pianos for the Ballet Caravan presentations in Chicago; he orchestrated it for Ballet Theatre.

Lincoln Kirstein had some pertinent things to say about *Billy the Kid* in his *Blast at Ballet:* "Instead of taking a picturesque cowboy legend and making it the tragedy of an individualistic, romantic desperado, *à la* early 'Western' serial movies [What does Kirstein mean, "early" Westerns? Go to any movie house today.] . . . which would have been the obvious thing to do, we saw the Kid's life as only a fragmentary, if symbolic, incident in the expansion of our vast frontier." Kirstein and Loring fully accomplished what they set out to do. There is nothing of the cowboy-movie treatment about *Billy the Kid,* which is authentic art in choreographic terms.

The details were carefully worked out. As an example, when Billy fires at a victim, he aims directly at the target and then executes a double turn in air symbolizing the flying bullet and the tension with which it has been released. When the victim falls, at the end of the double turn, Billy ends with a wicked kick. These movements are strong and meaningful. The scene of the gun battle, in which Billy, surrounded by two lines of fire, emerges alive, is also a dynamic piece of choreography. Form and design are present, and the action never degenerates into a rough and tumble mob scene. Much of the action is suggested rather than graphically depicted. Billy shades his eyes: he is in hiding; the men whirl about: they are shooting.

Loring himself was one of the best interpreters of the title role, to which he gave some nuances that have never been duplicated. After a killing, when he would strut in triumph with his back to the audience, he had a shoulder movement that actually sneered at the world, a movement far more expressive than anything he might have done with facial expression. Nobody else has achieved a comparable identification with the role, although there is little to complain about in the performances that John Kriza has given in recent years. His transformation from boy to tough killer is complete. He also has the athletic quality one expects from a desperado. Nothing of the esthete mars his dancing here. Marie-Jeanne, one of the shining lights of the American Ballet School in the Ballet Caravan days of the late thirties, was stunning in the role of the Sweetheart, which she created. Her style of dancing emphasized sharp, almost piercing gestures supported by a first-class technique. Annabelle Lyon brought more warmth and a softer quality to her interpretation. Alicia Alonso has provided the most touching characterization of the role. She seemed to be able to encompass the remoteness of a dream and the vitality of a warm, tender woman. Many dancers have danced the role well, but Alonso offered an extra dimension that made her Sweetheart unique. During Ballet Theatre's fifteenth anniversary season, Lupe Serrano did interesting work in the role. Although she suggested an exceedingly gifted dancer still in the formative stage, her approach was closer to that of Alonso than that of any dancer who has recently taken the part.

Bluebeard

It can be said that Fokine's creative career came to an end with *Bluebeard,* choreographed in 1941. He was to invent two more ballets, *Russian Soldier,* set to Prokofiev's *Lt. Kijé,* which received its *première* just four months before his death on August 22, 1942, and *Helen of Troy,* which had a single performance in Mexico City shortly after his death. But *Russian Soldier* was one of Fokine's least successful ballets, and there is little reason to believe that it ever will be restored to the repertoire. *Helen of Troy* was completely revised by Lichine.

Bluebeard, on the other hand, has never been out of the repertoire since its *première.* Audiences love it. It has humor, brilliance, and the constant goings-on of a three-ring circus. Fokine, in conceiving it, must have been inspired by the particular abilities of the great dancers he had at his

47

disposal, and he tailored each role to fit. Complex as the ballet is, however, its design is clear, and it could have been choreographed only by a master. In many respects *Bluebeard* is easy to underestimate. Because it is gay and lighthearted, many people watch it for its surface effects, missing the subtleties. *Bluebeard* should never be staged by a company unaware of Fokine's theories, for it can degenerate into long-drawn-out slapstick redeemed only by a few brilliant solos.

As Fokine conceived the ballet, every gesture and every step has a bearing on the dramatic line. *Bluebeard* must not be played for laughs; the laughs are there, and will come. Fokine never was interested in virtuosity for its own sake. In *Bluebeard* even a series of brilliant *fouetées* is employed to further an idea. Perhaps the dancer is intending to convey rage or anger. He is not filling in some empty measures to draw applause.

Fokine very seldom dealt with comedy. He intended *Bluebeard* as a *ballet-bouffe*—the choreographic equivalent of an Offenbach *opéra-bouffe*. He went to Offenbach for his idea, too. On February 5, 1866, Paris had seen the performance of a new Offenbach operetta, *Barbe-bleu (Bluebeard)*. It was a huge success. Meilhac and Halévy, the librettists, gleefully aided and abetted by the composer, had burlesqued the legend of Bluebeard. In his fine biography of Offenbach, Siegfried Kracauer points out the strong undercurrent of democratic feeling in the libretto. Those feelings "were expressed in the part played by Hortense Schneider—that of Boulotte, a simple peasant girl, whose unceremonious, almost rebellious attitude to King Bobèche shocked the court very greatly. . . . Bluebeard himself went so far as to assert that by his association with Boulotte he was introducing a new era in which 'palace and cottage' were united and made indistinguishable. Side by side with all this, and underlining it, is a satire on court life, the gay impudence of which was such that it almost led one to assume that such a thing as a court could only really exist in fairy stories. . . . In addition to this witty and epigrammatic tune ('A courtier must bow his shoulders') there were others which showed that it was merely second nature to Offenbach to ridicule the diabolical nature of Bluebeard. Nothing pleased him better than poisons that were really sugared water and murdered women who cheerfully survived."

All of this satire is in Fokine's ballet; and if the democratic tendencies mentioned by Kracauer are not much in evidence, that is because 1941 was a long way from 1866. In the first prologue, the old and decrepit King Bobiche comes in carrying an infant. The baby's name is Hermilia, and because she is not a boy she must be exiled. Bobiche and Count Oscar, his chancellor, put a necklace around her and place her in a basket that is to be floated on the river. The second prologue serves to introduce Count Bluebeard, a man who likes his women and takes them where he finds them. His beard is indeed blue—a bright, almost eye-blinding blue. He embraces all of the women in sight, disposes of four wives one after the other, and poisons the fifth. In this he is helped by his retainer, Popoloni.

The first act brings us to the palace of King Bobiche. Eighteen years have passed. Queen Clementine has an *amour* with one of her pages. The King, discovering them in a compromising position, orders the page hanged. Bobiche, who apparently spends his life spying on the Queen—and with good reason— catches her in several additional love affairs. Off go the miscreants to be hanged. Longing for his daughter, Bobiche orders his kingdom to be searched until she is found.

The first interlude follows. Oscar is on his way to seek the princess. He encounters the five lovers of the Queen on their way to be hanged. For a small consideration—all the money they have on them—Oscar releases them. They go their happy way and he goes his, considerably richer.

Act II takes place in the countryside. Peasants are dancing, and one of them is Floretta, really Hermilia. And with whom is she dancing? Prince Sapphire, who is disguised as a peasant. Boulotte enters, wildly jealous. She wants the prince. At that moment Popoloni enters, bringing the news that Bluebeard seeks a new wife. Bluebeard comes in and examines the live stock with a bored air. When his eye lights on Boulotte, his boredom disappears, and the balletic equivalent of smoke shoots from his ears. He selects her, and she is more than willing. They go off. Oscar and Popoloni engage in conversation. Oscar's eye lights on Floretta, and when he sees her necklace, he realizes that he has found Hermilia.

In the short second interlude, Bluebeard and Boulotte run into Oscar and Hermilia. One look is enough for Bluebeard. He makes up his mind to add Hermilia to his collection.

Act III takes place in a cellar in Bluebeard's castle. Popoloni is engaging in chemical experiments. Vaults are seen, one for each of Bluebeard's earlier wives, a sixth all ready to receive a new customer. Bluebeard enters and orders the death of Boulotte. She herself wanders in and immediately realizes what is brewing. She begs for pity and even tries to make love to old Popoloni, who, by a ruse, poisons her. Both Popoloni and Bluebeard make elaborate manifestations of grief. Bluebeard gallops off in search of Hermilia. But it turns out that Popoloni is really too soft-hearted to poison anybody: he brings Boulotte back to life. What is more, he has not allowed any of Bluebeard's previous wives to die. The graves open and out they come, eager to meet Boulotte.

The third interlude, sometimes omitted, brings Bluebeard to the ghosts of his supposedly murdered wives. They haunt him and he is overcome with guilt.

The fourth and last act is back at the court of King Bobiche. He and the Queen greet Hermilia. She looks unhappy; she misses Prince Sapphire, whom she wants to marry. But she does not know his name or that he is a prince; and when King Bobiche indicates that she is to marry a certain Prince Sapphire, she storms furiously about. Prince Sapphire enters. They look upon one another and fall into each other's arms. General happiness. In storms Bluebeard, demanding Hermilia—or else. He brings a rough crew with him to back up his demands. Bluebeard and Sapphire duel, and by an underhand trick Bluebeard stabs his opponent in the back. Things look bad for Hermilia, and also for King Bobiche, who is cowering behind his throne. This is the moment that Popoloni picks to confront Bluebeard with all his wives. The odds are too great for Bluebeard, who flees. They catch up with him and give him a trouncing. Then who returns but Queen Clementine's lovers? King Bobiche sees his chance. He dissolves all of Bluebeard's marriages and pairs the wives with the former lovers of his own Queen. Popoloni brings Sapphire back to life. Bluebeard decides to remarry Boulotte.

Bluebeard received its world *première* by Ballet Theatre at the Palacio de Bellas Artes, Mexico City, on October 27, 1941. It was repeated in New York on November 12 of the same year, with substantially the same cast, at the Forty-fourth Street Theatre. And what a cast! Consider: Anton Dolin (Bluebeard), Alicia Markova (Hermilia), Irina Baronova (Boulotte), George Skibine (Sapphire), Antony Tudor (Bobiche), Lucia Chase (Clementine). Others in the cast were Miriam Golden, Jeannette Lauret, Nora Kaye, Rosella Hightower, and Maria Karnilova (Bluebeard's wives), and, as the Queen's lovers, Dimitri Romanoff, Donald Saddler, Annabelle Lyon, Jerome Robbins, and Hugh Laing. One has to go back to Diaghilev's days to encounter another such star-studded assemblage. With so many great dancers, all in their prime (though Kaye, Hightower, and Robbins had not yet achieved any roles of solo importance), *Bluebeard* was bound to make an impression. One remembers the audience at the New York *première* goggling at the stage as though the crown jewels were on exhibition. Dolin swaggered, his blue beard waving lecherously in the air. Baronova was outstanding. Her dance in the vault was violent, yet showed a consistent purity of line and supreme execution. In the scene where Hermilia is first seen dancing with Prince Sapphire, Baronova's earthy, physical tantrums as she endeavored to win Sapphire's attention, were both dance and comedy of high order, and in addition provided a magnificent foil to Markova's detached, delicate, and lyric dancing. Skibine made the handsomest and most attentive of cavaliers. The sumptuous sets and costumes by Marcel Vertès also attracted much favorable comment.

But dancers alone do not make a ballet, and the fact that *Bluebeard* has survived is owing to Fokine. And if the plot of the ballet seems remarkably silly on paper, it works beautifully on stage. Even if an equivalent group of dancers may never again be assembled for it.

51

Bourrée fantasque

In 1932 George Balanchine created a ballet named *Cotillon*. Set to music by Chabrier, it was a popular repertory item for a while before it disappeared. It should be revived; there are far worse ballets in the repertoire. Balanchine probably retained a fond memory of the *Cotillon* score and of its composer, for his *Bourrée fantasque* (1949) not only was set to a Chabrier score, but also was named after one of his piano pieces.

Chabrier is an underestimated composer who still lacks the honor of a definitive study in English. Born in 1841, he was about forty years old before he left a civil service position to concentrate on music. The brilliant *España* of 1883 made him famous, but *España* is among the least typical of his works, and certainly not comparable in artistic worth to *L'Étoile* and *Une Education manquée* (a pair of stage works), or the *Pièces pittoresques* for piano. Chabrier was one of the great musical wits and one of the outstanding iconoclasts. Long before *les six* in Paris were fooling around with music-hall tunes and other brash ideas, Chabrier had set similar ideas on paper.

Balanchine selected four Chabrier pieces for his ballet. The *Marche joyeuse* serves as an overture. Then come the *Bourrée fantasque*, the Interlude from the opera *Gwendolyn* (which Balanchine calls "Prelude"), and the *Fête polonaise*. The ballet is in one act and three parts.

Bourrée fantasque is plotless, though each of the three sections has its own mood and treatment that attempt an approximation of the musical mood of the Chabrier pieces. After the overture the curtain rises to reveal several couples, who dance in ensemble. They retire to watch a *pas de quatre* danced by four girls. A tall girl and a short boy engage in something of a burlesque dance. More ensemble work, mixed with comedy, follows. The tall girl and the short boy return for more high jinks, and the rest of the company joins in.

The second movement, Prelude, is a long, lyric duet danced by a ballerina and her partner against the movements of eight girls. Some intricate patterns are employed. As in many of the Balanchine slow movements, one senses a slight story line, in which the partner seeks the ballerina, who dances in a maze formed by the supporting cast. In this instance, the lovers are not united, but walk off separately.

The concluding *Fête polonaise* is a lively, exhibitionistic movement in which the *corps de ballet*, a ballerina, and her partner indulge in effective athletics. Near the end of the ballet all of the participants from the preceding movements join the ensemble, and the work concludes with a typical Balanchine grand finale.

Bourrée fantasque received its first performance by the New York City Ballet Company at the New York City Center of Music and Drama on December 1, 1949. The principal dancers were Tanaquil LeClercq and Jerome Robbins; Maria Tallchief and Nicholas Magallanes; and Janet Reed and Herbert Bliss. The chic costumes were by Karinska.

After the first night there was general agreement that Balanchine had scored another success. The ballet obviously was not conceived as an earth-shattering masterpiece; it is full of fun and good spirits. A few dissenters, however, complained of the juxtaposition of slapstick and romantic elements. They pointed out with a certain justice that humor in ballet is a frail and precarious thing; that it is easy to get laughs from an audience by an obvious distortion of ballet steps, which takes no great ingenuity. They were referring, specifically, to the first movement of *Bourrée fantasque,* in which Tanaquil LeClercq and Jerome Robbins (later Todd Bolender) are seen in a rather grotesque burlesque on the formal *pas de deux.* Another disturbing element was the second movement. Having burlesqued the *pas de deux,* Balanchine follows it with a serious duet, extremely romantic in mood, a change that calls for an adjustment that some observers find difficult to make.

But most audiences find that *Bourrée fantasque* is not to be taken so seriously; and the sensational lifts in the last movement make up for some previous dull spots. In these lifts, Herbert Bliss made Janet Reed seem to sail through the air right over the orchestra; the ballerina's foot was pointed at the audience, and the dancers at times approached perilously close to the footlights. The ballet has remained popular ever since its *première.*

The Cage

Stravinsky's Concerto in D, composed in
1946, is a piece of absolute music for string
orchestra. It was not originally intended as
a ballet, but Jerome Robbins discovered
that it suited his purpose very well for *The
Cage,* and obtained permission to use it.

The central idea behind *The Cage* is the
act of the female of the species killing and
eating the male. It is well known that certain species of female spiders make short
work of their spouses (if spiders have
spouses) after the wedding ceremony is
over. The setting of *The Cage,* with long
strands enveloping the stage, suggests an
arachnid habitat. As the ballet develops,
one gets the idea that the central theme can
be expanded; that perhaps Robbins is using the spider to symbolize all womanhood.
What with concepts like Philip Wylie's
"momism" in the air, and the overwhelming preponderance of brilliant, well-

groomed perfect women over the poor, bumbling, foot-in-the-bucket male on any TV show you may dial, such an extension of the ballet is perhaps not as ridiculous as it might appear.

When the curtain rises on *The Cage,* the spiderlike strands initiate an unearthly, oppressive feeling. A group of women surrounds the Queen of the tribe. She gives birth to the Novice. Members of the tribe dance; so does the Queen. They look at the Novice, who moves, blinks at the light, and stirs. She starts to move upward, testing her legs and her talons. A man enters and seizes her, but she wrests herself away and kills him. This is her first blood, and she exults. Members of the tribe congratulate her.

Suddenly the tribe is startled. The members scuttle away. The Novice is caught by a male attacker. She fights him, but he is stronger; she feels strange impulses stirring, and the fight turns into a love duet. He is going to be the father of her children, and he consummates the act of love. Members of the tribe enter and see the two. The man tries to escape, but they swarm over him. The Novice is soon in the forefront of the attack. As the women hold him tight, the Novice drives her talons into his heart, then strangles him between her knees. The curtain comes down on the triumphant, malevolent figures of the Novice and her Queen.

The Cage received its *première* at the New York City Center of Music and Drama on June 10, 1951. The leading dancers in the New York City Ballet Company cast were Nora Kaye (the Novice), Yvonne Mounsey (the Queen), Michael Maule (the first Intruder), and Nicholas Magallanes (the second Intruder). The set was by Jean Rosenthal; costumes were by Ruth Sobotka.

Whatever the artistic merits of *The Cage,* there is no denying its theatrical effectiveness. It builds to a superb and exciting climax; its sharp, unconventional movements are imaginative; and as the Novice, Nora Kaye brought a degree of tension and sheer hatred which only a great actress could have achieved. Her angular motions at birth, with her hands gripping the air, were literally shocking; and her transformation, after the love scene, into an instrument of death was brilliantly carried off. Despite some critical mumblings about the symbolism of *The Cage* and its "artiness," not to mention its actual subject matter, the ballet has been a prominent part of the New York City Ballet's repertoire since its *première*.

Cakewalk

The cakewalk is a typically American dance with a typically American name. It probably is of Negro origin, and it reached the height of its popularity in the latter half of the nineteenth century. Its name is said to have been derived from the custom of giving a piece of pastry as a prize for the most intricate steps performed. Minstrel and vaudeville shows featured the strutting cakewalk, and the French were fascinated enough by the dance to adopt it into their reviews and musical comedies.

Cakewalk takes the old minstrel shows as a point of departure. The genesis of the ballet occurred during the 1946–7 Ballet Society season. At that time Ballet Society had presented a work called *Blackface,* with choreography by Lew Christensen to a score by Carter Harman. *Blackface* was not a success, and Robert Drew's *décor* and costumes were lying unused in a warehouse when the New York City Ballet Company decided to create a ballet around the old props. *Cakewalk* was the result. Except for the scenery and costumes, it had nothing to do with *Blackface*. Ruthanna Boris was the new choreographer, and a score was provided by Hershy Kay, who orchestrated music by Louis Moreau Gottschalk. Leading dancers at the *première,* on June 12, 1951, at the New York City Center of Music and Drama, were Janet Reed, Patricia Wilde, Yvonne Mounsey, Herbert Bliss, Frank Hobi, Tanaquil LeClercq, and Beatrice Tompkins.

The minstrel show used to be a typically American entertainment, with singers in blackface, one or more interlocutors, comedians, topical jokes and gags, dancing, magic acts, and singing. *Cakewalk* tries to re-create its spirit. A flossy entrance is made by the dancers in the Grand Introductory Walkaround. All move to their seats. A girl dances a Pathetic Ballad, in which the choreographer, as elsewhere, has burlesqued some of the old American dances. Then the Interlocutor executes his Sleight of Feet, a brilliant rapid dance that leaves him breathless. Two girls dressed as end men follow with a specialty dance called Perpendicular Points. They are succeeded by a girl dancing a Freebee to the accompaniment of clapping hands. The entire company joins in.

This ends the first of the three sections of the ballet. Part II introduces Louis the Illusionist and his two assistants. They invoke, in turn, Venus and the three Graces; a wild pony; Hortense (Queen of the Swamp Lilies); and Harolde (the poet). Part III presents the entire company in a vigorous, catchy cakewalk.

The ballet is a humorous evocation of a vanished period in American life. Ruthanna Boris, a clever choreographer, is adept with props, and she uses several for lighthearted gags that come off well. Fortunately, there also is a good deal of honest dancing, with Frank Hobi's Sleight of Feet and Patricia Wilde's Wild Pony dances taking honors for exciting virtuosity. Boris's extensive ballet background is very much in evidence all through *Cakewalk*. She has a comprehensive ballet vocabulary that she uses freely in ingenious combinations of steps which always flow easily. She has a decided penchant for small, feminine types of combinations with many beats and *pas de bourrées* and uses them more frequently than large broad movements.

It was a brilliant idea to use music by Gottschalk. Louis Moreau Gottschalk (1829–69) was an American-born pianist-composer who scored a tremendous success concertizing through Europe in the late 1840's. His piano pieces, based on Creole rhythms, also elicited admiration from such European musicians as Berlioz. At the height of his career, Gottschalk returned to America, where he gave an incredible number of concerts. He was our first touring pianist, and he must have been an exceedingly fine one. In public he played only his own compositions, some of which, such as *The Dying Poet,* graced every piano of the nineteenth century from Seattle to Atlanta. He was far in advance of his day when he used American folk material; and even his salon pieces are of interest for their Liszt and Thalberg-derived technical ideas (this was in the 1850's and in 1860's, remember). Hershy Kay's adaptation of the Gottschalk melodies for *Cakewalk* is as slick as a new Cadillac, and has been an important factor in the success of the ballet. ·

Caprichos

Herbert Ross, the choreographer of *Caprichos,* was inspired by a series of commentaries which Goya wrote for his *Caprichos,* a group of some seventy etchings under which the artist added pithy comments. One section of the *Caprichos* deals with human foibles, another with allegorical monsters.

Ross has drawn upon four unrelated etchings for his ballet. The first is named *Ya tienen asiento* ("These good girls have seats enough and nothing better to do with them than carry them on their heads"). No. 2 is *No te escaparás* ("No one ever escapes who wants to be caught"). No. 3 is *Tantalus* ("If he were more gallant and less of a bore, she would come to life again"). The last is *No hubo remedio* ("They are determined to kill this saintly woman. After judgment had been pronounced against her, she is dragged through the streets in triumph.

She has indeed deserved a triumph, but if they do it to shame her, they are wasting time. No one can shame her who has nothing to be ashamed of").

Goya was one of the great naturalists and one of the bitterest of artists. Ross has attempted to match in his choreography the lusty quality of the etchings. To accompany the ballet he chose Béla Bartók's *Contrasts* for piano, violin, and clarinet. His choreography is not, in the accepted sense, a ballet; it is rather a quartet of charades, almost a literal translation of the Goya scenes.

Ya tienen asiento presents two rather sluttish, even vicious, girls who dance around the stage, each with a stool. They seem to thrive on the misfortunes that others experience, and they form the link connecting the three otherwise disconnected episodes. In *No te escaparás* two men dance with a woman, using a pseudo-Spanish dance style, and finally seduce her. The two girls watch avidly. *Tantalus* is the most inventive of the episodes. A man mourns his dead wife. Suddenly she falls from nowhere into his arms. He attempts to bring her back to life, to dance with her, but she remains limp. In disgust he carries her off. This strange, weird *pas de deux,* in which the woman is a dead weight, ends in just the ghoulish way the choreographer had anticipated. *No hubo remedio* describes the burning at the stake of a saintly woman. The picture evoked is very literal, very cruel, and in its way, powerful. As an epilogue, a voice, heard through an amplifying system, calls out: *"El sueño de la razón produce monstruos"* ("The dream of reason produces monsters").

Caprichos was first presented by the Choreographer's Workshop at the Hunter College Playhouse, New York, on January 29, 1950. Ballet Theatre took the work into its repertoire at the Center Theatre, New York, on April 26, 1950. Helene Pons designed the costumes. In the Ballet Theatre cast were Charlyne Baker and Jenny Workman (*Ya tienen asiento*), Nana Gollner, Eric Braun, and Peter Gladke (*No te escaparás*), John Kriza and Ruth Anne Koesun (*Tantalus*), and Mary Burr, Jack Beaber, Jimmy Hicks, Vernon Lusby, and Ralph McWilliams (*No hubo remedio*). The musicians in the Bartók piece were Broadus Earle (violin), Joseph Levine (piano), and Alfred Gallodoro (clarinet).

This was Herbert Ross's second ballet. His first, not in the repertoire, had been a dance setting for a Paul White arrangement of sea chanties. Born in 1926, Ross entered the ballet world by way of the Broadway musical stage. He participated as a dancer, occasionally as an actor-dancer, in such hits as *Bloomer Girl, Beggars' Holiday, Look Ma, I'm Dancin'!* and *Inside U.S.A.* He has also choreographed dances for night-club acts and has written articles on dancing and ballet for publications here and abroad.

Ross later created another work for Ballet Theatre, *The Thief Who Loved a Ghost,* with sets and costumes by John Ward. This ballet was short-lived; it was closer to a dance-play than to a ballet, but it lacked the vitalizing force to make either good theater or good ballet.

Cirque de deux

How to translate "Circus for Two"? This is a tiny, clever ballet, the first that Ruthanna Boris composed. This young American choreographer, a member of the American Ballet in 1935, went on to dance leading roles in the ballets prepared for Metropolitan Opera productions during the short alliance between the opera house and the American Ballet. She then became a soloist with the Ballet Russe de Monte Carlo, took time out to appear in some Broadway shows, and finally formed a small dance group that has toured America.

Cirque de deux, created for the Ballet Russe de Monte Carlo, received its *première* at the New York City Center of Music and Drama on September 10, 1947. *Décor* and costumes were by Robert Davison. The programming was done in a manner designed to convey the flavor and intent of the ballet. It was *Cirque de deux,*

PRESENTING Miss Ruthanna Boris and Mr. Leon Danielian, AS-SISTED BY Miss Patricia Wilde and Mr. Frank Hobi.

The ballet has no specific story. The music consists of excerpts from the Walpurgis Night scene of Gounod's *Faust*. To many people this music has extra-musical associations, which was precisely why Boris chose it. "Go to any circus," she has written to the author of this book; "and you will find the trapeze artists swinging with *Walpurgis Night* as their background." And thus this saucy circus ballet was composed, as Boris says, "not *to* the music, but *on* the music. The ballet is simply a presentation—in the sense that any *pas de deux* is a presentation—of two 'stars,' male and female; a presentation of grace, agility, technique, and the personalities themselves. The two Pages, assisting, can be likened to the present and intangible aura of 'more glamorous are they who are served,' made tangible and physical. The Pages also, in a way, represent the audience, having their own definite functions within the form of the performance, but making their own personal observations *about* the performance when and where they have the opportunity.

"The whole ballet," Boris states, "is couched in circus terms, by means of suggestions and flavor. It is all intended as a 'romp,' in a strictly balletic sense, the humor being woven into the actual technique of dancing and, indeed, deriving its being from that very source, so that the audience may take from it as much or as little as they care to absorb. Like any communication, the ballet may mean something a little different to each one."

One of the really funny things about *Cirque de deux* is its use of a small rolling platform in an adagio for the ballerina. In classical dancing the partner hovers solicitously around the ballerina, supporting her, lifting her, helping her to turn. In the *pas de deux* of this ballet, the ballerina mounts the platform, strikes an attitude, and the partner slowly *wheels* her around while she is holding the attitude as beautifully as she can. It is all a spoof, gently and delicately done, with wit and flavor. The public has always liked it. In its way it is a classical *pas de deux*, tongue-in-cheek but not burlesque, firmly grounded on the traditional ballet vocabulary.

65

Con Amore

Sacred and profane—mostly profane—love
is the subject of *Con Amore,* a ballet that
could readily be subtitled "a romp in three
scenes." Lew Christensen selected three
bubbling Rossini overtures for the score,
and choreographed around it a tongue-in-
cheek plot of delightful incoherence.

The ballet, to a libretto by James Graham-Luhan, was first done at the War
Memorial Opera House, San Francisco, on
March 10, 1953, by the San Francisco Ballet. Principal roles were danced by Sally
Bailey, Nancy Johnson, and Leon Danielian. That company and the New York
City Ballet have an exchange program, and
Con Amore thus came into the latter's
repertoire on June 9, 1953, at the City Center of Music and Drama, New York, with a
cast headed by Sally Bailey, Nancy Johnson, Herbert Bliss, and Jacques d'Amboise.
Scenery and costumes by Esteban Francés

66

were supplied in 1954. *Décor* and costumes for the original production were by James Bodrero.

Certain manifestations of love are displayed in *Con Amore*. Scene 1, set to the Overture to *La Gazza Ladra*, is named "The Amazons and the Thief." A company of Amazons is seen drilling under their Captain and her Lieutenants. Amazons are not supposed to recognize love, and these sturdy females obviously are the cream of their species. But a thief suddenly appears and dances with them. He is a dashing specimen of manhood, and soon their hearts melt. Nobody's heart melts more than the Captain's. She will have him. At least, she wants him, but the thief will not have the love of either her or her companions. He tries to escape. His plight is hopeless, however. No matter where he turns, he is confronted by raised muskets. Will he give in? Not this hero. Defiantly he spurns them and kneels, baring his chest to receive a fusillade. Better death than dishonor. There is a sudden blackout as the Amazons begin to lift their guns.

Scene 2, "The Master's Return," is set to the Overture to *Il Signor Bruschino*. The action is entirely unrelated to that of the preceding scene. A fashionable lady's boudoir is shown. The mistress bids a fond farewell to the master, about to leave on a presumably long trip. Is she sorry to see him depart? We get the idea that she is not entirely prostrated with grief. He marches out. No sooner has he gone than she primps herself, obviously waiting for somebody. Sure enough, a rake knocks at the door. This is not the man she is expecting, and she tries to get rid of him, but he takes out an expensive piece of jewelry. This changes matters considerably. Before he can follow up her change of mood, a knocking is heard (the Rossini score has some "knocking" measures, and the choreographer has taken full advantage of them). The lady pushes the rake into a hiding place and greets the newcomer. He is a sailor, apparently just off the boat from at least a ten-year cruise without the benefit of feminine companionship. He chases her around the room, everything but fire coming from his nostrils. Once more there is a knocking at the door, and the lady pushes him into the hiding place already occupied by the rake. Entrant No. 3 turns out to be a student, nose immersed in a book. He is not especially interested in the lady; love to him is the most academic of subjects. She has to pursue him. The rake and the sailor find this most distasteful. They emerge and maul the young student. The husband picks this moment to return. He enters and looks at them, stunned, as the stage blacks out.

Scene 3 is "A Triumph of Love," danced by the participants of the first two scenes and also by a female Eros, armed with bow and arrow as all good Cupids are. The music is the Overture to *La Scala di Seta*. Eros is the *deus ex machina* of this story. When the blackout lifts, we see the thief preparing to be shot by the Amazons. We also see the husband chasing the three men in his wife's boudoir. There is also some byplay of slapstick nature, in which a forest is denuded of its leaves for camouflage purposes. Eros sets everything right. She shoots her arrows left and right. The thief and the Captain of the Amazons fall in love. The rake and the sailor pair off with the Amazon Lieutenants. Husband and wife are reunited. Which leaves the student —who looks at Eros with a wild surmise, drops his book, and starts chasing her.

The plot is fairly complicated, but Christensen handles it with clarity in a nonchalant, offhand manner. The result is an attractive light ballet without pretensions. The music works nicely with the action; the sets are ingenious; the choreography is charming. What could have been lowdown slapstick has been transformed by Christensen's deft treatment into a popular repertory item. The athleticism of Jacques d'Amboise as the thief has been a major factor in the ballet's success. This young man with the incredible elevation is given every opportunity to stay in the air. He has taken full advantage of it. Janet Reed and Jane Mason have danced charmingly as the Mistress; and Yvonne Mounsey and Patricia Wilde have been effective as the Captain of the Amazons.

Concerto barocco

Concerto barocco is another of those Balanchine works succinctly described in the program as "Classic Ballet." It is set to Bach's Concerto in D minor for Two Violins, and has disturbed some people to whom the music of Bach and other "abstract" composers is sacred and inviolate. Balanchine's attitude is different: he does not feel that he has tampered with the music. Bad music, he thinks, often inspires bad dancing. The corollary is that good music will inspire good dancing. People who come to *Concerto barocco* are interested in the ballet, and the ballet will try to interest them through terms of dance alone. Balanchine has much in common with Stravinsky in his view of the functional relationship between music and dance. To a composer of neo-classic music, the classic, abstract ballet is the purest form of dance; at least, it is so to Stravinsky. And to a creator of neo-classic ballets, classic, abstract music is the perfect medium. No story is told either in music or dance. In both the emphasis is on style, purity, and clarity, whereas a choreographer with a romantic or sensational view toward ballet would ordinarily avoid classical music as too severe for his purposes.

Balanchine sees classical dancing as a counterpoint to classical music, and he thinks that there is no reason why the two should not be juxtaposed, provided that the choreographer refrain from adding a story or otherwise pushing the music beyond its proper limits. The key to the success or non-success of such a procedure is the taste of the choreographer. We have seen what happened, in the thirties, when choreographers happily went through symphonies of Beethoven and Brahms, superimposing nonsensical stories that cheapened and degraded the music to which they were allied. No wonder the musical purists raised a storm, and rightly!

By avoiding any semblance of a story, by concentrating on nothing but movement—movement allied to the movement of music, phrase by phrase—Balanchine has escaped the artistic sins of his predecessors; and Bach's "pure" music comes out allied to "pure" dance. The ideal, of course, is to have music expressly composed for a ballet. Failing that, we must trust to the musicality of a choreographer not to wrench from its emotional and technical context the music he has chosen. A jazzy dance sequence to a Bach score would be vandalism, and this is said knowing full well that Bach availed himself of most of the dance forms current in his day. But the emotional *milieu* of Bach's dance and that of jazz are eternally separated.

In *Concerto barocco* the movements are severely stylized (though they do not lack lyricism) and are tied very closely to the structure of Bach's music. As a new musical strand enters, it is echoed by a new complex on the stage; as the contrapuntal lines unfold, they are graphically spelled out in equivalent choreographic patterns. Balanchine probably did not wish to mirror the music with absolute precision, but there is enough correlation to keep the dancers very close to a choreographic translation of Bach.

Concerto barocco

There are three movements, one for each movement of the Concerto. The first movement, *Vivace,* presents a *corps de ballet* of eight girls against which are placed the two girl soloists (one for each violin of the Concerto). In the second movement, *Largo ma non tanto,* the ballerina and her partner dance with, and in contrast to, the *corps de ballet.* The third movement, *Allegro,* is brisk and energetic, and Balanchine has devised strongly rhythmic steps for it.

Practice clothes are used in the current productions; nothing is present to distract attention from the choreography. With the exception of one series of sensational slide steps executed on a diagonal across the stage by the ballerina and her partner, the choreography is orthodox and of the *danse d'école,* entirely neo-classic, and scrupulously insistent on keeping away from anything that might be construed as doing violence to Bach's ideas.

Concerto barocco was first presented by the American Ballet at the Hunter College Playhouse, New York, on May 29, 1941. Sets and costumes were by Eugene Berman. In the cast as solo dancers were Marie-Jeanne, Mary Jane Shea, and William Dollar. The Ballet Russe de Monte Carlo revived the ballet on September 9, 1945, but did not use the Berman *décor.* This performance was given at the New York City Center of Music and Drama, with Marie-Jeanne, Patricia Wilde, and Nicholas Magallanes in the leading roles. The Berman *décor* was restored when the New York City Ballet Company took *Concerto barocco* into its repertoire on October 11, 1948, at the City Center. Marie-Jeanne, Ruth Gilbert, and Francisco Moncion were the leading dancers. On September 13, 1951, the *décor* was dropped, presumably for good, in favor of practice clothes and a blue cyclorama. The dancers this time were Maria Tallchief, Diana Adams, and Nicholas Magallanes.

All of the dancers who have participated in *Concerto barocco* since its *première* have seemed to be acutely conscious of the respect due Bach and Balanchine. They dance it with severe and unsmiling faces, as though taking part in a religious rite. One has noted with interest, too, how the duo of Maria Tallchief and Diana Adams falls into the work. These two dancers could hardly be less alike. Tallchief is sharp and precise, and works with steel-spring movements; Adams is lyric, willowy, considerably softer. Yet both are such fine artists, so dedicated to the music and Balanchine's treatment of it, that their physical differences seem to disappear. They, like the ensemble, approach *Concerto barocco* as though it were a ritual.

Coppélia
or the Girl with the
Enamel Eyes

 Arthur Michel Saint-Léon (1815–1870), who today is known to the public only by *Coppélia,* was one of the most important dance figures of his day, a highly successful choreographer, an accomplished dancer, and important theorist whose influence was felt in many European centers. He was also a violinist, a fine musician and, to the envy of many young bloods of the Second Empire, for a time the husband of Fanny Cerito, the enchanting ballerina. He was a busy man, traveling from city to city as a guest choreographer; and often he was too busy to choreograph. Instead he would stage one of his old ballets under a new name. He also occupied himself with the problems of dance notation: in 1852, he delivered himself of a treatise on the subject with the blockbusting name of *La Sténochorégraphie.*

Saint-Léon not only designed the choreography of *Coppélia,* one of the oldest ballets to have held a permanent place in the repertoire (its *première* took place at the Paris Opéra on May 25, 1870), but also had an active share in the book. The story was based on a tale by E. T. A. Hoffmann, the German ultra-romanticist who held such sway over his generation. Saint-Léon worked on the plot with Charles Nuitter. The score composed by Léo Delibes turned out to be his ballet masterpiece, just as the choreography was Saint-Léon's finest effort. Part of the great importance that *Coppélia* was to have for future ballet history was its musical contribution, for in this work Delibes showed that a ballet score was not necessarily merely an accompaniment for dancing, but could be an equal partner. Before the Delibes ballets it would have been difficult to isolate a great ballet score. Gluck's *Don Juan* (1761) and Beethoven's *The Creatures of Prometheus* (1801) are among the very few exceptions. The 1841 *Giselle,* for example, is an indestructible ballet, but not even its greatest admirer would go on record as saying that Adolphe Adam composed much more than a hack score for it.

It is interesting to note that the basic theme of *"Der Sandmann,"* the Hoffmann story that Nuitter and Saint-Léon adapted for *Coppélia*—that of a doll coming to life—also found a place in *Les Contes d'Hoffmann,* Offenbach's brilliant opera, in which, in the first act, Hoffmann falls in love with the mechanical doll created by Coppélius.

At the *première* of the ballet a girl in her teens (some authorities give the age as fifteen, others as sixteen) danced the leading role. This was Giuseppina Bozacchi, called in as a replacement when Adele Grantsova, the popular Russian ballerina, found herself unable to be in Paris at the time. Poor Bozacchi, after dancing eighteen performances, was marooned in Paris during the Prussian siege, and died of fever brought on by malnutrition. The following year, Léontine Beaugrand made a name for herself in the role.

A critic named Elias de Rouze reviewed the *première* for the *Revue et Gazette Musicale.* He found Delibes's music *"vive et joli,"* though not always of great originality, but *"plus agréable.*" The music for the second act especially he thought gracious, rhythmic, well orchestrated, elegantly written. "The great success," he continued, "belonged to the Italian dancer Mlle. Bozzacchi [*sic*], a child of sixteen, frolicsome, sprightly, with eloquent eyes, an expressive face, a supple body, with legs of steel. She dances very well. Her points are precise, clean, rapid. . . . She has above all that which ordinarily is not achieved except through age and experience—grace." De Rouze goes on to prophesy a great career for her. "When at the age of sixteen one achieves such a success, one will go far."

The critic of *Le Figaro* also had nice things to say about the music: "a distinguished, piquant and colorful score, excellently orchestrated. . . . It is extremely difficult to write for ballet with a certain amount of artistry, taste, and style. M. Delibes has avoided the commonplace in a piece where it had every right to be encountered." The critic of *Le Menestrel* speaks of Bozacchi, giving her age as fifteen. "The title of child prodigy should be devised for her had it not been abused in so many other cases. Although scarcely fifteen years old, she is already a very skillful dancer. What is better still, in our opinion, is that she is a graceful and witty actress. Add to that a well-proportioned, dainty little body, and that she promises to have the prettiest face in the world. If she fulfills all of her first promises, she will be a power in the profession."

The little Bozacchi must have made an enchanting Swanilda. The role calls for a mixture of childishness, naïveté, flirtatious love, and mock-heroic dramatics. Swanilda is an utterly adorable, empty-headed butterfly.

As conceived by its creators and generally done today, *Coppélia* has two acts and three scenes. The curtain rises on a scene in a small European town several hundred years ago. Dr. Coppélius comes out of his house, looks at a young woman who is reading a book on his balcony, and goes back inside. Swanilda enters, looks up at the girl, who is called Coppélia, engrossed in the book, tries to attract her attention, but gets no reply. Swanilda becomes definitely annoyed. She then watches her lover, Franz, come down the street and blow a kiss at the girl.

Now Swanilda is more than annoyed. She confronts Franz and accuses him of being faithless. Much byplay, tears, stamping of feet. Franz tries to comfort her, assuring her that nobody else has taken his heart. Swanilda refuses to listen. She leaves as a group of young people enter, but returns when all dance a mazurka, in which she participates, though she still is angry at Franz.

The burgomaster enters. He tells them that at a celebration the following day, the lord of the manor will present dowries to any couples who will get married at that time. He then asks Swanilda directly if she will marry Franz. There follows some byplay with an ear of wheat, in accord with an old European belief that the grain will supply the answer as to whether a lover is faithful. Swanilda claims that the ear of wheat is silent; she breaks off her engagement to Franz. He leaves angrily. Everybody dances in a czardas. Night comes on, and all leave the stage. Dr. Coppélius comes out, ostentatiously locking his door. He gets mixed up with a boisterous band of young people and drops the key. The stage is empty again. Swanilda and some friends enter, and she finds the key. What a chance to discover the identity of the literary young lady who lives in the house! The girls disappear into the house. Enter Franz, lugging a long ladder. Because Swanilda has thrown him over, he is going to try to meet Coppélia, the other young lady of his dreams. As he is climbing the ladder, an agitated Dr. Coppélius rushes in, chases him away, sees the door to his house open, and darts within. Franz, picking up where he had left off, replaces the ladder and resumes his climbing.

Act II takes place inside Dr. Coppélius's house. The room is full of life-like, life-size dolls that Swanilda and her friends examine with curiosity. After a moment or two, Swanilda pokes her head into the alcove wherein sits the mysterious Coppélia and discovers that the seemingly studious girl who spends all her time reading is also a doll. Somebody jars a doll dressed as a Chinese. He dances until his clockwork runs down. They wind up all the dolls, who dance while the girls watch with rapture. Suddenly a furious Dr. Coppélius enters. The girls flee—all but Swanilda, who runs into the alcove where Coppélia is kept Franz comes through the window. Dr. Coppélius seizes him. Franz explains that he is in love with Coppélia. They talk, and Dr. Coppélius pretends to listen with interest, even friendship. He pours a well-doctored drink for Franz, then another and another. Franz becomes gloriously drunk and finally passes out. Dr. Coppélius rubs his hands in anticipation and drags a mighty tome from a shelf. He turns the pages, looking for a formula. He then goes to the alcove and examines his Coppélia—only he does not know that, instead of the doll, Swanilda is sitting there. He wheels her into the room, makes a few magical gestures over her and Franz, obviously trying to transfuse Franz's life-force into the doll. Swanilda, making believe she is Coppélia, responds to the gestures. She awkwardly rises, and Dr. Coppélius believes that she has come to life. She dances, stiffly at first, then with fluid grace. She begins to tease Dr. Coppélius, who pleads with her to behave. He puts a Spanish shawl over her; she dances a bolero. A Scottish scarf, and she dances a jig, more and more strenuously, ending up by kicking the book of formulas and running wildly around the room. Franz revives, and Dr. Coppélius pushes him out. Swanilda, after creating havoc in the room and upsetting all the dolls, dashes out after Franz, but he returns with Swanilda's friends, and they all watch the proceedings with glee. Finally all run out, including Swanilda and Franz. Dr. Coppélius, seeing the figure of Coppélia lying in his room divested of clothes, realizes that he has been deceived.

The second scene of this act (often it is given as a third act) takes place in a meadow on the festival day. Franz and Swanilda approach the lord of the manor to receive their dowries and be married. Dr. Coppélius storms in, accusing the lovers of damaging his life's work. Swanilda, realizing the justness of his claim, is willing to offer him her dowry, but the lord of the manor gives Dr. Coppélius a bag of gold and sends him off. A series of divertissements follow. According to the libretto:

. . .

The Bell-ringer alights first from the car.

He summons the morning hours.

They appear, quickly followed by wild flowers.

The bell rings! It is the hour of prayer. Aurora vanishes, chased by the hours of Day.

These are the working hours, and the young girls and reapers begin their work.

The bell rings again! It announces a wedding, and Hymen appears, accompanied by a little Cupid.

All at once the air is rent with discord and sounds. It is war, it is discord. Arms are raised and flames of fire illuminate the darkened sky. But soon all is calm again. The bell which a few moments before was calling to arms, makes the glad sound for the return of peace. Discord is dispelled and with the evening hours and night begin pleasures and joys.

Franz and Swanilda then dance an *adagio*. The people join with them in a happy, energetic dance to end the ballet.

The United States first saw *Coppélia* on March 11, 1887, at the Metropolitan Opera House. It was done by a group that worked with Theodore Thomas's American Opera. Marie Giuri and Felicita Carozzi danced the leading roles (the role of Franz was often danced by a woman in the last century). In 1910 Pavlova created much excitement in the press by her performance of Swanilda. The Ballet Russe de Monte Carlo was responsible for a large-scale revival at the Metropolitan Opera House on October 17, 1938. Alexandra Danilova was the ballerina, and people still talk about her Swanilda. It was indeed a characterization against which all others must be measured. In these performances Igor Youskevitch and Frederic Franklin, two dancers ideal for the role, alternated as Franz.

A somewhat cut version was introduced by Ballet Theatre and staged by Simon Semenoff at the Metropolitan Opera House on October 22, 1942. Irina Baronova was the magnificent Swanilda, Anton Dolin the Franz.

Coppélia has been in the Sadler's Wells repertoire since 1933. The first two acts, staged by Nicholas Sergeyev, had been done on March 21, 1933 at the Sadler's Wells Theatre. A revival on April 15, 1940, restored the third act. Then, on March 2, 1954, an entirely new production staged by Ninette de Valois entered the repertoire. It was this version that America saw for the first time on September 21, 1955, at the Metropolitan Opera House. Osbert Lancaster provided the sets and scenery. In the cast were Nadia Nerina (Swanilda), David Blair (Franz), and John Hart (Dr. Coppélius).

The production was a delight, and fully merited the excited press it received. Nadia Nerina appeared to be put together like a doll, looked like a doll, and danced like a darling. She may not have had that saucy temperament which was the exclusive property of Danilova, but who has? Nerina is a charmer in her way.

Coppélia probably contains more dancing for the ballerina than any other three-act work. The first and second acts are full of solo work, and the last has a strenuously difficult *pas de deux*. While *Coppélia* is not as long as *Swan Lake* or *Sleeping Beauty*, it must be remembered that the Swan Queen and Princess Aurora do not have to dance in every act, and also have long stretches of pantomime.

The lightness and gaiety of *Coppélia* are inclined to make some people underrate the ballet or think that the dancing is easy. No assumptions could be farther from the truth. *Coppélia* is difficult to dance, and the work is a balletic masterpiece, probably the dancing-est and most charming piece in the repertoire when produced with care. How much of the original has been retained nobody knows. Most versions are "after" Lev Ivanov, the choreographer of the Imperial Ballet in Petipa's day. The Sadler's Wells production has been adapted from Ivanov and Enrico Cecchetti, and has been produced by Nicholas Sergeyev, a Russian who was *régisseur* at the Maryinsky Theatre. But the original music is French, and the story has a flavor that is certainly more French than Russian. No drawn-out processions or elaborate pantomime sections, such as abound in Russian ballet, are present.

A footnote to the popularity of *Coppélia:* Diaghilev never staged it for his great company because, as he said, it and *Sylvia*, also with music by Delibes, were "too hackneyed for Paris."

Daphnis and Chloe

(Daphnis et Chloë)

Always more talked-about than performed, the ballet *Daphnis and Chloe* has never been a permanent repertoire item. The only completely successful thing about it has been its musical score, one of Maurice Ravel's supreme works. Ever since Isadora Duncan had made a one-woman Hellenistic revival, classical matters had been very much the artistic rage. In 1909 Diaghilev engaged Ravel to compose the music for a ballet to be created around the classical tale of Daphnis and Chloe. Fokine originally had suggested the idea; he had long dreamed of doing a Greek ballet. Ravel, who had met Diaghilev in 1906, before the Ballets Russes days, set to work on a libretto submitted by Fokine, visualizing "a vast musical fresco, concerning itself less with archaic fidelity than with fidelity to the Greece of my dreams, which in many ways resembled that imagined and depicted by the French artists of the end of the eighteenth century."

Diaghilev expressed doubts about the score when he finally received it in 1912 (Ravel, at the same time, was expressing doubts about the choreography that Fokine was devising for it). *Daphnis and Chloe* was announced for the fall season, but unfortunately the Ballets Russes failed to prepare it as well as they might have. The company was busy on Nijinsky's *L'Après-midi d'un faune,* and the absorbed Diaghilev showed little interest in *Daphnis.* Serge Grigoriev, *régisseur* of the company, believes that Diaghilev gladly would have abandoned Ravel's music had matters been less advanced. *Daphnis* was given toward the end of the season, much to Ravel's disgust. From that point on, though Fokine was especially fond of it, the ballet was in and out of the company's repertoire. "I have come to the conclusion," Grigoriev has written in his book about the Ballets Russes, "that there are lucky ballets and unlucky. *Daphnis and Chloe* was an unlucky ballet. Somehow it could never stick in our repertoire . . . yet it had lovely music, settings, costumes, and choreography. There seemed to be some malignant fate overhanging it."

It took the dancers a long time to work into *Daphnis and Chloe.* They certainly did not have it pat on opening night at the Théâtre du Châtelet, Paris, June 8, 1912. The leading dancers at the *première* were Tamara Karsavina, Vaslav Nijinsky, and Adolph Bolm. Pierre Monteux conducted. The sets and costumes were by Léon Bakst.

Even the great Karsavina needed personal coaching, just as Stravinsky had had to come to her aid for *The Firebird* two years before. Ravel attended the rehearsals, counting and beating time for the ballerina. On the morning of the performance itself, Ravel and Karsavina were working backstage on some tricky problems. "There was nothing Olympian about Ravel," Karsavina wrote in *Theatre Street.* "Obligingly he would come to my help in the difficult rhythmic passages of his score. There were many stumbling-blocks in the music of *Daphnis and Chloe.* . . . There was a dance in it for me in which the bars followed a capricious cadence of ever-changing rhythm. Fokine was too maddened, working against time, to give me much attention; on

81

the morning of the performance the last act was not yet brought to an end. Ravel and I at the back of the stage went through— 1,2,3—1,2,3,4,5—1,2, till finally I could dismiss mathematics and follow the pattern of the music." Victor Seroff, in his biography of Ravel reports that when the *corps de ballet* ran into the predicament of 5/4 time in the finale, the composer came to their rescue by suggesting they omit the customary counting of 1,2,3,4,5—1,2,3,4,5 and substitute the syllables of Diaghilev's full name: Ser-gei Dia-ghi-lev. Ravel was ever resourceful.

Nijinsky may not have danced his best at the *première*. His head was probably still full of *L'Après-midi,* which had caused a great scandal in Paris because of its alleged lewdness, and of which he nominally was the choreographer, though it was no secret that a great many fingers had been in that choreographic pie. Virtually everybody in the company had been busily at work to make it a success, and Fokine blamed Nijinsky for giving all of his time to *L'Après-midi,* to the detriment of Ravel's ballet. When the season ended, Fokine resigned in protest.

The story that Fokine evolved for *Daphnis and Chloe* follows the Greek myth of the shepherd Daphnis and his beloved Chloe, as found in the works of Longus. A detailed synopsis of the ballet is printed in the score above the related musical action. The following is my own translation:

A meadow at the edge of a sacred grove. Hills in the distance. At the right, a grotto, at the entrance of which, carved in rock, are the figures of three nymphs in an archaic sculpture. A little toward the back, at the left, a large rock shaped vaguely in the form of Pan. . . . A clear spring afternoon. When the curtain goes up, the scene is empty.

Young men and girls enter carrying baskets of presents intended for the nymphs. Little by little the stage fills. The people make obeisance before the altar of the nymphs. The young girls enfold the pedestals with garlands. A religious dance follows. In the rear Daphnis is seen, preceded by his flock. Chloe joins him. They go toward the altar and disappear at a turning, re-enter at front, and prostrate themselves before the nymphs. The dance is interrupted. Sweet emotion [of the dancers] on viewing the couple. The young girls entice Daphnis and surround him with their dance. Chloe feels the first attacks of jealousy. At this moment she is dragged into the dance of the young people. The cowherd Dorcon appears, particularly bold. At the end of the dance he tries to embrace Chloe. Innocently she offers her cheek. But with a brusque gesture Daphnis pushes aside the cowherd and tenderly approaches Chloe. The young people interpose. They place themselves before Chloe, and gently remove her. One of them proposes a dance contest between Daphnis and Dorcon. A kiss from Chloe will be the prize for the victor. Dorcon dances grotesquely. The audience ironically imitates the *gauche* movements of Dorcon, who finishes his dance amid general laughter. Daphnis dances lightly and gracefully. All invite Daphnis to receive his reward. Dorcon advances, but is chased away by the people, to the sound of laughter. The laughter breaks off when a radiant group forms around Daphnis and Chloe. The people retire, taking Chloe away. Daphnis rests, immobile, in an ecstasy. Daphnis stretches out in the grass, his face in his hands. Lyceion enters, approaches the young shepherd, bows her head, and puts her hands over his eyes. Daphnis thinks it is a trick of Chloe. But he recognizes Lyceion, and puts her aside. She dances. As if by accident she lets one of her veils drop. Daphnis rolls over and rests on his shoulders. Ironically she dances again, slower, until the end. Another veil glides to earth; it too is picked up by Daphnis. Resentfully she leaves, mocking, leaving the young shepherd troubled.

He hears the clash of arms, cries of war, in the distance. In the background women run, pursued by pirates. Daphnis thinks of Chloe, who is perhaps in danger, and leaves hastily to help her. Chloe runs in, distracted, looking for a hiding place. She kneels before the altar of the nymphs, beseeching their protection. A group of brigands enters, sees Chloe, and carries her off. Daphnis enters, searching for Chloe. He discovers on the ground a sandal that she has lost in the struggle. Full of despair, he curses the divinities who had not protected the young girl, and he falls unconscious at the entrance of the grotto.

A mysterious light envelops the landscape. A little flame suddenly burns brilliantly over the head of the statues. The nymphs come to life and descend from their pedestals. They begin a slow and mysterious dance. They stoop over Daphnis and dry his tears. They revive him and lead him toward the rock. Little by little the form of Pan becomes apparent. Daphnis prostrates himself before him. Everything grows dark.

A dim light. It is the camp of the pirates. A hilly corner. Behind, the ocean. At right and left, rocks. A ship is seen nearby. The pirates are seen running here and there loaded with booty. Torches violently light up the scene. Bryaxis orders the captive brought out: Chloe, her hands tied, is brought out by two pirates. Bryaxis orders her to dance, which she does in a supplicating manner. She attempts to flee. She is brought back with violence. Desperately she continues her dance. Again she tries to escape. She is again brought back. She abandons herself to despair, thinking of Daphnis. Bryaxis wishes to carry her off. She pleads with him. The pirate chief triumphantly lifts her. Suddenly the atmosphere becomes charged with foreboding elements. In various places, illuminated by invisible hands, fire breaks out. Fantastic beings leap and run. Goat-feet surge from all sides and surround the pirates. The earth opens. The mighty shadow of Pan is seen over the distant mountains in a menacing gesture. All the pirates flee in a frenzy.

The scene changes to that of the first part of the ballet. Nothing is heard but the murmur of rivulets of dew dropping from the rocks. Daphnis is stretched out in front of the grotto of the nymphs. Little by little the dawn breaks. Birds are heard singing. In the distance a shepherd passes with his flock. Another shepherd is seen. Enter a group of shepherds in search of Daphnis and Chloe. They discover Daphnis and raise him. Anguished, he looks for Chloe's face. She finally appears, surrounded by shepherdesses. They fall into each other's arms. Daphnis sees the crown Chloe is wearing. His dream was a prophetic vision: the intervention of Pan is clear.

The old shepherd Lammon explains that Pan has saved Chloe in remembrance of the nymph Syrinx, with whom he was in love. Daphnis and Chloe mime the story of Pan and Syrinx. . . . Their dance gets faster and faster and, in a dizzy whirl, Chloe falls into the arms of Daphnis. Before the altar of the nymphs he swears his faith. A group of young people dressed as bacchantes enters, shaking tambourines. Daphnis and Chloe tenderly embrace. A group of young men spreads over the scene. A joyous tumult. General dance.

America never saw *Daphnis and Chloe* as its creators conceived it. Diaghilev announced it for the first American tour of the Ballets Russes, but it apparently was never given. (Ravel's glorious score, of course, immediately passed into the concert repertoire—especially the second suite he selected from it.) Catherine Littlefield staged the work for the Philadelphia Ballet on March 31, 1936, and it was presented by the same company at the Lewisohn Stadium in New York on July 30 of that year.

The Sadler's Wells Ballet revived *Daphnis and Chloe,* with

choreography by Frederick Ashton, at Covent Garden, London, on April 5, 1951. John Craxton did the scenery and costumes. In the cast were Margot Fonteyn (Chloe), Michael Somes (Daphnis), and John Field (Dorcon; spelled "Dorkon," more correctly, in the Sadler's Wells program; but why "Lykanion" for Lyceion?). The same principals appeared in the ballet when it was presented at the Metropolitan Opera House, New York, on September 25, 1953.

Ashton's choreography had little in common with Fokine's. "He was convinced," writes Mary Clarke in her book about Sadler's Wells, "that it would no longer be right to approach the work in the same spirit as Bakst and Fokine had done, for the eyes of 1951 are not the same as those of 1912, and Ashton wanted his ballet to be a contemporary restatement of an old story, not a resuscitation of an earlier presentation of that story. A recent holiday among the Greek islands had convinced him that the myths and legends and even the gods of ancient Greece were still very much present in the atmosphere and in the lives of the people, and he wanted, above all, to suggest this timeless quality."

He did not hesitate to make changes in the story, either. In the original version of 1912, for example, Daphnis is completely faithful to Chloe and spurns the advances of Lyceion. In Ashton's choreography Daphnis, far from spurning her, engages in a violent love affair with her. Ashton, too, has completely eliminated the mimed story of Pan and Syrinx. And, far from striving for a reconstruction of classical Greek dress, he has costumed his dancers in modern clothing. The men wear khaki trousers, the women simple skirts and bodices that could be worn anywhere in the Western world today. The new choreography attempts a lyric line without any toe work or pyrotechnics. A sort of neo-Grecian effect is obtained, especially in the first solo of Daphnis. Chloe's dances are tender and intimate. The weakest section of the ballet is the general dance at the end, where the men and women, flapping colored scarves, recall graduation exercises at a dancing school.

Margot Fonteyn made an unbelievably lovely Chloe. She has

85

a plastic quality not always achieved by highly trained ballet dancers, and which distinguishes the great dancing artist from the mere ballerina. With this inner communion, so to speak, Fonteyn is still a forceful and convincing actress. She has matured artistically since she was first seen in this country in 1949. Today she is one of this generation's supreme dancers.

According to Mary Clarke, the London *première* was received calmly by the audience and "very cooly by an ungrateful Press." Nor were New York audiences overwhelmed by Ashton's *Daphnis and Chloe,* though everybody agreed that it was wonderful to see such a fabled ballet on the stage once again. Had not Sadler's Wells brought it, America might still be waiting. The complicated score (which needs a chorus) alone might make a production prohibitive for a company on this side of the Atlantic. One of the facts America must face is: no subsidy, no ballets like *Daphnis and Chloe.*

Designs with Strings

 A graduate of the School of American Ballet, John Taras had had drilled into him a knowledge of and respect for the classical tradition. As a student of Fokine and as a dancer with Ballet Caravan, the Littlefield Ballet, the American Ballet, and Ballet Theatre, he learned the workings of a ballet company from a dancer's-eye view. He has composed several ballets, of which *Designs With Strings* is the only one now in the active repertoire. It was first performed by the Metropolitan Ballet, a British organization, at Wimbledon, England, on February 6, 1948. Ballet Theatre introduced it to America at the Center Theatre, New York, on April 25, 1950. Irene Sharaff designed the costumes. The dancers at the American *première* were Diana Adams, Norma Vance, Lillian Lanese, Dorothy Scott, Erik Bruhn, and Holland Stoudenmire.

Taras set his ballet to the second movement of Tchaikovsky's Trio in A minor as rearranged for piano and strings. The Ballet Theatre program quoted a short statement by Beryl de Zoete from the *New Statesman and Nation:* "There is no plot, but as dancers are not robots their contacts in dance as in life are inevitably productive of sentiment—one might almost say of sentimental situations—and you may detect a ghost of a drama, which, like the emotions of certain chords and harmonic progressions in music, you are free to interpret as you will."

Designs With Strings is strongly Balanchine-derived, though a rather soft lyric quality of its own also comes through. It is an unpretentious piece for six dancers—four girls and two boys. Quality of movement rather than virtuosity is required. As no set is necessary, and as the costuming is simple, a ballet company will find that *Designs With Strings* is a handy work to have in the repertoire. It poses few production problems except the need for imaginative lighting.

Dim Lustre

 Says the note in the program: "A whiff of perfume, the touch of a hand, a stolen kiss release whirls of memories which take the rememberers back briefly to other moments and leave them not exactly as they were before." With this somewhat Cabellian statement as a clue, the action of *Dim Lustre* can easily be understood though, as with many Tudor ballets, all kinds of subtleties become clear only after repeated viewings.

The names of the characters also furnish a clue: A Reflection; Another Reflection; It Was Spring; Who Was She?; She Wore a Perfume; He Wore a White Tie; and so on. The device sometimes is exasperating; one wonders if it really is necessary. But a ballet stands or falls on what the dancers do, not on what they are named, and one gladly puts up with this Tudor idiosyncracy when he creates works as beautiful as *Dim Lustre*.

This is a very elegant and sophisticated

ballet—a stunning ballroom scene inhabited by aristocrats who relive all kinds of memories in flashbacks. Although Tudor is known to compose slowly, *Dim Lustre* was an exception. He created it on short notice—in sixteen days. The ballet is in one act, with music by Richard Strauss—the *Burleske* for piano and orchestra, a most *gemütlich* score, full of Viennese life and sparkle, with several langorous, slow sections that can be described only as *Schmalz*—but good *Schmalz*.

The action is slim. Little incidents recall to the minds of one of the dancing couples events from the past. The ballerina is kissed on the shoulder by her partner; instantly there comes to her mind the memory of a boy who kissed her once on a spring day, years ago (*It was Spring*). His vision comes and goes. A touch on the man's shoulder recalls to him the memory of a summer day when he danced with three pretty girls (*Who Was She?*). He relives the moment when he tried to kiss one of them but was prevented by the others. He comes back to the present with a wrench. He dances with his partner. She drops her handkerchief, and as he returns it to her the perfume reminds him of another lady, a very glamorous one, in his past (*She Wore a Perfume*). His necktie reminds her of a man with whom she once had an affair *(He Wore a White Tie)*. At the end of the ballet, the couple look at each other with the realization that their memories are more precious to them than their love, that they are not for one another.

Tudor uses all kinds of devices to make his points. As usual, he telescopes time by a sort of flashback movie technique. Each memory is introduced by the appearance of the dancer's double seen as a mirror image (an actual dancer) accurately reflecting the other's movements. As the images vanish, the episodes that are relived are danced on a semi-dark stage. At the conclusion of each episode the lights are brought back to normal and the couple resume their activities in the present time. This is tricky to manage, and is one reason why the ballet was out of the repertoire for some seasons. If the mirror-image sequences are not rehearsed so that the synchronization is perfect, the result can be sloppy. If an unskilled electrician is handling the lights, the result can be disastrous.

Dim Lustre is not only a series of duets. The featured couple is surrounded by other dancing couples who weave in and out of their lives. Tudor's use of space and floor patterns is a model of professional craftsmanship. He has designed the movement largely on a diagonal line, which makes for a certain degree of smartness. And all of the movements are prevailingly lyrical. This is a *dancing* ballet that is a joy to watch. It is strongly Proustian, a sort of balletic *Remembrance of Things Past,* done with the attention to detail and characterization that only a master like Tudor has been able to maintain in our time.

Ballet Theatre presented the *première* of *Dim Lustre* at the Metropolitan Opera House on October 20, 1943. The cast consisted of Nora Kaye (The Lady With Him), Hugh Laing (The Gentleman With Her), Muriel Bentley (A Reflection), Michael Kidd (Another Reflection), John Kriza (It Was Spring), Rosella Hightower (She Wore a Perfume), Antony Tudor (He Wore a White Tie), Janet Reed, Albia Kavan, and Virginia Wilcox (Who Was She?). An ultra-smart period setting, with crystal chandeliers and costumes ranging in color from pale beige to deep burgundy, with the principals set off in white, was designed by Motley.

Like most original casts, this one was tailor-made to the specific requirements of the dancers involved. In Nora Kaye and Hugh Laing, Tudor of course had two of his ideal interpreters. Though *Dim Lustre* is much lighter in texture than most other Tudor ballets, Kaye and Laing experienced no trouble in shedding heavy dramatics in favor of a sophisticated, light approach. The movements are fluid and rapid. The ballerina, with her long white gloves and high feather headpiece, has to skim smartly over the stage. Tudor never before or after has covered space with such rapid patterns. Kriza was given one of the most difficult variations Tudor ever created for a male dancer—turns and leaps at lightning speed. He made something of a *tour de force* of it, dancing brilliantly without sacrificing the feeling that

91

a romantic springtime dream was in progress.

The ballet has been intermittently in the repertoire. During the summer of 1955 Tudor started to rework *Dim Lustre,* and it was restored to Ballet Theatre's repertoire during the following season.

The Duel

 In 1615, Claudio Monteverdi composed his
Il Combattimento di Tancredi e Clorinda.
Its text, taken largely from Book XII of
Torquato Tasso's *Gerusalemme liberata,*
recounts the tale of the Crusades in which
Tancred slays the Saracen girl he loves.
That, substantially, is the story of William
Dollar's ballet, *The Duel.*

Dollar, a veteran American dancer and
choreographer who has been associated at
one time or another with virtually every
leading company here, originally created
the work for Roland Petit's Ballets de Paris.
It received its *première* at the Théâtre
Marigny, Paris, on June 28, 1949. Colette
Marchand, the original Clorinda, repeated
her performance on October 6, 1949, at the
Winter Garden in New York. But the ballet
is no longer seen in the original form. As
done by the Petit group, under the name of
Le Combat, it was a *pas de deux;* no other

dancers appeared on stage. When the ballet, which is set to music by Raffaello de Banfield, entered the New York City Ballet Company repertoire, it was expanded to include a background of three male dancers in addition to the two leading roles. Costumes for this production were designed by Robert Stevenson. The date of the *première* at the New York City Center of Music and Drama was February 24, 1950. In the cast were Melissa Hayden (Clorinda), William Dollar (Tancred), Val Buttignol, Walter Georgov, and Shaun O'Brien. Francisco Moncion has since succeeded Dollar in the role of Tancred.

The Duel is also in the repertoire of Ballet Theatre, where it is called *The Combat*. Thus Dollar's work is perhaps the only one in ballet history to have been in the repertoire of two major American companies at the same time, having two different titles, costumes, sets, and choreographies (there are some differences in the two versions), but with the same score, story, and choreographer. Ballet Theatre's production was first seen in London, at the Royal Opera House, Covent Garden, on July 23, 1953. It used scenery and costumes by Georges Wakhevitch; the leading dancers were John Kriza and Melissa Hayden.

"The ballet," says the Ballet Theatre program note, "suggested by Canto III and Canto XII of Tasso's poem, *Jerusalem Delivered,* takes place in the days of the Crusades. The opening scene tells of the first encounter of Clorinda, the pagan girl, and Tancred, the Christian warrior. A stage blackout indicates a lapse of time, and the following scene shows their final meeting —a mortal combat. Only after he has wounded her fatally does Tancred discover that his masked assailant is the girl he loves."

Ballet Theatre's production is hampered by awkward costuming and a fussy approach. In the New York City Ballet performances, the simpler costumes, which do not detract from the dancers' movements, allow one to concentrate on the pure dance elements. The role of Clorinda allows much opportunity for a dancer who can attain a brittle, steel-like intensity. Dollar has kept his patterns clear and direct (a little more direct in the New York City Ballet version), has invented movements that have something of the sweep of pageantry about them, and has provided a lyrical and even tender outlet for his leading dancers. *The Duel* is a strong ballet with a forceful climax done with dignity and honesty. And in the battle scenes one feels the struggle empathically; these are not stock choreographic motions, but a highly stylized and successful account of body against body, steel against steel.

The action poses no problems to the observer. Tancred is seen leading his warriors. Clorinda enters in full armor and engages one of Tancred's men. She overcomes him and dances over his body. Her helmet had fallen off during the battle, and Tancred sees that she is a woman. He salutes her respectfully. She leaves. There is a blackout. Tancred enters and does a warlike dance. Clorinda next takes the stage. She too is fully armed for battle. She beats off two Crusaders who attack her. She then has her fatal battle with Tancred. Wounded to death, she tears off her helmet. Tancred, horror-stricken when he recognizes her, tries to comfort her last moments.

Fall River Legend

"Lizzie Borden took an axe, and gave her mother forty whacks." Agnes de Mille based *Fall River Legend* on the Lizzie Borden murder case. "While in no way attempting to tell that fearful story factually," the choreographer tells us, "in fact departing radically from history, it explores the passions that lead to a violent resolution of the oppressions and turmoils that can beset an ordinary life."

Agnes de Mille composed the ballet for Ballet Theatre in 1948. (She has not, as of 1955, created a later ballet for any company.) *Fall River Legend* is different from her previous works, such as *Rodeo* and *Three Virgins and a Devil* or the dances in *Oklahoma!* Perhaps de Mille felt that she had exploited her particular brand of humor as far as it would go, and decided that she was ready for a serious ballet. *Fall River Legend* could not be more serious. Lizzie

Borden was a young lady who lived at 92 Second Street, Fall
River, Massachusetts. On August 4, 1892, it was alleged, she
assaulted and killed her father and stepmother with an axe. She
was brought to trial—a marathon trial that lasted ten months,
after which she was acquitted. There was a strong feeling that
she was guilty, however, and how the jury reached the decision
it did was a cause for widespread speculation.

With that part of the case, *Fall River Legend* has no interest.
Indeed, the central character is condemned and hanged. Taking
the murder case as a peg, and without using names, de Mille has
attempted to explain what made Lizzie act as she did. A psychi-
atric report, in short, from childhood to the grave, in a prologue
and eight scenes. Freud knew not what he spawned.

The Prologue of *Fall River Legend* shows the Accused standing at the foot of the gallows. Near her is the Pastor. Facing her
is the speaker for the jury. Spectators are present. The speaker
reads off the bill of particulars: "A true bill . . . The house in
which the murders were committed was the house in which you
were born . . . You, there, with your father and mother lived
happily." The scene changes to the house, and Scene 1 shows the
Accused as a child. Neighbors pass by. The child dances happily.
(Throughout this scene, the Accused is watching and partici-
pating, through of course all this is a figment of her imagination,
and nobody sees her.) The child is frightened by a severe, dom-
ineering woman. They obviously detest one another. The child's
mother suddenly becomes ill, apparently from a heart attack.
She is led into the house as the child trembles. The mother soon
recovers, and the three of them—father, mother, child—represent the happiest of families. But the mother dies of a second
attack, and the woman who has so frightened the child becomes
her new mother.

The next scene takes place after twenty-five years. The Ac-
cused now takes the stage as a direct performer in the tragedy.
We see her sitting miserably between her father and stepmother.
This is not a happy family; all three are repressed, taut, hateful.
The Accused feels unwanted and cast out. She tries without
success to attract the attention of her parents, but whatever she

wants to do is forbidden by her stepmother. She goes into the yard and meets the pastor. She is attracted by his kindness and sympathy. Her father orders her in. She sits, as before, then goes out and returns with an axe. The stepmother looks at her, horrified, but the Accused has nothing on her mind except to chop some wood. Which she does, and returns to the brooding house.

Scene 3 takes place in the street outside the house. The Accused watches happy couples go by. She is impelled to her back yard, where she sees the axe. She recoils, but it is obvious that thoughts have entered her mind which do not involve chopping wood. The pastor enters, gives her a bouquet, and asks her to a picnic. Her parents break up the friendship, the stepmother whispering poisonous things into the pastor's ear. Goaded to a frenzy, the accused disobeys her parents and goes off with the pastor.

For the first time, in Scene 4, she is part of the community, away from her parents. She listens to the pastor preach, participates in the dancing, and has a wonderful time until her stepmother appears. Then, noticing her whispering to the people, the Accused attacks her stepmother, thus playing right into the older woman's hands. The Accused is led home, having alienated the pastor and the people by what to them is her irresponsible conduct. They now believe the reports her stepmother has been spreading about her. In Scene 5, the stepmother disappears into the house. Now the Accused knows what she must do. She gets the axe and goes in. Her parents jump up, transfixed; and as the Accused covers her face, there is a blackout.

In Scene 6 the murders have just been committed. Nothing is left to the imagination: the room is a mess, with blood all over the floor, and when the Accused enters, she has blood over her. Her mother appears in a vision. This is a rather horrifying scene. The Accused, in her imagination, has reverted to childhood, and her mother takes the girl into her arms. Then she notices the blood, which the girl unsuccessfully tries to hide. The mother sees what has been happening, chides her, gently slaps her, and glides away—but with a loving backward look.

In Scene 7 the Accused runs into the arms of the neighbors,

who have been aroused by the commotion. She is accused of murder. The last scene is the gallows. Memories pass before her. The pastor comforts her. Finally she is left alone, and then is hanged until she is dead.

Morton Gould composed the score for *Fall River Legend*. It received its *première* by Ballet Theatre at the Metropolitan Opera House on April 22, 1948. The principal dancers were Alicia Alonso (The Accused), Muriel Bentley (Her Stepmother), Peter Gladke (Her Father), and John Kriza (Her Pastor). Costumes were by Miles White, and the ingenious sets were created by Oliver Smith. De Mille had designed the role of the Accused with Nora Kaye in mind, but Kaye was ill at the time of the *première*. The role alternated between Alonso and Diana Krupska until Kaye was well enough to take over.

Fall River Legend suffers from over-literalism. It is hardly a subtle ballet, and the emotional points the choreographer wished to make are constantly repeated at length, as though the audience were too insensitive to get the exquisite nuances. The ballet is long on melodrama and short on choreographic invention. That, added to the limited balletic vocabulary de Mille has at her disposal and the echoes of many ideas that Tudor previously had achieved more successfully, leaves *Fall River Legend* less than a complete artistic entity. We are expected to feel sorry for the Accused, but it is hard to work up sympathy for a creature so obviously and sentimentally contrived.

Fancy Free

A ballet about a trio of sailors on the town
was bound to hit American audiences with
peculiar impact in 1944. The United States
Navy, which had won a great victory at
Guadalcanal only about five months before,
was preparing itself for the mighty strikes
at Japanese islands. On April 18, 1944, the
day that *Fancy Free* received its *première*
by Ballet Theatre at the Metropolitan
Opera House, groups of sailors were operating a few blocks away, in the Times
Square area, their minds very much on the
subject that the ballet was illustrating.
They were Our Boys, fighting men all; and
who would begrudge a fighting man a little
relaxation? Leonard Bernstein had been
commissioned to do the score, and it was
such a hit that the following season he was
represented with a tremendous Broadway
success, *On the Town*—a musical comedy
that, not absolutely by coincidence, dealt

with sailors loose in New York for an evening's fun. And the man responsible for the dances in *On the Town* was Jerome Robbins, the choreographer of *Fancy Free*.

It was Robbins's first ballet, and seldom has a first attempt met with such success. *Fancy Free* was American all the way through (including its cast). It had a jazzy insouciance, a swaggering adolescence, a large amount of good, clean fun, and a most happy inability to take itself too seriously. It was definitely not the work of an amateur, choreographically speaking. Although it was Robbins's premier attempt, it was the product of a thoroughly experienced dancer and man of the theater. Young as he was, Robbins had danced in the Broadway theater before entering the *corps de ballet* of Ballet Theatre; and with that company he had worked himself up to leading roles. He had also studied music and knew a lot about stagecraft.

Oliver Smith's clever scenery brilliantly set the mood of *Fancy Free*. Completely stylized, it brought the City of New York on stage—skyscrapers in the background, a lamppost, a beat-up saloon seen from the exterior as well as interior. It is a warm summer evening, and a bored bartender is having trouble finding an interest in life. Three sailors appear, fresh off the boat, ready for an evening's amusement. Which amusement, of course, concerns girls. They adjust their uniforms, make plans, and enter the bar for a little lubrication before the serious work of the evening. They choose up to see who will pay for the beers. One of them is swindled—apparently he always is, for the other two have a pre-arranged code—and ponies up. They wander outside and poke gum into their mouths. Suddenly they are electrified. A girl is passing by; and, as they used to say in the armed forces, this is indeed a girl. The sailors scramble for her, and a bit of a fracas ensues. She stalks haughtily away, followed by two of the boys. The other starts to return disconsolately to the bar.

But before he reaches it, he bumps into another pretty girl. They make friends, and he asks her in for a drink. At the bar he modestly describes the terrible battles he has been through, his sufferings, and his heroism. They dance together, then sit down again. At this moment his two friends enter with a girl in tow—

the girl they have chased. It turns out that the two girls are friends. They squeak at each other and make a great to-do. All sit at a table, and it is a bad piece of mathematics. Three boys plus two girls means that somebody is going to be short, and it isn't one of the girls. Two of the couples dance; the third boy decides to cut in. It looks as though there might be trouble. Instead of having a free-for-all, however, the boys decide to have a dancing competition, agreeing that the loser will clear out.

The first boy to dance is an acrobatic type. He is all over the place, ending with a leap to the surface of the bar. The second has a more lyrical dance to offer; he is the sensitive type. The third shoots the works in a hot Latin American number. Unfortunately the girls can't make up their mind about the merits of the dances. The boys take matters into their own hands, and a real Donnybrook ensues, with the sailors pummeling themselves in a wild melee of arms and legs. While all this is going on, the girls simply walk out and leave them flat. When the boys wake up to the fact that they are alone, they look embarrassed, shake hands, and make up. They have a beer; and the one who always pays, pays. Out into the street, under the lamppost, they wander. They have sworn off girls—now it's all for one and one for all. In comes the most beautiful gal of all. She is everything a sailor could want—a Broadway princess, all curves and allure. Do they look at her? You bet your life they do! But, mindful of their resolution, nobody makes a move after her. She disappears down the street. Human blood and bone can stand no more. One of the sailors makes a dash after her, and the others frantically follow.

Jerome Robbins himself was one of the sailors at the *première*. The others were Harold Lang and John Kriza. The girls were Muriel Bentley and Janet Reed. Rex Cooper was the bartender, and Shirley Eckl the vision who comes into the sailors' eyes at the end of the ballet.

The ballet has been a constant fixture in the Ballet Theatre repertoire ever since its *première*. This is something of a record for a contemporary ballet—eleven consecutive years at the point of writing. *Fancy Free* has held up very well. It has not dated;

and if it does not always have the impact that it had in 1944, the fault through the decade has not been the ballet, but that of some of the dancers interpreting it. For Robbins obviously created the work with certain dancers in mind, and several late-comers have lacked the personality of those in the original cast. Not too long after the *première* Robbins left Ballet Theatre to concentrate on choreography. He has been in and out of Broadway ever since, and also has contributed some much-talked-about ballets to the contemporary repertoire. He is a highly talented choreographer, and his works are always received with interest; but never again has he distilled the particular blend of Americanism, humor, ingenuity, and sheer animal spirits which he created in *Fancy Free*.

La Fille mal gardee

 Attempts to translate the title of *La Fille mal gardée* into English have produced such unhappy results as "Naughty Lisette" and "The Wayward Daughter." The oldest ballet now in the repertoire, the only extant work of the famous choreographer Jean Dauberval (1742–1806), it was originally produced at Bordeaux in 1786. How much that is actually Dauberval's has come down to us is anybody's guess. Probably very little. And nothing of the composer's other music has survived; at least, none of it appears to be in print. He was Johann Wilhelm Hertel (1727–89), a German composer of operas, concertos, and other long-forgotten works. His contribution to *La Fille mal gardée,* by which alone he lives (not too securely; it is not a very inventive score, though it has a few pleasant moments) is not even listed in the 1955 edition of *Grove's.*

La Fille mal gardée

Dauberval's real name was Jean Bercher. He did much to further the theories of Noverre, with whom he had studied, and in *La Fille mal gardée* he created a little masterpiece that remains astonishingly vital and up-to-date. *La Fille mal gardée* is a comedy, and Dauberval has come to be known as the father of the comic ballet. So popular did this ballet become that even the hinterland of the New World saw a production of it in the early years of the nineteenth century. This took place at the famous old Park Theater, in New York, on July 6, 1839. A certain Mme Lecomte danced the leading role. The critics said that she was too fat.

La Fille mal gardée, in most ballet repertoires of Europe throughout the nineteenth century, was especially popular in Russia, under the title of *Vain Precautions*. Alexandre Benois, in his *Reminiscences of the Russian Ballet*, writes nostalgically of Virginia Zucchi's appearance in it at St. Petersburg in 1885. Benois had a real Zucchi-crush; he was a fifteen-year-old schoolboy at the time. "Zucchi's second triumph on the Imperial stage was her appearance in *La Fille mal gardée*. This was the ballet that had delighted the Imperial family in Krasnoye Selo, and it was now chosen by the management for Zucchi's debut in her new engagement. . . . *La Fille mal gardée* is a naïve story in the style of a *bergerie* of the eighteenth century, but, thanks to Zucchi and in spite of the faded *décor* . . . the performance seemed actually to exude the fresh fragrance of fields and meadows and to create a full illusion of the charm of country life." In later years Benois, perhaps still starry-eyed over Zucchi's appearance in it, was said to have classed *La Fille mal gardée* on a level with such ballets as *Giselle, Coppélia,* and *Sylvia*. But then, the ballet was a tradition in Russia. Charles-Louis Didelot had staged it there, according to Serge Lifar, in 1817. As Didelot was a pupil of Dauberval, he probably was careful to treat the ballet with great respect.

La Fille mal gardée tells the story of two lovers, Lisette and Colin. Lisette is the daughter of Mother Simone, a wealthy widow who owns a large farm and has no use at all for Colin. She catches them dancing and chases him away. Lisette then gets a good lecture on the importance of choosing a proper husband. Lisette's friends appear, everybody dances, and Colin joins the fun when Mother Simone is not around. When she does return, she chases him away once more. Lisette goes into a tantrum and her mother sternly places before her a butter churn. She starts to work, and who turns up but the impetuous Colin? Much flirtatious byplay (of course, Mother Simone is elsewhere), and they dance with a long ribbon that Colin produces.

A neighbor enters. He is Thomas, fat and rich, and he wants his son Alain to marry Lisette. Alain, no great intellect, has only one interest in life—catching butterflies. He is never without a butterfly net, and is constantly chasing a bug across the stage. Mother Simone and Thomas discuss the marriage and come to a satisfactory understanding. Lisette is brought forth and introduced to Alain. They suddenly realize what is going on, and to say that both are scared would be to put it mildly. An interlude follows, in which all troop to the notary, Lisette dragged by her mother, Alain chasing butterflies. A change of scene brings us to a harvest, where Mother Simone and Thomas dance. She ogles him; perhaps she can capture him? They dance off, and Colin, who has come on the scene, dances with his beloved Lisette. Alain meanwhile is chasing butterflies. A thunderstorm comes up, and everybody flees, Colin making off with Lisette.

The following act takes place in the interior of Mother Simone's house. It is all very domestic. The mother spins and Lisette reads. She is dying to get the key to the house from her mother, especially as that rascal, Colin, has his face at the window. She dances for him, making her mother play the tambourine. Harvesters are admitted by Mother Simone; they stack huge sheaves of wheat against a wall. Mother Simone goes out with the harvesters, not forgetting to lock the door, at which point the sheaves part and Colin comes out. He makes ardent protestations of love, and at first Lisette is frightened. He wins her over, and they trade scarves to pledge their love. Mother Simone is heard approaching. Lisette hastily hides Colin in a hayloft. Mother Simone, however, sees the scarf, knows that

Colin has been around, and gives Lisette a good what-for. On the entrance of Thomas and Alain to conclude the marriage arrangements, she pushes Lisette into the hayloft. Farmers, a notary, and other observers watch while Mother Simone and Thomas make the final arrangements. Then Mother Simone gives Alain the key to the hayloft and tells him to fetch Lisette. He opens the door, and there stand Lisette and Colin, their hair embroidered with pieces of hay. Of course, everybody thinks the worst despite the explanation of the young couple. As there is no other logical way out, and as the notary is present, Mother Simone agrees that the lovers may be married. A concluding scene presents a festival to celebrate the wedding.

The last scene is sometimes cut. *La Fille mal gardée*, indeed, has been staged several ways. Originally it was in two acts and three scenes; as presented today it generally is done in several consecutive scenes. Until Michael Mordkin revived the work on November 12, 1938 at the Alvin Theatre, New York, almost one hundred years had passed since America had seen a version of it. The last previous recorded performance apparently took place during a Fanny Elssler tour, at her farewell New York performance, on July 1, 1842. Pavlova announced it for her 1913–14 American season, but there is no record that she ever danced it in this country. In Mordkin's revival, Lucia Chase danced Lisette, Dimitri Romanoff was seen as Colin, and Mordkin was Mother Simone (a role generally danced by a man). Ballet Theatre later took over this production, with a new choreographic arrangement by Bronislava Nijinska, and in its new form offered it at the Center Theatre, New York, on January 19, 1940. In the cast were Patricia Bowman (Lisette), Yurek Shabelevsky (Colin), Alexis Kosloff (Alain), and Edward Caton (Mother Simone). Dimitri Romanoff replaced Shabelevsky shortly after the first performance. Later on, in Ballet Theatre performances (with the work renamed *Wayward Daughter*), Irina Baronova and Ian Gibson were to delight American audiences as Lisette and Alain. Still later, in 1942, *La Fille mal gardée* again turned up in Ballet Theatre programs. Same cast, same production—but it was called *Naughty Lisette*. Sets and costumes for all of the Ballet Theatre productions were by Serge Soudeikine.

When Ballet Theatre revived the work for its fifteenth anniversary season, in the spring of 1955 at the Metropolitan Opera House, it was given under its original title, *La Fille mal gardée*. Ballet Theatre was fortunate in its casting on this occasion. Alicia Alonso, one of the great classic ballerinas of our time, was the most adorable of Lisettes, completely relaxed and natural in her acting, nonchalantly accomplishing superb technical feats with elegance. John Kriza was ideal as Colin. He made the lover alive and believable. Eric Braun, as Alain, had superb elevation, *batterie,* and turns. His dancing, however, did leave something to be desired; it lacked the elegant finish of the other two principals. There was no doubt that he could mount tremendous distances into the air. What would happen when he finally came down—that was another question.

Filling Station

Filling Station is described by its creators not merely as a ballet, but as a "ballet-document." Why the "document"? Possibly because the ballet was a deliberate attempt to re-create the American scene. When it received its *première* on January 6, 1938, by Ballet Caravan at the Avery Memorial Theatre in Hartford, Connecticut, little or nothing had been done along those lines in ballet. *Billy the Kid,* probably the most "American" of the ballets in the repertoire, did not come along until some eight months later, on October 16. In 1938, there was much talk about the emergence of a national American school in all of the arts. Much activity was in progress; many names were under discussion.

Virgil Thomson, who composed the score for *Filling Station,* was not, generally speaking, one of those names, though *Four Saints in Three Acts,* which had received performances in 1934, had created a good deal of comment, much of which was highly patronizing (*"Pigeons on the grass, alas"*). The curious thing is that Thomson was quietly doing things in the so-called American genre some time before the other composers of his generation woke up to the potentialities of the native idiom (always excepting the strange figure of Charles Ives). Thomson's *Hymn Tune Symphony*, completed in 1928, contains elements that many people think were invented by Copland, who did not get around to composing this type of music until after the success of *El Salón México* and *Billy the Kid* in the late thirties. Copland, indeed, freely admits that he has been influenced by Thomson. In its time the latter's *Filling Station* came as a revelation to many listeners. It avoided the spiked dissonances that were the vocabulary of the serious composer. It had Satie-like elements and refused to take itself seriously. It was theatrical, frankly superficial, and quoted irreverently from sources in the American folk tradition (*Hail, hail, the gang's all here,* or *We won't get home until morning*).

Lincoln Kirstein supplied the plot of *Filling Station* and the choreographer was Lew Christensen. The synopsis of the ballet, as set forth in the original Ballet Caravan program, reads:

America has so many kinds of people in so many parts of the country, with so many local stories, that it is difficult to find a contemporary fable to fit a modern Hero. But everyone who has ridden in an automobile recognizes the typical, self-reliant, resourceful and courteous Filling Station Mechanic as a friend indeed. . . . We call him Mac. He keeps his washroom spick and span. The chromium on his gaspumps gleams. His road maps are neatly stacked to be given away on request. His friends are two truck drivers, Roy and Ray, chased by a State Trooper who warns them against speeding and over-loading. A distressed Motorist inquires the route he has lost. His wife and children burden him down with demonstrations of domestic bliss. A rich young couple from the country club stagger in and turn the filling station into a dancehall. A nervous gangster finds himself involved in murder. Mac summons the State Trooper. The station is emptied, and Mac, finding himself alone again, spreads his tabloid and turns on his radio, waiting for whatever will turn up next.

Ballet Caravan, in which Lincoln Kirstein had an interest, had been founded in 1936, and was the protoype of the New York City Ballet Company. Kirstein's relationship with Thomas went back several years before Ballet Caravan days. In 1933, Thomson had introduced Kirstein to Balanchine in Paris. Kirstein, in a program note to *Filling Station* for the New York City Ballet, states that it was Thomson's encouragement in the very earliest days of his, Kirstein's, interest in ballet, when he was still a Harvard undergraduate, that provided the necessary impetus. *Filling Station,* says Kirstein, was "an attempt to make an American ballet out of an American myth." Paul Cadmus, engaged to create the costumes and scenery, was inspired by comic-strip colors and patterns. The ballet was given during two consecutive tours of the American Ballet Caravan in South America. It received over three hundred performances. Then it dropped from the repertoire for several years until its revival by the New York City Ballet Company, at the New York City Center of Music and Drama, on May 12, 1953.

At the Hartford *première* the cast included Lew Christensen (Mac), Eugene Loring and Erick Hawkins (Ray and Roy), Ray Weamer (State Trooper), Harold Christensen (Motorist), Anne Campbell (His Wife), Fred Danieli (Rich Boy), Gisella Caccialanza (Rich Girl), and Dwight Godwin (Gangster). The New York City Ballet revival, which also used the Cadmus sets and costumes, presented Jacques d'Amboise (Mac), Edward Bigelow and Robert Barnett (Roy and Ray), Stanley Zompakos (Motorist), Shaun O'Brien (His Wife), Edith Brozak (His Child), Janet Reed (Rich Girl), Michael Maule (Rich Boy), Walter Georgov (Gangster), and John Mandia (State Trooper).

The ballet was nostalgically received on its revival. In its early days it had attracted a great deal of serious attention. Kirstein let the world know that the ballet could be considered the American answer to *Sleeping Beauty* and *Swan Lake,* with Mac representing an American Prince Charming. As Anatole Chujoy points out in his study of the New York City Ballet: "He never said it in so many words, but one got the distinct impression that

111

Kirstein hoped that the comic-strip-like *Filling Station* would replace for American spectators the fairy-tale ballets of other companies." Christensen, though using an American theme with American prototypes, was careful to express his action in movements stemming from orthodox ballet technique. He thus demonstrated that classic ballet was not incompatible with light theater entertainment. Time has dimmed the initial impact of *Filling Station,* which today appears a little naïve and one-dimensional, but it stood for much in 1938, and its importance is hard to overestimate.

The success *Filling Station* enjoyed in its revival was in part owing to canny casting. Jacques d'Amboise received one of his best roles as Mac, the strong, amiable youth whose mission in life is to please his customers. Christensen has created for this part long, broad, easygoing movements that keep the dancer in the air a good deal of the time. D'Amboise, an athletic dancer with considerable elevation, nonchalantly spun through the air with the greatest of ease, showing no more visible effort than a garage attendant checking oil and water. Janet Reed, one of the finest soubrettes before the public, brought out all the humor of the rumba *pas de deux* with Michael Maule, not finding it necessary to play for obvious laughs. Her wit was sharp, her dancing gracious. Some of the humor elsewhere is forced, especially in the episodes where the child demonstrates her eagerness to use the station's facilities. Humor in one decade has a habit of becoming flat in the next.

The Firebird
(L'Oiseau de feu)

One night Igor Stravinsky went to bed and (in complete accordance with all success stories and fairy tales) woke up famous. The day after the *première* of *The Firebird* on the evening of June 25, 1910, at the Paris Opéra, Stravinsky was a made man. To that happy circumstance he owed an assist to the laziness of Anatol Lyadov.

For Lyadov originally had been commissioned by Diaghilev to compose the score to the ballet. He dawdled until the then unknown Stravinsky was brought in. Stravinsky had aroused Diaghilev's enthusiasm with an orchestral scherzo named *Fireworks.* Another link between them was the composer's interest in painting, sculpture, and the arts in general. Alexandre Benois, in his reminiscences, has stated that what Diaghilev and other officials of the Ballets Russes especially admired about Stravinsky was "the absence of the slightest dogmatism

113

—the dogmatism which, whatever his admirers and adepts may say, later on dried up and froze his creative power. In general, if Stravinsky did sometimes shock us with his typically 'Russian abruptness' and a slight tendency to be cynical, he had nevertheless a charming spontaneity and that 'sentimental reaction' which is the best source of inspiration."

And so Stravinsky was called in and set to work on *The Firebird*. He was highly flattered. Throughout the winter of 1909 he worked hard on the ballet, constantly in touch with Diaghilev and Fokine, who was the choreographer. Fokine, reports Stravinsky in his memoirs, "created the choreography of *L'Oiseau* section by section as the music was handed to him. I attended every rehearsal with the company, and after rehearsals, Diaghilev, Nijinsky (who was not, however, dancing in the ballet) and myself generally ended the day with a fine dinner washed down by claret."

Stravinsky was a little unhappy about the casting, "which was not what I had intended. Pavlova, with her slim, angular figure, had seemed to me infinitely better suited to the tale of the fairy bird than Karsavina, with her gentle feminine charm, for whom I had intended the part of the captive princess. Though circumstances had decided otherwise than I had planned, I had no cause for complaint, since Karsavina's rendering of the bird's part was perfect, and that beautiful and gracious artist had a brilliant success in it."

The composer was still under the influence of Rimsky-Korsakov in this score. *The Firebird* deals with a Russian legend (Balakirev had once planned an opera on it, and the figure of Kastchei appears in Rimsky-Korsakov's opera *Kastchei the Immortal*). Stravinsky, however, went Rimsky-Korsakov more than one better. Like his predecessor, he made use of Russian folk songs. Unlike him, Stravinsky treated the musical material in anything but a literal fashion. *The Firebird* abounds in rhythmic invention and harmonic usage far in advance of anything to come from Rimsky-Korsakov's pen. Small wonder, then, that the score of *The Firebird* was such an integral factor in the

114

ballet's success. All Europe knew that a major musical figure had arrived.

The Firebird is a prime example of Diaghilev's theory that musician, choreographer, painter, and dancer should work in close co-operation while creating a ballet. Fokine may have been the first to come up with the basic idea; he had always wanted to compose a ballet based on a Russian fairy tale. He evolved most of the scenario, working closely with various members of the company, especially Serge Grigoriev, the *régisseur,* who obtained several collections of Russian fairy tales. When Diaghilev told them of Lyadov's defection and that Stravinsky had been substituted as the composer, there was what Grigoriev has called "an ominous silence." The Diaghilev company, if they had heard of Stravinsky at all, knew of him only as a promising beginner. But Diaghilev was not to be deterred.

Alexander Golovin was entrusted with the sets, and the company went into rehearsal. Everybody knew that *The Firebird* was going to be a success, even if Alexandre Benois took exception to Golovin's *décor.* "The greatest experts in stage planning," he wrote in his *Reminiscences of the Russian Ballet,* "could not have made head or tail of that maze of approximation. It seemed like a huge, chequered carpet, blazing with color but devoid of any depth. . . . Golovin's costumes were even less successful. . . . The result was that Fokine's choreographic ideas, performed by the artists in working clothes at rehearsals, seemed to be extremely fantastic and eerie, but on the stage everything was submerged in uniform, sumptuous luxury." There also was the trouble that inevitably accompanies a new, complicated score of genius. "From the moment they heard the first bar," Grigoriev recalls, "the company were all too obviously dismayed at the absence of melody in the music" —absence of melody in *The Firebird!*—"and its unlikeness to what they were used to dancing at the Maryinsky. Some of them indeed declared that it did not sound like music at all."

It was found necessary to keep Stravinsky on hand to clarify the difficult points of his score. Stravinsky would sit in the re-

hearsal studio "demolishing" the piano, banging out the
rhythms, humming loudly in his typical composer's voice, and
not caring whether or not he hit the right notes. Grigoriev, for
one, found it invigorating to watch such a display of temperament, and he believes that Fokine may have been inspired by
Stravinsky's presence. "Also the extraordinary music led Fokine
to the invention of original steps, which the dancers could not
but enjoy and be amused at." When the ballet was finished and
danced through before Diaghilev and his friends, it made a deep
impression, rough as the product was at the time.

Gabriel Pierné, the well-known French composer, conducted
the opening-night performance. He and his musicians had some
trouble at rehearsals, and again Stravinsky had to be called
in to explain the niceties of his music. *The Firebird* was in rehearsal right up to the opening curtain. At the one and only
dress rehearsal, the lighting was chaotic, and Fokine was in a
frenzy of anxiety. Diaghilev came to his rescue by promising to
operate the switchboard himself, which he did. Among Grigoriev's worries was Fokine's idea, on which he insisted, of having
two live horses on the stage. When the curtain went up, one
horseman dressed in black on a black horse was to cross the
stage from one corner, a horseman in white on a white horse
from another. They symbolized night and day. Diaghilev supported Fokine's notion, probably figuring that the horsemen
would produce an unexpected effect on the public. He was
right. "The public," Grigoriev writes, "was certainly astonished
by the horses, and Fokine was duly delighted." To Grigoriev's
unbounded happiness, the animals did not last beyond the second performance (nor have they ever returned).

The *première* was a triumph. Tamara Karsavina was the
toast of Paris after it saw her Firebird. Fokine himself danced
the Tsarevich, and Alexis Bulgakov was seen as Kastchei (Enrico
Cecchetti did not dance this role at the *première,* as has so often
been claimed). Vera Fokina danced the role of the Tsarevna.
Next day the Parisian press went wild, as the Parisian press will
do on covering an artistic event of unprecedented importance.

The Firebird is in one act. The plot, a composite of several

Russian fairy tales, takes place in a mysterious forest. Prince Ivan, the Tsarevich, is seen, hunting. He is frightened by the appearance of the Firebird and runs off. She dances, brilliantly and in an otherworldly fashion; and the Prince steals on to watch her. As she finishes the dance, he captures her. She pleads for mercy, they dance together, and he gives the creature her freedom in return for one of her feathers. After she leaves, twelve maidens enter and are joined by another, the Tsarevna. When Ivan greets them, they tell him to flee, for he is on the grounds of Kastchei, the mighty enchanter. Ivan, in love with the Tsarevna, refuses to leave. Suddenly the stage darkens and fills with the demons and retainers of Kastchei, who capture Ivan. The enchanter enters and attempts to cast a spell over the Prince. Ivan waves the Firebird's feather, and she comes to his aid. She dances wildly among the demons until they fall to the ground in an exhausted sleep, whereupon the Firebird leads Ivan to a hollow tree. He pulls out a casket in which reposes an egg. Kastchei is less than happy at this turn of events, for the egg contains his soul. He clutches at it, but Ivan hurls it against the ground. Kastchei dies, and the maidens are released from his enchantment. The maidens, a group of young men, and Ivan's beloved hail him as their deliverer.

America first saw the ballet in the very first American performance by the Diaghilev Ballets Russes at New York's Century Theatre on January 17, 1916. The leading parts were danced by Xenia Maclezova, Leonide Massine, and Enrico Cecchetti. Ernest Ansermet conducted the orchestra. During the American ballet renaissance in the thirties, several productions of *The Firebird* were seen. Col. W. de Basil's Ballet Russe brought its version to the Majestic Theatre in New York on March 20, 1935. Alexandra Danilova danced the title role, and also in the cast were Tamara Grigorieva, Leonide Massine, and David Lichine. In the Original Ballet Russe presentation, at the Fifty-first Street Theatre on December 6, 1940, the Firebird was Irina Baronova and the Tsarevna was again Grigorieva. Paul Petroff and Igor Schwezoff were the other principals. Both productions used sets and costumes by Natalie Gontcharova. A revival by

Ballet Theatre at the Metropolitan Opera House on October 24, 1945, used choreography by Adolph Bolm and sets and costumes by Marc Chagall. The cast included Alicia Markova, Anton Dolin, John Taras, and Diana Adams.

This was not a successful revival. The New York City Ballet Company later purchased the Chagall sets, which provided the necessary spark for a version by Balanchine. The new *Firebird* was first done on November 27, 1949, at the New York City Center of Music and Drama. Maria Tallchief, Francisco Moncion, Edward Bigelow, and Pat McBride were the dancers. Perhaps another factor in Balanchine's revision was Stravinsky's reservation about the original Fokine choreography, which he thought complicated and overburdened with detail. It was the composer's belief that the dancers experienced too great difficulty co-ordinating their steps and gestures with the music, with a consequent esthetic discord.

Balanchine's restaging discarded many of the elements in the original Ballets Russes production. He used not the 1910 score, but a suite arranged by Stravinsky—a suite that omitted about a third of the original material and used a considerably smaller orchestra. Balanchine also discarded some of the plot, notably the section dealing with the egg containing Kastchei's soul. The restaging achieved a mixed reception in New York, although it was conceded that as a tour-de-force Tallchief's Firebird was remarkable. The big fuss about the ballet came from England, where the critics screamed sacrilege: "tabloid version . . . unconvincing . . . mistimed . . . loses its point" and, the greatest insult they could dredge up, "Hollywood!"

Four years after the British gazed with such horror on the Balanchine revival, they bowed low to the ground to honor the Sadler's Wells revival, first seen at the Edinburgh Festival on August 23, 1954. This production aimed at reproducing the original Diaghilev *Firebird*. Natalie Goncharova, who had made the sets and costumes for Diaghilev after the Golovin sets were destroyed, was commissioned to do the same for Sadler's Wells. Serge Grigoriev, who had played such a prominent part in the inception of the ballet back in 1910, staged the new production

with his wife, Lubov Tchernicheva. She had been one of Diaghilev's principal dancers and ballet mistress. The great Karsavina, living in England, coached Margot Fonteyn in the title
role. And Ernest Ansermet, who had been associated with the
ballet in its early days, conducted. In addition to Fonteyn, others
in the Edinburgh cast were Michael Somes, Frederick Ashton,
and Svetlana Beriosova.

New York greeted this production at the Metropolitan Opera
House on September 20, 1955. The same quartet of dancers—
Fonteyn (Firebird), Somes (Ivan), Beriosova (Tsarevna), and
Ashton (Kastchei)—appeared. Many observers at this American
première felt like archaeologists who had come upon an ancient
structure in a perfect state of preservation. Criticism, in a way,
would be impertinent. There was no denying that Fokine's *Firebird* had somewhat dated; and a dance in which the maidens
rolled apples across the stage had some of the audience in titters.
On the other hand, *The Firebird* as thus seen had a wonderful
freshness and sweetness, an indescribable charm, and some beautiful moments of sheer dance. Some defects in actual performance could have been pointed out. Somes swaggered not too
convincingly, and Ashton played a little too much for laughs:
as Fokine conceived Kastchei, the enchanter was certainly not
a burlesque figure. To balance this was Fonteyn's magical, fluttering Firebird, a golden vision soaring above the earth. Beriosova as the Tsarevna was sweet, demure, and elegant, a fairy-
tale princess about whom adults dream. The production was
mounted with typical Sadler's Wells extravagance, and in the
final tableau the entire company was on stage. *The Firebird* as
done this way is magnificent theater. It should be in the repertoire as long as ballet lasts.

The Four Temperaments

 The Four Temperaments is subtitled "A Dance Ballet Without Plot." According to its choreographer, George Balanchine, the work "is an expression in dance and music of the ancient notion that the human organism is made up of four different degrees, and it is from the dominance of one of them that the four physical and psychological types—melancholic, sanguinic, phlegmatic, and choleric—were derived."

A fuller explanation is given in Robert Burton's endlessly fascinating compendium of medieval medical lore, *The Anatomy of Melancholy*. Those who would like to read up on the entire subject should consult *The Anatomy*, MEM. II, Subs. 2. It starts as follows:

A humour is a liquid or fluent part of the body, comprehended in it, for the preservation of it; and is either innate or born with us, or adventitious and acquisite. The radical or innate is daily supplied by nourishment, which some call *cambium,* and make those secondary humours of *ros* and *gluten* to maintain it . . .

Blood is a hot, sweet, temperate, red humour, prepared in the meseraick veins, and made of the most temperate parts of the *chylus* in the liver, whose office is to nourish the whole body, to give it strength and color, being dispersed by the veins through every part of it . . .

Pituita, or phlegm, is a cold and moist humour, begotten of the colder part of the *chylus* (or white juice coming out of the meat digested in the stomack) in the liver; his office is to moisten the members of the body, which, as the tongue, are moved, that they be not over dry.

Choler is hot and dry, bitter, begotten of the hotter parts of the *chylus,* and gathered to the gall: it helps the natural heat and senses, and serves to the expelling of excrements.

Melancholy, cold and dry, thick, black, and sour, begotten of the more faeculent part of nourishment, and purged from the spleen, is a bridle to the other two hot humours, *blood* and *choler,* preserving them in the blood, and nourishing the bones. These four humours have some analogy with the four elements, and to the four ages in man.

Thus the four temperaments. The ballet, set to the Theme and Four Variations by Paul Hindemith, was produced in 1946. Balanchine and Lincoln Kirstein had commissioned the score in 1940 for the Latin American tour of the American Ballet in 1941. Anatole Chujoy, in *The New York City Ballet,* states that the two men had proposed to call the ballet *The Cave of Sleep,* and that Pavel Tchelitchev was commissioned to do the *décor* and scenery. But "the ballet was not mounted at that time because of the dissatisfaction of the composer with Tchelitchev's sketches. He felt that the visual impression offered him, however beautiful, was overwhelming, and contained ideas extraneous to his original program."

In the meantime, Hindemith's score had received its *première* on September 3, 1944, in Boston, Richard Burgin conducting an ensemble of Boston Symphony players for the performance. Then in 1946 a new *décor* was commissioned from Kurt Seligmann. Ballet Society was formed by Balanchine and Lincoln

Kirstein that year, and *The Four Temperaments* was on the initial program of the society, given at the Central High School of Needle Trades, New York, on November 20, 1946. Chujoy describes the auditorium of the high school as "a huge, barn-like hall, cold and uninviting . . . as impersonal as a railroad station." No great inspiration for dancers, this, but the program went on as scheduled, though the audience could hear the scenic men nailing the sets into place. Dancing in the *première* were Beatrice Tompkins and José Martínez (Theme); Elise Reiman and Lew Christensen, Gisella Caccialanza and Francisco Moncion, William Dollar, Georgia Hiden, Rita Karlin, and ensemble (Melancholic Variation); Mary Ellen Moylan, Fred Danieli and ensemble (Sanguinic Variation); Todd Bolender and ensemble (Phlegmatic Variation); Tanaquil LeClercq, William Dollar, Todd Bolender, and ensemble (Choleric Variation).

Seligmann's sets and costumes were rather overpowering and tended to obscure the motions of the dancers. In the current production of the New York City Ballet Company, the sets and scenery have been discarded, and *The Four Temperaments* is performed by dancers in plain black practice clothes. The ballet entered the New York City Ballet repertoire on October 25, 1948. Maria Tallchief, Todd Bolender, Tanaquil LeClercq, and Herbert Bliss were the leading dancers.

The Four Temperaments is plotless and in five parts. The first section, Theme, presents three couples who move in accord with the musical statements. The first variation, Melancholic, is slow and features a male dancer, solo, who later is joined by several girls. The second variation, Sanguinic, is in waltz tempo, with a male and female dancer supported by a group of four secondary dancers. The third variation is Phlegmatic, in which a male dancer, alone at first, engages in a lively dance with four girls. In the fourth variation, Choleric, a ballerina has a brief solo and then is joined for a spirited conclusion by the rest of the ensemble.

Not as super-objective as many Balanchine ballets, *The Four Temperaments* makes an effort to reflect the subject in the type of motion selected for it. The ballet has been conceived in something of a neo-classic style (despite its frequent romantic touches), and has been assembled with the clockwork precision that Balanchine, above all living choreographers, knows so well how to attain. The movements and patterns are sharp, clear, and logical; but the planning has heart as well as skill behind it. *The Four Temperaments* has been an admired part of the New York City Ballet Company repertoire ever since its *première*.

Gaîté Parisienne

In *Gaîté Parisienne* Leonide Massine created what is probably the most popular
and the most-performed ballet ever presented in America. Since its *première* in
1938, it has never been out of the Ballet
Russe de Monte Carlo repertoire (and it
never has been performed by any other
ballet company). It is a good-natured romp,
backed by sparkling Offenbach music (brilliantly arranged and orchestrated by Man-
uel Rosenthal), full of lively dance, and
with a story line that seems irresistible to
ballet audiences everywhere. If everything
else has failed, *Gaîté Parisienne* at the end
of an evening is guaranteed to send any
audience homeward happy.

Massine had a flair for comic ballets like
this, and it is unfortunate that he did not
create more of them instead of wasting his
time with such now-forgotten symphonic
ballets as *Choarteum* and *Seventh Sym-*

phony. A sure workman and an experienced man of the theater, Massine was able to keep things moving clearly, steadily, and entertainingly. Nobody is going to pretend that *Gaîté* is the ultimate in choreographic art, but it is a good deal better than some more ambitious attempts by less gifted creators.

Gaîté Parisienne is in one act. The action takes place in a large, luxurious Paris restaurant. Waiters and cleaning girls are busily preparing the room for the evening's customers. The flower girl enters in a flurry, flirts with the waiters, and sets up her stand. The glove seller also gets ready for business. The restaurant begins to fill up. One of the central characters of the ballet, the Peruvian, makes a whirlwind entrance. This is obviously his first trip to Paris, and he must have been hearing stories about the city. He is out for a good time, and he has the money to see that he gets it. He buys a flower from the flower girl, and then, attracted by the good looks of the glove seller, lets her fit him with a pair of gloves.

The baron enters, and the flower girl makes a play for him. The baron, however, is more interested in the glove seller, and asks her to dance. The Peruvian, meanwhile, is flitting from one girl to another, wriggling with delight and anticipation. Some soldiers and an officer enter and dance with the girls. La Lionne, an elegant and haughty beauty, makes a dramatic entrance. All the men flock to her, causing annoyance to her escort, the duke. The party now is becoming lively. The Peruvian flirts with the glove seller, and the baron is displeased. Nor does the duke like the way La Lionne is taking up with the dashing young officer (*all* officers in the ballet world are young and dashing; it's an unalterable law). A general fight breaks out, during which the Peruvian crawls under a table, trembling. Finally the restaurant is cleared. The baron and the glove seller, now friends again, return for a charming *pas de deux*. Once again the restaurant fills up. The can-can girls perform and the crowd is wild with excitement. Now it is time to go home, and everybody finds a friend for the night. The glove seller and the baron, La Lionne and the officer, the flower girl and the duke disappear into the night. The Peruvian? He had thought that he was dated up with the glove seller, and he stands disconsolate as he is left alone.

The world *première* of *Gaîté Parisienne* took place at the Théâtre de Monte Carlo on April 5, 1938. In the cast were Nina Tarakanova (Glove Seller), Eugenia Delarova (Flower Girl), Jeannette Lauret (La Lionne), Leonide Massine (Peruvian), Frederic Franklin (Baron), and Igor Youskevitch (Officer). The book, *décor,* and costumes were by Count Étienne de Beaumont. At the American *première,* at the Metropolitan Opera House on October 12, 1938, Alexandra Danilova was the Glove Seller and Lubov Rostova took the part of La Lionne. The other principals were the same.

The role of the glove seller turned out to be one of the most popular of Danilova's portrayals. It seemed to be made to order for her, and she danced it constantly until her departure from the Ballet Russe de Monte Carlo in 1953. Danilova, of course, was more than a dancer; she was a legend—one of the last active figures of the great Diaghilev days (she was dancing with the company as early as 1924). Invariably she was partnered by the dashing, eternally youthful Frederic Franklin. As they danced the waltz, it was a second-Empire evocation in which Danilova was the most coquettish of *cocottes,* Franklin the most ardent and aristocratic of lovers. At the point of writing (1955), Franklin is still dancing the role of the Baron. And it does not take a particularly long memory to recall Massine's exploits as the Peruvian. Nobody since has come near his characterization, though (lest we be accused of being like the old gentleman in the corner who mumbles about Sothern and Marlowe) it cannot be denied that Leon Danielian, who currently dances the role, has had his own contribution to make to it.

Gala Performance

Gala Performance is a satirical ballet that also happens to be humorous. The two do not always go together. Humor, as defined by Webster, is the faculty of discovering, expressing, or appreciating the ludicrous or the incongruous. Satire is the act of holding up abuses, vice, shortcomings to reprobation or ridicule. Swift's *A Modest Proposal* is a satire that is not very humorous; Shakespeare's *Much Ado* is humorous without being satirical.

Humor is a difficult thing to express in ballet in an adult fashion. There can be, and often is, humor of movement. Ballet is a highly stylized art form using a specific vocabulary of movement. When a dancer gets into position, certain things are expected; and when those certain things are altered, the results can be funny, much as if a sprinter, halfway down the track, suddenly decided to finish the race on his hands

127

and knees. Thus, in ballet, when the dancer makes strenuous preparations for a series of rapid turns, creating an empathic response in the audience, and then slowly revolves once with an air of having accomplished a rare and precious thing, the result is funny (as it was when André Eglevsky did it in a Robbins work no longer in the repertoire). Unfortunately many choreographers have abused this device, relying on obvious laugh-getters such as impossibly awkward poses and actual pratfalls.

Or there can be humor of situation, entirely permissible in a ballet that tells a story. The success of this sort of humor, of course, depends on the novelty or literacy with which the story is told. Tudor's *Judgment of Paris* (also highly satiric) and Massine's *Gaîté Parisienne,* which is rather straight ballet, are authentically funny, deriving their humor from a specific set of circumstances in the libretto.

Antony Tudor's *Gala Performance* is humorous both in movement and in action. And it is highly satiric, holding, as it does, the mirror up to the foibles of three ballerinas, each representing a specific *école de danse*. The action takes place around the turn of the century. *Gala Performance,* in one act, is really divided into two sections, both set to music by Prokofiev. Part I uses the first movement of the Piano Concerto No. 3 in C. Here we are backstage, where dancers are getting ready for a performance just before the curtain goes up. Members of the *corps de ballet* come out and begin to loosen up. Dancers wander on and off, flexing their legs. Everybody is agog with anticipation, for this is the night that three great ballerinas—La Reine de la Danse, from Moscow; La Déesse de la Danse, from Milan; and La Fille de Terpsichore, from Paris—will all be in one ballet.

As everybody watches with grand respect, the Queen haughtily walks forth. She examines the girls, then orders one of them to remove a necklace (said jewelry obviously will conflict with the jewelry *she* is wearing). The Daughter of Terpsichore bounces in, all frills and flutter. She is introduced to her Russian rival, and the greeting lowers the temperature of the surrounding air about fifty degrees. The Goddess from Italy makes the most dramatic entrance of all. Conscious of her great superiority, she walks as though she is honoring the floorboards. She expects homage from everybody; it is her due. She is introduced to the company, and she gives her instructions to the conductor and ballet master just as her two colleagues before her have done. The conductor, who by now has three completely different sets of instructions, nods in agreement. What else can he do? Last-minute preparations take place, the girls of the *corps de ballet* get into position, the lights come up, and the evening's entertainment is about to begin.

Tudor has used the four short movements of Prokofiev's *Classical Symphony* for Part II of *Gala Performance*. After a brief blackout, the scene reveals the stage as seen by the audience. The dancers have positioned themselves and start the ballet. The first movement is the Russian ballerina's dance. With great aplomb and self-satisfaction she performs some complicated turns in the grand manner; and if, once in a while, she is a little sloppy in her execution, who can cavil in the presence of such style? She takes bow after bow; finally she has literally to be peeled from the wings to make room for the Italian ballerina.

All is hushed as the Italian ballerina comes forward as slowly and inevitably as the rising tide. She curtly nods to the conductor and does a slow dance, mostly involving her *pointes* and her ability to hold a pose *en pointe*. She too takes all the bows she can get, thoughtfully ordering the stage cleared so that her partners will not be flustered. Quite different is the French ballerina's dance. This little girl is all over the place in a series of *grands jetés*. Never motionless, she has her partner gasping, and this extends to the bow-takings, for she is always off-stage when he is looking for her to share the applause. Bashfully, each time, he has to retire.

The fourth movement brings the ballerinas together. Each tries to outdo the other, though the Italian ballerina, with godlike indifference to the mortals around her, carries on as though she were alone. In a magnificent madhouse, each ballerina executes her own specialty, with not a glimpse at the ensemble that is supposed to be supporting her. The stage is inundated with flowers at the end of the finale. The Italian ballerina manages to scoop up most of them, though she has a hard fight on her hands. Several curtain calls follow, the three ballerinas still trying to get to the favored spot on the stage.

Gala Performance received its *première* at Toynbee Hall, London, by the London Ballet, on December 5, 1938. The three ballerinas were Peggy van Praagh (La Reine de la Danse), Maude Lloyd (La Déesse de la Danse), and Gerd Larsen (La Fille de Terpsichore). The male roles were taken by Hugh Laing (Partner to La Fille) and Antony Tudor (Partner to La Déesse). Scenery and costumes were by Hugh Stevenson. Ballet Theatre gave the first American presentation at the Majestic Theatre, New York, on February 11, 1941. Scenery and costumes were by Nicolas de Molas. In the cast were Nora Kaye (La Reine), Nana Gollner (La Déesse), Karen Conrad (La Fille), and Hugh Laing and Antony Tudor in their original roles.

Gala Performance not only is a deliciously satirical spoof on ballet of the late nineteenth century, but it holds good for our own day. The backstage scene could take place before tomorrow's performance by any ballet company—the nervous tension, the last-minute suggestions, the undercurrent of uncertainty of what will happen once the curtain goes up. Petty rivalries and superstitions (the latter an occupational disease; every dancer not only has a pet superstition of her own, but also generally shares those of everybody else) are still part of the ballet life.

So are the three ballerinas whom Tudor has symbolized. The Russian ballerina is a great virtuoso. Style, line, nuance, sensitivity—these completely escape her—but she is a great virtuoso. She is engrossed with trick turns and other stunts: anything to bring an immediate response from her dear, devoted public. (She is not much different from some of the guest ballerinas from Europe thrust into our companies from time to time.)

Then we have the Italian ballerina—beautiful, haughty, aloof. Everybody was born to be her servant. She is as cold as absolute zero; all she is concerned about is the details of her work. Every movement and gesture is definite, and definitely calculated. She is a stylist rather than a virtuoso, but she has lost sight of the main objective. On the other hand, the French ballerina is a constantly active young lady who moves around so much because she does not have the technique to do anything else (a paradox; but repose is one of the hardest things to achieve in any art). She has good elevation, and she favors one step just to show it off. Her entire variation is based on a simple combination of *grands jetés,* and she exudes an ersatz kind of charm until she almost slides across the stage in it. In all truth, she is not a very good dancer, and tries to make up in personality what she lacks in technique.

Unfortunately in recent years there has been a tendency to "ham" up *Gala Performance* to a point at which it is burlesque and not satire. Which, patly enough, reinforces Tudor's original ideas about the braininess and artistic inclinations of a typical ballerina, who will take off like any other thoroughbred unless restrained by a strong bridle in the form of a ballet-master with teeth (a mixed metaphor that will have to do until a better one comes along).

When *Gala Performance* first entered the Ballet Theatre repertoire, and when Tudor was on hand to bare his teeth, some superb characterizations were seen. Nobody really has succeeded Karen Conrad as the French ballerina. She had more than enough natural elevation for the *grands jetés* with which the role abounds, and she could manage the fussiness of style without being fussy (the only way to handle the part). With a minimum of gesture and stage business she made the part hilarious.

Among the outstanding Italian ballerinas have been Miriam Golden, Nana Gollner, and Alicia Alonso. The best Russian ballerinas have been Nora Kaye and Nina Stroganova. The last-named has not been seen in this country for some years, but her part in *Gala Performance* was memorable. Her training was very close to the school that was being satirized by Tudor, and one had the uneasy feeling that perhaps she was living the role, not merely acting it.

The men, as so typical of the 1900 period, are, in *Gala Per-*

formance, relegated to a role little more than props. They support (when their ballerinas will let them), bow out, and retire. One of the funniest—and somehow touching—moments of *Gala Performance* occurred when Tudor himself, as partner of the Italian ballerina, realized that he no longer was needed. He turned his back to the audience and walked away, conveying by his whole bearing the impression that he wished he were able to vanish on the spot and be spared the embarrassment of having to walk what seems an endless distance off stage. The other men in *Gala Performance* also have their troubles, and only at a few fleeting moments do their ballerinas deign to recognize them as being among the living.

Giselle

 Although not the oldest ballet in the repertoire—*La Fille mal gardée* holds that honor—*Giselle* is the oldest one with a history of continuous performance. *La Fille* was missing for almost one hundred years, whereas *Giselle* has been before the public continuously since 1841. It is *the* romantic ballet; it supplies the ballerina's Ophelia, complete with mad scene. Every actor wants to do Hamlet, every ballerina Giselle; and every great ballerina has danced the role. Name almost any great female dancer of the last hundred years and you have named a great Giselle. Under the ministrations of a lesser dancer *Giselle* can degenerate into sentimental and even ludicrous tosh. Its story is no intellectual contribution, nor is its musical score one to claim immortality (though it works well enough with the stage action). But, given a Giselle with style and acting ability, with the genius to make believable the plight of a young woman who dies of a lovesick heart and later saves her lover from death, the ballet can tear your heart out.

Giselle, as said above, is *the* romantic ballet—a term hard to pin down with any exactitude, but recognizable for all that. It is a flower of the romantic period that produced the Byronism of Liszt, the operas of Weber, the paintings of Delacroix. It deals with a never-never land, where the maidens are all beautiful and the men all handsome. It was a rebellion against the stately formalisms of the classical period, and it invoked the world of fairies and demons. It was the age of the virtuoso—Thalberg and Liszt on the piano, Paganini on the violin, Taglioni in the ballet. It was an age when people drowned themselves in sentiment. Of all this *Giselle* is part.

The genesis of the ballet can be traced in a letter, translated by Cyril Beaumont, that Théophile Gautier wrote to Heinrich Heine on July 5, 1841, one week after the *première* (the entire letter can be found in *The Romantic Ballet as seen by Théophile Gautier,* a fascinating little book published by Beaumont in 1932). "My dear Heinrich Heine," writes Gautier, "when reviewing, a few weeks ago, your fine book, *De l'Allemagne,* I came across a charming passage—one has only to open the book at random—the place where you speak of elves in white dresses, whose hems are always damp; of nixies who display their little satin feet on the ceiling of the nuptial chamber; of snow-colored *wilis* who waltz pitilessly, and of all those delicious apparitions you have encountered in the Harz mountains and on the banks of the Ilse, in a mist softened by German moonlight"—Gautier was a true romantic and a child of his age—"and I involuntarily said to myself: 'Wouldn't this make a pretty ballet?'

"In a moment of enthusiasm I even took a fine large sheet of white paper, and headed it in superb capitals: *Les Wilis.* Then I laughed and threw the sheet aside without giving it any further thought, saying to myself that it was impossible to translate that misty and nocturnal poetry into terms of the theater, that richly sinister phantasmagoria, all those effects of legend and ballad so little in keeping with our customs. In the evening, at the opera, I met, at a turning of the wings, the witty man who knew how to introduce into a ballet, by adding to it much of his own wit, all the fairy caprice of *Le Diable amoureux* of Cazotte, that great poet who invented Hoffmann in the middle of the eighteenth century.

"I told him the tradition of the *Wilis*. Three days later the ballet *Giselle* was accepted. At the end of the week, Adolphe Adam had improvised the music, the scenery was nearly ready, and the rehearsals were in full swing. You see, my dear Heinrich, we are not yet so incredulous and so prosaic as you think we appear."

The "witty man" referred to by Gautier was Jules Henri Vernoy de Saint-Georges, a busy scenarist and librettist who quickly worked up a book for *Giselle*. Gautier in his letter goes on to summarize the plot, in detail. "There, my dear poet," he concludes, "that, more or less, is how M. de Saint-Georges and I have adapted your charming legend, with the help of M. Coralli, who composed the *pas,* groups, and attitudes of exquisite novelty and elegance. For interpreters we chose the three graces of the Opéra: Mlles Carlotta Grisi, Adele Dumilâtre, and Forster. Carlotta danced with a perfection, lightness, boldness, and a chaste and refined seductiveness, which places her in the first rank between Elssler and Taglioni; as for pantomime, she exceeded all expectations; not a single conventional gesture, not one false movement; she was nature and artlessness personified. True, she has Perrot the Aerial for husband and teacher. Petipa was graceful, passionate, and touching; it is a long while since a dancer has given us so much pleasure or been so well received. . . . As for the scenery, it is by Cicéri, who is unequaled for landscapes. The sunrise that marks the conclusion is wonderfully realistic. La Carlotta was recalled to the sound of the applause of the whole house. So, my dear Heine, your German *Wilis* have succeeded completely at the French Opéra."

A note about the dancers. Carlotta Grisi, La Carlotta, was one of the favorites of the romantic age, together with Marie Taglioni and Fanny Elssler. A superb dancer from her teens, she was made a celebrity by *Giselle*. She was, at the time of the

Giselle première, married to Jules Perrot. He is the "Perrot the Aerial" mentioned by Gautier, and he was one of the most famous male dancers and choreographers of the nineteenth century. Perrot wanted very much to stage *Giselle,* but it was Jean Coralli, the staff choreographer of the Opéra, who did the dances. Perrot, however, though Gautier is silent on the point, contributed many ideas to Coralli, and probably choreographed all of Grisi's dances. Another point on which Gautier is silent is his love affair with Grisi, which eventually led to her separation from Perrot. The Petipa referred to above is Lucien, who danced the role of Albrecht. He was the brother of the more famous Marius, choreographer of the Tchaikovsky ballets. Pierre Cicéri was a popular landscape painter of the day. Mlles Forster and Dumilâtre were members of the Opéra ballet. Others in the cast, not mentioned by Gautier, were Eugène Coralli as Wilfrid, M. Simon as Hilarion, and Mlle Roland as Berthe.

Giselle is in two acts. The first takes place in a village on the Rhine. Peasants are busy: it is vintage time. Hilarion, a gamekeeper, enters. He approaches Giselle's cottage, hears somebody coming, and hides. Albrecht, Duke of Silesia, and his squire, Wilfrid, enter. Albrecht doffs his royal cape to reveal the peasant clothes he is wearing. To the peasants he is known as Loys, and he has hidden his royalty because he is, like Hilarion, in love with Giselle. Wilfrid beseeches Albrecht to leave. Albrecht refuses, giving him his cape and sword to conceal. After Wilfrid departs, Albrecht knocks at the door of Giselle's cottage. He playfully hides, and when Giselle appears, looking around, she finds an empty stage. She dances, knowing full well that Albrecht is watching (and not knowing that Hilarion is also a more than interested spectator). Albrecht comes out of hiding and they sit on a bench. He vows eternal love to her. She picks a daisy: he loves me, loves me not. The daisy ends on a "not," whereupon Giselle (whose heart is certainly much stronger than her head) begins to cry. Albrecht consoles her, and they dance. Hilarion furiously strides forth and separates them, swearing that *he* loves her. Giselle spurns him, and he departs, blood in his eye.

Village girls enter. They dance, and Giselle joins them. Albrecht follows. Berthe, Giselle's mother, comes forth, worried, and tells Giselle to stop dancing because of her frail heart. Berthe also warns her daughter that if she dies she will become one of the wilis.* Berthe breaks up the dancing and takes Giselle into the cottage. The stage is empty. Hilarion approaches, determined to find a way to show Giselle that she is being deceived. Hearing a hunting horn, he hides. Enter the Prince of Courland, his daughter Bathilde, and a retinue including Wilfrid. Seeking refreshment, they knock on Berthe's door. Girls bring out a table, two chairs, goblets, wine. Giselle comes out. She bows in awe to the nobility, but is especially fascinated by Bathilde's accoutrements: she never has seen such clothes. Bathilde is amused, a little touched, and also struck by Giselle's beauty. She takes off her necklace and gives it to the peasant girl. Then the prince and princess go into the cottage to rest.

Hilarion comes from his hiding place. He has discovered Albrecht's cape and sword. At this moment a group of peasant boys and girls enters and prevails on Berthe to allow Giselle to dance. This she does, being joined by Albrecht. It is now Hilarion's moment. He pushes the lovers apart and brandishes Albrecht's sword, the sign of nobility. Giselle refuses to believe it, but Albrecht knows the game is up. When the prince and princess come out, they see Albrecht dressed in peasant clothes. Why? Albrecht kneels before Bathilde, and when the agonized Giselle protests—even attacks Bathilde—she is told that Albrecht and Bathilde are betrothed.

Giselle's mad scene follows. She flings to the ground the necklace Bathilde has given her. She faints. On reviving, she pitifully wanders across the stage, her feet dismally echoing the steps that she and Albrecht had happily danced. Her mind wanders. Seeing the sword, she seizes it and stabs herself. Hilar-

* In German fairy mythology, a wili is a girl who dies before her wedding day and is doomed to dance all night in the forest after death. Night after night the wilis dance, hounding to death all who cross their path.

ion for the first time realizes the unutterable harm he has wrought. Giselle dies; and Albrecht, first trying to kill Hilarion, falls across her body, sobbing. Hilarion flees, horror-stricken, and the peasants grieve.

The second act opens on a forest glade just before midnight. Giselle's grave is seen bathed in a white light. Three hunters enter with a lantern and proceed to amuse themselves with a dice game. As midnight approaches they get restless and leave the haunted glen. So does Hilarion, who is despondently wandering about. An eerie silence, and then Myrtha, Queen of the Wilis, enters. She dances—a cold, brilliant, dispassionate dance —and summons the wilis. All dance and turn toward Giselle's grave. Giselle rises and dances. At the end of the dance, when the stage is deserted, Albrecht and Wilfrid enter. Albrecht dismisses Wilfrid and bows in misery before the grave. Giselle appears, flitting past him like a vision. He pursues her, dances with her, follows her into the depths of the forest. Hilarion enters, to be confronted with Myrtha and all of the wilis. He is condemned to death and hurled into a lake. Albrecht is next to be condemned. Giselle pleads for his life, but Myrtha is adamant, whereupon Giselle points to the cross on her grave. When Albrecht takes refuge under it, Myrtha is helpless. But she has other cards to play. She orders Giselle to dance, and the newest of the wilis cannot refuse. Albrecht leaves the protection of the cross to dance with her. Again they plead; again their plea is refused. They continue to dance, and Albrecht grows exhausted. Soon he will die. But day approaches, and the wilis vanish back to their graves. Albrecht, saved, falls across the tomb into which Giselle has vanished forever.

Giselle began to make the rounds immediately after its *première* at the Théâtre de l'Academie Royale de Musique, Paris, on June 28, 1841. About five months after its first performance it was in the New World. At least, a *Giselle*-inspired ballet was given at the Olympic Theater, New York, on November 1, 1841. It was "a melodramatic ballet" entitled *Giselle or the Doomed Bride,* and it probably had no perceptible relation to the *Giselle* that Paris had seen. Mr. and Mrs. Wells, Mrs. Watts, and Mrs. Baldock, whoever they may have been, were the dancers, and they shared the bill with a farce named *Bob Short*. A production undoubtedly truer to the spirit of the original took place at the Park Theater on February 2, 1846, as danced by Augusta Maywood and "Mons. Frederic." The following April 13, also at the Park Theater, saw the appearance of the American ballerina Mary Ann Lee as the hapless heroine. Lee, partnered by a dancer with the somewhat American name of George Washington Smith, had probably introduced a fairly definitive *Giselle* to America in a performance given in Boston at the Howard Athenaeum on January 1, 1846. She had studied with Coralli in Paris, had seen *Giselle* many times, and was probably a really accomplished dancer.

Of course the ballet was bound to end up in the Diaghilev repertoire, though the impresario felt (as he had felt in the case of *Coppélia*) that it was too well known to Parisian audiences. He held out for a while, but the men on his staff finally talked him into it. Tamara Karsavina and Vaslav Nijinsky were given the leading parts, Alexandre Benois did the sets, and Fokine rehearsed the company. June 18, 1910, saw the Paris *première* by the Ballets Russes. Serge Grigoriev later said that Diaghilev had been proved right in predicting that *Giselle* was not what the Paris public would wish to see danced by Russians, that it found *Giselle* old-fashioned and lacking excitement.

Benois, in his *Reminiscences of the Russian Ballet,* had some pertinent remarks to make about *Giselle:* "It is in some respects an ideal ballet, for it is short . . . but comprehends nevertheless the whole gamut of human feelings. The subject is, within limits, both reasonable and unreasonable. A measure of fancy has been found and is so presented that it compels our belief. It is the same measure we find in our favorite fairy-tales; they are beloved by us because they fulfill the same demands. Further, the choreographic story of *Giselle* has this advantage over many other ballet stories, that one of its chief elements is *the dance.* Thanks to this, *Giselle* remains something incomparable and inimitable." Benois points out that *Giselle* had been intended by Diaghilev specifically for Pavlova, and that Karsavina got the role only when Pavlova did not rejoin the company for the 1910 season. "I must confess," he writes, "that in those days this seemed to be something of a risk. Karsavina was just beginning the serious work of perfecting herself, and it seemed to us that she was a long way behind Pavlova. Our prejudice was so great that we somehow forgot the enormous success that she had scored during the previous season. However, Karsavina stood the test with the greatest brilliance and from the moment she created the role of Giselle she almost outshone Pavlova." Pavlova, of course, had already danced Giselle at the Maryinsky Theater with thrilling impact. Their names were followed by those of Spessivtzeva, Markova, Fonteyn, Alonso, and the other great Giselles of this century.

The role of Giselle, it need not be stressed, is perhaps the most difficult in the repertoire, rivaled only by the Odette-Odile combination in *Swan Lake*. To dance Giselle properly, the ballerina must be a superlative and extremely subtle actress. Otherwise, bathos. Given a great dancer, the ballet, after a century, continues to stand up amazingly well *as a ballet*. The dances are woven in and out of the action with remarkable fluency, and throughout the two acts there are almost no extraneous divertissements. This is not to imply that the choreography lacks moments of breath-taking brilliance, but to say that they are so skillfully arranged as to be always parts of the whole.

During the village scene in the first act, for example, Giselle has a solo that starts out innocently enough but is climaxed by a succession of *ballonnés* and *attitudes en avant* while hopping on one *pointe* in a diagonal across the stage; this is followed by a series of fast turn combinations. This is a technical feat under any circumstances, but from where the audience sits it must not appear to be a virtuoso stunt, and the dancer must keep the pyrotechnics within the gentle characterization of Giselle. She is not a grand ballerina performing brilliantly, but a shy country girl very much in love. Some ballerinas within recent memory have done everything but stand on their heads to impress the audience; but they are not great Giselles. Only the pure in artistic heart can successfully attempt the role.

America has seen many Giselles through the years. After Mary Ann Lee, there were such dancers as Hermine Blangy (1846), Henrietta Vallée (1847), Julia Turnbull (1847), Caroline Rousset (1851), Léontine Pougoud (1853), Celestine Franck (1858), Lizzie Schultze (1864), and Katti Lanner (1870). Pavlova was seen in a revival at the Metropolitan Opera House, New York, on October 15, 1910; this abridged version had Michael Mordkin as Albrecht. For about twenty-five years, America went *Giselle*-less. Then, in June 1934, a condensed version was given at Radio City Music Hall, with choreography by Florence Rogge. Nina Whitney danced the title role.

Three years later Mordkin revived *Giselle* for his own ballet; the work was danced by Lucia Chase (Giselle), Dimitri Romanoff (Hilarion), Viola Essen (Myrtha), and Mordkin himself (Albrecht). The Ballet Russe de Monte Carlo introduced its version to New York at the Metropolitan Opera House on October 12, 1938. This version, restaged by Serge Lifar, with scenery and costumes after Benois, was danced by Alicia Markova (Giselle), Serge Lifar (Albrecht), Marc Platoff (Hilarion), and Alexandra Danilova (Myrtha). Later Igor Youskevitch took Lifar's part.

A more definitive revival was presented by Ballet Theatre on January 12, 1940, at the Center Theater, New York. Anton Dolin, who was responsible for the restaging, attempted a reconstruction of the Russian version first produced in Moscow in 1842. Lucinda Ballard created the costumes and scenery. The leading dancers were Dolin (Albrecht), and Annabelle Lyon (Giselle). When Markova joined Ballet Theatre in 1941, she took over the title role in her incomparable manner. No other ballerina of our time has brought to the role comparable pathos, delicacy, and understanding. A new Ballet Theatre version, staged by George Balanchine, was first presented at the Broadway Theater, New York, on October 15, 1946. Alicia Alonso and Igor Youskevitch were the leading dancers. New scenery and costumes were supplied by Eugene Berman. Alonso

141

and Youskevitch made one of the most nearly perfect couples that this generation has seen in *Giselle*. Her ideas about the role were mature and intense. She brought to it a subjective, introspective quality that only a Markova could have equaled, and she performed some technical feats that Markova never has cared to attempt. Youskevitch, who may well be the greatest *danseur noble* of our time, provided the most sympathetic portrayal of Albrecht that New York has ever seen.

Giselle entered the Sadler's Wells repertoire on January 1, 1934, at the Old Vic Theatre, London. It underwent several modifications thereafter. American audiences are familiar with the Covent Garden production of June 12, 1946, which uses sets and costumes by James Bailey. At the American *première*, on September 19, 1950 at the Metropolitan Opera House, Margot Fonteyn danced the title role, Michael Somes was the Albrecht, and Pamela May danced the role of Myrtha. Moira Shearer also was seen as Giselle during that season, and her characterization attracted as much favorable comment as Fonteyn's. Hers was a youthful, appealing Giselle of uncommon beauty and lyricism.

André Eglevsky in APOLLO (Stravinsky-Balanchine)

Francisco Moncion, Nicholas Magallanes, and Maria Tallchief
in ORPHEUS (Stravinsky-Balanchine)

Alicia Markova in L'APRÈS-MIDI D'UN FAUNE

ABOVE: Eugene Loring (striped pants) as Billy in the Copland-Loring Ballet Caravan BILLY THE KID (with Erick Hawkins, Lew Christensen, Michael Kidd)

BELOW: John Kriza as the young Billy (Ballet Theatre)

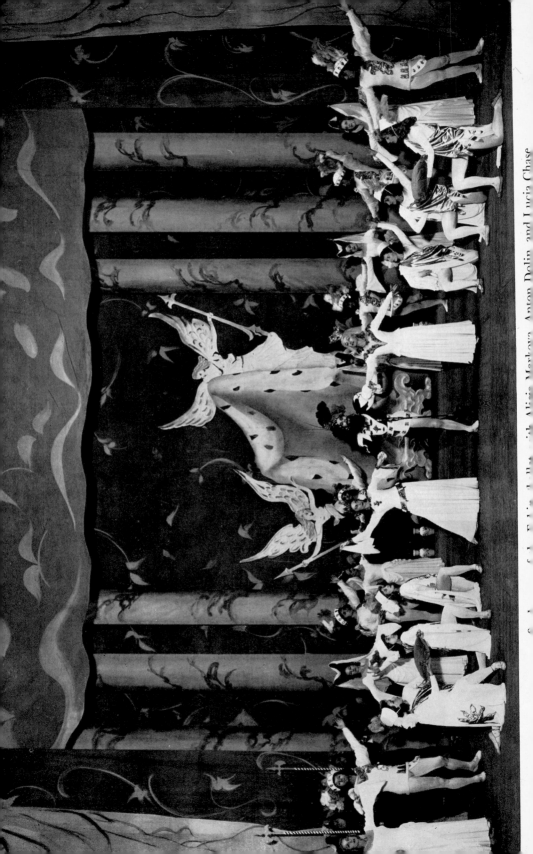

A scene from the ballet *Bluebeard*, with Alicia Markova, Anton Dolin, and Lucia Chase

Tanaquil LeClercq, Todd Bolender, and others
in the Chabrier-Balanchine BOURRÉE FANTASQUE

Members of the New York City Ballet in THE CAGE (Stravinsky-Robbins)

Alexandra Danilova in COPPÉLIA (Ballet Russe de Monte Carlo)

Frederic Franklin and Danilova in COPPÉLIA

Michael Somes as Daphnis in the Ravel-Ashton DAPHNIS AND CHLOE (Sadler's Wells)

Hugh Laing and Nora Kaye in the Strauss-Tudor DIM LUSTRE (Ballet Theatre)

Antony Tudor, Hugh Laing, Agnes de Mille in the revival of
Tudor's JUDGMEŃT OF PARIS (Ballet Theatre, 1955)

The original FANCY FREE (Bernstein-Robbins): Janet Reed, Muriel Bentley, Harold Lang, Jerome Robbins, John Kriza (Ballet Theatre)

Janet Reed and others in the New York City Ballet production of
FILLING STATION (Thomson-Christensen)

THE NUTCRACKER: the New York City Ballet revival,
with Maria Tallchief and André Eglevsky

Tamara Karsavina and Adolph Bolm in the Diaghilev Ballets Russes production

THE FIREBIRD—I

Tamara Karsavina
(left) coached
Margot Fonteyn
(right) for the 1954
Sadler's Wells revival.

Margot Fonteyn in the Sadler's Wells Ballet revival

THE FIREBIRD—II

Francisco Moncion and Maria Tallchief in the Balanchine adaptation (New York City Bal

Irina Baronova in LA FILLE MAL GARDÉE (Ballet Theatre)

Leonide Massine as the Peruvian in GAÎTÉ PARISIENNE
(Ballet Russe de Monte Carlo)

GALA PERFORMANCE:

...tory: Tudor, Nora Kaye (Russian ballerina), Alicia Alonso (Italian ballerina), Norma Vance (French ballerina), Hugh Laing (Ballet Theatre)

GISELLE: Alicia Markova and Anton Dolin

ELLE: Alicia Alonso (center), with Sonia Arova and Igor Youskevitch (Ballet Theatre)

Nicholas Magallanes in the Britten-Ashton ILLUMINATIONS (New York City Ballet)

John Kriza, Leo Duggan, Eric Braun, Ivan Allen in
the Gould-Robbins INTERPLAY (Ballet Theatre)

George Skibine and Marjorie Tallchief in the Rieti-Bellini-
Balanchine NIGHT SHADOW (Marquis de Cuevas' Grand Ballet)

Allegra Kent in the Ives-Balanchine IVESIANA (New York City Ballet)

PETROUCHKA: Alicia Markova, Nicholas Beriosov, Leonide Massine
(Ballet Russe de Monte Carlo, late 1930s)

PETROUCHKA: Lucia Chase, Dimitri Romanoff, Michael Kidd (Ballet Theatre)

PILLAR OF FIRE (Schoenberg-Tudor), with original Ballet Theatre cast—
Annabelle Lyon, Antony Tudor, Lucia Chase, Nora Kaye, Hugh Laing

A STREETCAR NAMED DESIRE (North-Bettis): Christine Mayer, John Kriza, Nora Kaye,
George Tomal, Scott Douglas (Ballet Theatre)

PRODIGAL SON: Francisco Moncion in the
New York City Ballet production (Prokofiev-Balanchine)

GRADUATION BALL
(Strauss-Dorati-Lichine):
Ruth Ann Koesun
and David Lichine
(Ballet Theatre)

RODEO: Opening scene (ABOVE) of the Copland–de Mille ballet, with scenery and costumes by Oliver Smith
Closing scene (BELOW) front, center—Allyn McLerie and John Kriza

ROMEO AND JULIET: Alicia Alonso and Hugh Laing in scenes from the Delius-Tudor version, with scenery and costumes by Eugene Berman (Ballet Theatre)

SCHÉHÉRAZADE: version of the Bakst scenery and costumes (about 1932) for René Blum's Ballets de Monte Carlo

SLEEPING BEAUTY: Rowena Jackson and Brian Shaw
(from the NBC-TV Sadler's Wells performance, December 12, 1955)

THE BLUEBIRDS

Karen Conrad and
Ian Gibson
(PRINCESS AURORA,
early Ballet Theatre days)

SOUVENIRS: Todd Bolender and Jane Mason;
scenery and costumes by Rouben Ter-Arutunian (New York City Ballet)

Tanaquil LeClercq, Barbara Bocher, Todd Bolender in the
Copland-Robbins PIED PIPER (New York City Ballet)

SWAN LAKE—1: Robert Helpmann and Margot Fonteyn (Odile) in Act III of the Sadler's Wells full-length version

SWAN LAKE—II: Act II of the Sadler's Wells production; scenery and costumes by Leslie Hurry;

Lupe Serrano and Erik Bruhn
(middle 1950s)

Alicia Alonso and Igor Youskevitch (early 1950s)

Alicia Markova and
Anton Dolin (early 1940s)

SWAN LAKE—III: THREE SWAN QUEENS AND THEIR PRINCES

LES SYLPHIDES: Lupe Serrano in the Ballet Theatre version

Tanaquil LeClercq and Francisco Moncion

SYMPHONY IN C: NEW YORK CITY BALLET VERSION OF THE BIZET-BALANCHINE BALLET

Patricia Wilde and Herbert Bliss

THEME AND VARIATIONS: Igor Youskevitch in the Ballet Theatre production; scenery and costumes by Woodman Thompson

Graduation Ball

 Graduation Ball is the only ballet by David Lichine which has remained a repertoire item. It is a lighthearted (and somewhat lightheaded) piece of fluff, but there is nothing offensive about it, and it includes some charming dances. Also, the score is a big help. Antal Dorati went through a good deal of the Johann Strauss literature, selected a few bits that are little heard (the *Waldmeister* Overture, among others), attached them to such popular excerpts as the *Acceleration Waltz, Perpetuum Mobile,* and *Tritsch-Tratsch Polka,* re-orchestrated them, and ended up with an utterly charming piece of music.

Lichine has made very few humorous excursions. In his ballets he generally has been at close grips with mighty problems, and he generally has been thrown by them. *Graduation Ball* finds him relaxed. Behind him, Lichine, a Russian-born dancer and

143

choreographer, has a tradition extending to the Ida Rubinstein and Pavlova companies, as well as to the early days of the Ballet Russe de Monte Carlo. This background of classical training is suggested in *Graduation Ball,* the product of a choreographer who knows all the tricks and is thoroughly experienced with classical ballet movement.

As the curtain rises, we see a group of Viennese school girls getting ready for a party. They have invited the boys of a local military academy. The girls are in a tizzy, running around with a borrowed powderpuff, adjusting each other's hair and gowns. The old, ugly headmistress (danced by a man) bustles around, adding to the confusion. A march is heard. Sure enough, the boys are on the march, the ballroom their objective. In they come, one-two, one-two, led by an old, dignified, and ultra-severe general. Halt, attention. The general presents himself to the headmistress, and the two of them retire, leaving the boys lined up on one side of the room, the girls on the other.

They bashfully look at one another. How to break the ice? One of the girls, stars in her eyes, tentatively approaches the formation. They immediately stand at attention. Then a group of boys elects a sacrificial goat and pushes him toward the girls. The ice is not merely broken; it has melted before you can say "Johann Strauss Junior." Everybody dances. With the return of the general and the headmistress, the formal part of the entertainment begins. First a drummer boy performs a smart dance. A lyrical *pas de deux* follows; then a dance-step competition. Two girls try to outdo each other in the number and grace of *fouettés* (that most exciting and athletic of all dance steps) they can manage. In a final *perpetuum mobile* everybody whirls around. The general and the headmistress have developed a little romance of their own, and are caught in a rather compromising position. The party goes on a little more, and then the general calls a halt. He lines up the boys and marches them off. But one young rascal sneaks back for an appointment with his girl. The headmistress catches him and sends him away with a box on the ear.

Graduation Ball can degenerate and, alas, has often degenerated into a slapstick affair. When it was first seen in this country, it was alert and charming. The original *pas de deux,* named "Giselle and the Scotsman," was a nostalgic period piece. Lichine later replaced it with a more objective and virtuosic duet conceived for Alicia Alonso and Richard Reed. The Drummer's Dance also has some ingenious bits. The twirling of the drum sticks is quite a feat when done with the steps that go with it. And the dance-step competition is an exciting divertissement. The *fouettés,* combined with the double turns on the point in every conceivable position (arabesque, attitude, second, etc.), are exhilarating when correctly performed. If *Graduation Ball* has failed to hold its own artistically (though it still is one of the most popular ballets before the public) that is because the type of performance currently accorded it ranks far below the brio and excitement given by the original cast.

Graduation Ball received its world *première* by the Original Ballet Russe de Monte Carlo at the Theatre Royal, Sydney, Australia, on February 28, 1940. Alexandre Benois provided the costumes and scenery. The same company presented the American *première* at the Philharmonic Auditorium, Los Angeles, on October 10, 1940, and the New York *première* at the Fifty-first Street Theatre, New York, on November 6, 1940. The cast contained Borislav Runanine (Headmistress), Igor Schwezoff (General), Tatiana Riabouchinska (Leader of the Junior Girls), David Lichine (Leader of the Cadets), Nicolas Orloff (Drummer Boy), Tatiana Stepanova and Michel Panaieff (Giselle and the Scotsman), Tatiana Leskova (Impromptu Dance), and Alexandra Denisova and Genevieve Moulin (Dance-Step Competition).

On October 26, 1944, *Graduation Ball* entered the repertoire of Ballet Theatre at His Majesty's Theatre, Montreal, Canada. The first New York performance was given at the Metropolitan Opera House on October 8, 1944. This production had scenery and costumes by Mstislav Dobujinsky; current (1955) programs give no credit for costumes and sets. The Ballet Theatre cast was again headed by Lichine and Riabouchinska. Others were Alpheus Koon (Headmistress), John Taras (General), John Kriza (Drummer Boy), Rosella Hightower (Impromptu Dance), and Marjorie Tallchief and Margaret Banks (Dance-Step Competition). At this performance a classic *pas de deux* was substituted for "Giselle and the Scotsman," the *pas de deux* that previously had been used. Here Alicia Alonso was given the opportunity to reveal the temperament and artistry that were, in a few years, to place her among the ranking ballerinas of the period. Her partner was Richard Reed. As danced by them, this *pas de deux* was one of the most striking in contemporary ballet, building to a magnificent climax with an intricate lift and turn in air that had one breathless. Over the years the dance has lost some of its excitement, mostly because there were no Alonsos to take over after she left the role.

As a team in the dance competition, no two dancers have been able to match the brilliance, brio, and speed of Denisova and Moulin, who created the parts. Nearest to approach them were Marjorie Tallchief and Margaret Banks, excellent technicians with the right flash and flair, but neither temperamentally nor physically as well-matched as the original dancers. Since then the competitors have been quite uneven. Thus the basic idea of the sequence misses fire, for after the first brief engagement (there are several) it is clear that there is really no competition at all.

John Kriza, when he wanted to be, was the best Drummer Boy of all. Sometimes, however, he has been inclined to overplay, lose control, and exaggerate the stylized movements. Rosella Hightower was brilliant in the Impromptu Dance, and especially skillful in the way she handled the character implications and pantomimic sections of the role. No subsequent dancer made much of an impression until Barbara Lloyd assumed the part. Lloyd's humor is not as infectious as Hightower's, but she handled the acting artistically and danced with complete freedom, bouncing around the stage in the Impromptu Dance and performing the most difficult beats and turns as though they were nothing out of the ordinary. By far the best of the Generals was Igor Schwezoff, a man of Alpine height who, with one twitch of his eyebrows, could have the house roaring with laughter.

146

Helen of Troy

The original idea was that *Helen of Troy* be prepared as a companion piece to *Bluebeard*. With this in mind, Michel Fokine, who had choreographed the story of the much-married gentleman, set to work on the legend of the Greek gods. Shortly after completing *Helen of Troy* in Mexico City, Fokine died on August 22, 1942. The work had one performance in Mexico City on September 10, 1942. It was not a success, and never got beyond that single performance. The ballet was thereupon turned over to David Lichine, who used the original scenery and costumes designed by Marcel Vertès. The work in its new form received its *première* by Ballet Theatre in Detroit, Michigan, on November 29, 1942. Leading roles were danced by Irina Baronova (Helen), André Eglevsky (Paris), Jerome Robbins (Hermes), and Simon Semenoff (Menelaus). The New York *pre-*

mière took place at the Metropolitan Opera House on April 3, 1943. Vera Zorina replaced Baronova in the title role; the cast was otherwise the same.

Lichine and Antal Dorati prepared the libretto (Dorati also arranged the musical score from pieces by Offenbach), which has to do with a certain well-publicized incident among the ancient Greeks. The ballet is in a prologue and three scenes. In the Prologue, Paris is guarding his sheep. He dances for them, and these remarkable sheep applaud. Hermes wanders in, chewing an apple. He tells Paris that the three goddesses he has in tow are there to be judged. Paris is to say which is the fairest: Hera, Pallas Athena, or Aphrodite? Paris decides for Aphrodite, as even a blind man would have, for Hera is a determined spinster type, and Pallas Athena a bookish one who constantly has her nose buried in a weighty tome. Aphrodite is not only pretty—she also promises Paris that he shall have for a wife the most beautiful woman in the world. She gets the golden apple, her prize for winning, and leads Paris out. His pet lamb follows. Hermes, chewing his apple, has been an interested observer. To end the prologue, he himself pulls down the curtain.

The first scene takes place at the court of King Menelaus in Sparta. His wife, Helen, the most beautiful woman in the world, dances for him. Paris enters and falls in love with her. She is interested; Menelaus, old and decrepit, is no suitable partner for her. Paris manages to dance with Helen. He would like to abduct her, but too many courtiers are present. However, Calchas, the high priest, takes a fancy to the pet lamb that has accompanied Paris, and chases it. He is followed by the entire court. Menelaus has fallen asleep, his head on Helen's shoulder, and Hermes takes her place. Helen and Paris dance together, vowing their love. The courtiers return. Calchas goes into a trance and tells Menelaus that his borders are being invaded. The old King hastily gets into armor and leads his troops to battle. Hermes, the author of all this mischief, gets Helen to give Paris the key to her room.

In an entr'acte, which follows immediately, Orestes, also in love with Helen, persuades the head chambermaid to disguise him as a woman so that he may slip into Helen's chamber.

Scene 2 takes place in Helen's apartment. She is ready for bed when Orestes, who has mingled with the other ladies in waiting, tears off his disguise and pleads his love. Hermes walks in, reading a book. When he sees what is going on, he gets rid of Orestes and tells Helen that Paris is waiting. The two lovers embrace passionately. When their ardor gets a little overpowering, Hermes places a screen in front of them and proceeds placidly to knit. The pet lamb has followed Paris into the bed-chamber; it too hides behind the screen. In comes Menelaus, dressed in a nightgown. He has returned from the wars. He peers suspiciously at Hermes, even more suspiciously at the screen. Paris sneaks out, followed by Helen, who has disguised herself in the lamb's coat. Menelaus chases them while the poor lamb shivers in its underwear. The entire court appears. There is a wild hurry-scurry, which Hermes directs with a policeman's whistle. Paris and the lamb escape, Menelaus falls exhausted on the floor, and Helen laughs.

In another entr'acte, Menelaus bewails his sorry state. His handkerchief is soaking wet with tears. Ladies of the court iron it and give it back to him.

The final scene is a port. Ladies dance before the ocean, and a pet faun dances with them, causing some consternation. (This is a parody of *L'Après-midi d'un faune*.) The court gathers. Paris and Helen, outward bound, enter. Hermes comes up in a ship. The lovers escape the weeping Menelaus and set sail for Troy. Hermes amuses himself by playing with a yo-yo.

Many observers have wondered why *Helen of Troy* remains in the repertoire. Its farce does not come off very well, the situations are strained, and the comedy is of a low order. The idea of an apple-chewing, yo-yo-playing Hermes may have originally seemed hilarious to his creators, but as worked out, the idea is rather less than funny. The role of Paris has a little more meat in it; Lichine built the part around André Eglevsky, who could always perform remarkable turns. When Eglevsky left the company, Igor Youskevitch stepped into the role. Lately it has been danced by Erik Bruhn, thus confounding those skeptics who thought that once Eglevsky and Youskevitch left *Helen of Troy* it would be put aside for an eternal rest.

Illuminations

 The *première* of *Illuminations,* at the New York City Center of Music and Drama on March 2, 1950, was a very festive affair. It was the opening program of the International Theater Month, sponsored by UNESCO. Lincoln Kirstein and Rosamond Gilder, the latter a representative of the American National Theater and Academy (ANTA), addressed the audience. The performance was dedicated to Great Britain, and the British Ambassador was present to see the new ballet by Britain's Frederick Ashton. *Illuminations,* specifically created for the New York City Ballet Company, was Ashton's first work for an American group. (Sadler's Wells reciprocated by inviting Balanchine to stage *Ballet Imperial* for them.) It was also the first time Ashton had used such a strongly literary base upon which to create a ballet. The consensus was that he succeeded handsomely.

151

He chose for music Benjamin Britten's *Les Illuminations,* a setting for soprano or tenor and string orchestra of ten poems by Rimbaud. Britten had composed the score in 1939. The ballet is described in the program as "A sequence of danced pictures (*tableaux dansantes*), or charades, in which images suggested by Rimbaud's poems and symbolic incidents from his violent life are interwoven on the musical pattern."

The ballet is divided into nine sections: Fanfare ("Alone I hold the key to this savage side-show"); Dreamtown ("Suburban Bacchantes weep . . . barbarians dance nocturnal rites . . ."); Phrase (". . . I have hung golden chains from star to star . . . and I dance"); Antiquity (". . . Supple son of Pan . . ."); Royalty; Anarchy ("A man and a woman proclaim they would be king and queen"); Being Beauteous; Sideshow; and Farewell ("Departure amid novel sounds, and love"). The principals in the cast were Nicholas Magallanes (Poet), Tanaquil LeClercq (Sacred Love), and Melissa Hayden (Profane Love).

Rimbaud (1854–1891) was one of the strange geniuses of literature. He was in jail at fifteen; during much of his life he was little more than a tramp. He nearly died of hunger in Paris, but was befriended by Verlaine, who encouraged him. The two young poets lived together for a while. They had an argument on a trip, and the furious Verlaine shot Rimbaud. He went to jail for it. Rimbaud wrote no poetry after the age of nineteen. He lived in Germany and Italy, and then vanished from sight for sixteen years, which he spent as a soldier in the Dutch army, a deserter, and a wanderer in the jungle. Toward the end of his life he settled in Abyssinia, where he became a prosperous merchant and politician and chieftain of an African tribe. He returned to Europe for an operation on his knee and died after his leg was amputated.

Rimbaud was one of the first of the surrealist poets. In *Les Illuminations* he makes the soul of a poet—his own soul, for the poetry is largely autobiographical—the protagonist. He uses the word "illuminations" in the sense of an illuminated manuscript or, as he himself translated it, "Painted Plates." Wallace Fowlie, an authority on Rimbaud, thinks that the poems of

Illuminations light up a secret catastrophe we can only guess at. Britten has set ten of the poems (most of them are prose-poems) in their entirety in the original French, and sections of them are sung while the ballet is in progress.

Ashton's cast includes the Poet, the Dandy, the King and Queen, and Sacred and Profane Love. The central figure is the Poet, who, when first seen, is trying to wake some people on the stage. He urges them to dance, and the key to the action is contained in Rimbaud's lines: "The savages dance ceaselessly in the festival of night. And for one hour, I went down into the surge of a Bagdad boulevard where groups sang of the joy of new work, in a torpid breeze, moving about without being able to elude the fabulous phantoms of mountains where people had to find themselves again. What good arms, what precious hour will return to me that place from whence come my sleep and my slightest movements?"

The Poet is left alone. He throws golden dust into the air and dances. This ballet sequence illustrates the lines in *Les Illuminations* which read: "I stretched out ropes from spire to spire; garlands from window to window; golden chains from star to star; and I dance." In the section of the ballet named Antiquity, corresponding to *Antique* in the poem, the Poet dances with two women. One is in white—Sacred Love—and one is sensuous and abandoned—Profane Love. Rimbaud's lines for *Antique* are: "Graceful son of Pan! Under your brow crowned with flowers and with berries, your eyes, precious balls, move. Spotted with dark streaks, your cheeks look hollow. Your fangs glisten. Your chest is like a lyre and ringing sounds are heard moving in your white arms. Your heart beats in that abdomen where your double sex sleeps. Walk at night and gently move this thigh, then this other thigh and this left leg."

Sacred Love retires while the Poet dances to these lines with Profane Love. A parade then enters, and a couple is crowned king and queen. This is a satiric sequence to Rimbaud's poem entitled *Royalty:* "One fine morning, in a country of very gentle people, a handsome man and woman cried out in the public square. 'My friends, I want her to be queen.' 'I want to be

queen.' She laughed and trembled. He spoke to his friends of
a revelation, of a period of trial ended. They swooned over one
another. In effect, they were monarchs for an entire morning,
when crimson draperies were hung over the houses, and for
the whole afternoon, when they walked toward the gardens of
palms."

The Poet breaks up the ceremonies, placing the crown on his
own head. Profane Love enters and tries to attract him, but he
repulses her. He sleeps, and Sacred Love dances with four men.
Rimbaud's poem is grotesque: "Standing before snow, a being
of tall beauty. Death whistles, and rings of muffled music cause
this worshiped body to rise up, expand and tremble like a
ghost; scarlet and black wounds break out in the superb flesh.
The very colors of life deepen, dance, and stand out from the
vision, in the yard. Fears rise and threaten, and the persistent
taste of those things encumbered with the whistle of life and
the raucous music which the world, far behind us, throws to our
mother of beauty. She flinches and stands up. Oh! our bones
are reclothed with a new, amorous body. Oh! the ashen face,
the emblem of horsehair, the arms of crystal! The cannon upon
which I must fall, in the medley of trees and light air!"

This is all a dream of the Poet. When he wakes, he throws
away his crown. People come upon the stage—the same people
he had roused to dancing in the first scene. They maltreat him
in the section of the ballet called Sideshow. Rimbaud's poem,
which gives a clue to the action, is named *Parade:*

"Well-built fellows. Some of them have exploited your worlds.
Without cares and in no hurry to use for creation their brilliant
faculties and their knowledge of your consciences. What mature
men! Eyes deadened, like a summer's night, red and black, tri-
colored, of steel spotted with stars of gold; faces deformed, ashen,
pale, burning; wild hoarseness. The cruel demeanor of decorations!
—There are some young fellows—what would they think of Faunt-
leroy?—with frightening voices and dangerous resources. They are
sent to the city to give themselves airs, rigged out disgustingly *de
luxe.*

"Oh! the most violent Paradise of the enraged smile! No comparison with your Fakirs and other scenic antics. In improvised

costumes and in the style of a bad dream, they recite plaintive poems and perform tragedies of brigands and spiritual demi-gods such as history or religion never have seen. Chinese, Hottentots, gypsies, fools, hyenas, Molochs, old insanities and sinister demons are mixed up with their popular, maternal tricks, with poses and bestial tenderness. They would interpret new plays and songs 'of good girls.' Master jugglers, they transform the place and the people and use magnetic comedy. Their eyes flame, their blood sings, their bones expand, tears and red rivulets stream. Their joking or their terror lasts a minute or for months.

"I alone have the key of this wild circus."

The last sentence here is also the one that Ashton has used as a clue to his first scene. In the final scene the Poet is captured and lifted high. He asks Profane Love for help. She derides him, remembering the time he spurned her. She tells one of the men to shoot him, which he does (this recalls the episode in Rimbaud's life when he was shot by Verlaine). He is wounded in the arm. He steps over a now repentant Profane Love and walks away, toward a vision of Sacred Love. Rimbaud's poem is *Depart:*

"Seen enough. The vision met itself in every kind of air.

"Had enough. Noises of cities in the evening, in the sunlight, and forever.

"Known enough. The haltings of life. Oh! Noises and visions.

"Departure in new affection and sound."

Ashton has occasionally attempted a bit of surrealism to match the quality of the verse—in his dance of Profane Love, for example, giving the dancer only one toe slipper, leaving the other foot bare. Cecil Beaton's costumes try to match the extravagance of the verbal imagery and of the choreography. Whether or not they are in the best of taste is a moot point. In any case, Ashton and Beaton set themselves a difficult task. It is not always easy to extract a central meaning from writing as eccentric, symbolistic, and concentrated as Rimbaud's. *Illuminations* as a ballet may have weak points, but it is a noble attempt.

Interplay

Jerome Robbins found a perfect score for *Interplay*, his second ballet, in Morton Gould's *American Concertette*. Gould's piece for piano and orchestra was first presented on a radio program, with José Iturbi as soloist, on August 25, 1943. It was a jazzy, good-humored work, slick as a Norman Rockwell magazine cover, melodious, expertly constructed. (Thanks to its success as a ballet score, *American Concertette* is no longer known by its original name, but is always referred to as *Interplay*.) The Robbins ballet, composed in 1945, is also good-humored, jazzy, slightly rambunctious, and very American.

Pinning down exactly what constitutes the American element in any native work of art is not easy. The breeziness of *Interplay*, its rhythmic bounce and sly spoofing of classical ballet, its pronounced jazz elements and red-blooded athletics result in a creation that could have been produced nowhere but in America. It pays lip service to the choreographic amenities, much as high-school kids pay lip service to their teachers, but underneath displays an impatience with, and even a mockery of, the balletic *status quo.*

The name *Interplay* was carefully chosen. Robbins, an exuberant young man, tried to present in a ballet the interplay between modern and ancient dance forms in this country. He used a small group for it—four boys, four girls, dressed in leotards with a short tunic (none of your tutus here). A backdrop and wings of cloth in various primary colors are used in lieu of scenery. As Robbins conceived the movements, the dancers are young, exulting in their youth and animal spirits. They are teen-agers happily and innocently romping. The four boys are first seen horsing around (to use the apt slang expression). When the girls enter, they pair off with the boys. The name of the first of the four movements is "Free Play," and the movements are just that, with the dancers playing games, dancing in jazz-like motions, and coming up to the footlights, where they become black silhouettes. "Horseplay" is the second movement. It contrasts the archaic style of the gavotte with the abandoned steps of jazz. The third movement is "Byplay," a blues largely built around a duet by one of the couples. In the last movement, "Team Play," two of the boys choose sides, and each side goes into a huddle. Then there is an athletic competition in which each side attempts to outdo the other.

The program note for *Interplay* calls it "a short ballet in four movements in which there is a constant play between the classical ballet steps and the contemporary spirit in which they are danced." In the hands of a tasteless choreographer the work could have been merely vulgar. Robbins has avoided the pitfall, and succeeded in creating a delightfully mischievous, almost impish, ballet. Its tongue-in-cheek quality extends even unto itself: *Interplay* does not take itself too seriously.

This is not an easy ballet to dance. Satire is always hard to achieve, and Robbins's constant alternation of classic and jazz elements imposes real demands on the dancers, who must main-

tain a simple line and yet master complicated choreography and
extremely difficult feats of virtuosity.

Interplay first saw the light of day at one of Billy Rose's *Concert Varieties* at the Ziegfeld Theater, New York. June 1, 1945,
was the date, and the dancers were Robbins, Janet Reed, John
Kriza, Michael Kidd, Muriel Bentley, Rozsika Sabo, Bettina
Rosay, and Erik Kristen. Tibor Kozma played the piano solo.
The set was designed by Carl Kent. On October 17 of the same
year, with the composer conducting, *Interplay* entered the Ballet Theatre repertoire. There the dancers were Janet Reed,
Harold Lang, John Kriza, Muriel Bentley, Rozsika Sabo, Mil-
dred Herman, Tommy Rall, and Fernando Alonso (substituting
for Michael Kidd). Oliver Smith designed the set. *Interplay* was
an instant success, and has not been out of the repertoire since.
It went into the repertoire of the New York City Ballet Company on December 23, 1952, in a performance that was less than
distinguished. Somehow the Balanchine-trained dancers of this
company could not unbend sufficiently to make *Interplay* the
witty and flexible thing it can be.

The only dancer of the original Ballet Theatre cast still to be
seen in *Interplay* at the time of writing is John Kriza. Otherwise
the cast has changed many times over. Replacing the girls never
has seemed to pose much of a problem. Eager young things with
vitality, secure techniques, and a sort of typically American
jazzy co-ed quality can be found in abundance. Curiously, however, a good man is harder to find for *Interplay*. Since Tommy
Rall and Harold Lang were around, there never has been a
group of men capable of conveying in an equivalent degree the
lighthearted humor and brashness of the dancing and at the
same time negotiating its considerable technical difficulties.

Ivesiana

 When George Balanchine wishes to stage
an experimental ballet, he goes to the right
kind of music. His *Opus 34* had used a do-
decaphonic score by Arnold Schoenberg.
His *Ivesiana,* as its title suggests, uses music
by Charles Ives, that remarkable composer
who may well have been the only authentic
musical genius that America has produced.

Ives, who died on May 19, 1954, had a
career that somewhat resembled that of
Wallace Stevens in poetry. Both were successful businessmen, and both turned out a
large number of original works in a highly
modern idiom. Ives was, if the term is not
too contradictory, a sophisticated primitive.
His music revels in all kinds of wild harmonies; as is well known, he was experimenting with polytonality and other devices
before the turn of the century. His rhythms
are of unparalleled complexity, and some
of his music poses such technical problems

that it is unplayable. And yet, under all this, lies a basic emotional simplicity, the "primitive" side of his character. He is the first American composer to employ seriously the hymn tune, patriotic anthems, popular songs that flourished after the Civil War. He was constantly weaving them into his music.

Balanchine, attracted by this novel composer, and particularly by his rhythmic innovations, chose a series of six unrelated orchestral pieces for his choreographic suite, and attempted several experiments in dance composition. He called the ballet *Ivesiana* for the same reason that Tchaikovsky called one of his suites *Mozartiana*—because (so states the note in the New York City Ballet program) "it is not the narrative or pictorial values of the music that has inspired him but the quality of the music of Charles Ives."

The six Ives pieces that Balanchine originally used (he has changed the second movement twice since then) were *Central Park in the Dark* (1907), *Hallowe'en* (composed in 1911; the first of the *Three Outdoor Pieces,* of which *Central Park in the Dark* is the third), *The Unanswered Question* ("a cosmic landscape," composed before 1908), *Over the Pavements* (1913), *In the Inn* (1911), and *In the Night* (1906). All of this music has been recorded on long-playing discs, though some of it has been discontinued from the LP catalogues and may be hard to find.

In classical terms *Ivesiana* is as unballetic a work as Balanchine has ever composed. The final movement, for example, has the entire cast entering on their knees from the wings, shuffling along until the center of the stage is reached. Martha Graham has used this device from time to time, but never with a stage full of people. The general feeling is that of a strict ballet disciplinarian who has suddenly turned to the Central European school and to Martha Graham for inspiration. The result, not always convincing, adds up to something like an *avant-garde* piece of the twenties.

Ivesiana received its *première* by the New York City Ballet Company at the New York City Center of Music and Drama on September 14, 1954. The first section, *Central Park in the Dark,* was danced by Janet Reed, Francisco Moncion, and an ensemble of twenty. Large groups seem to move aimlessly, groping in the dark to the murmurous music. Certain pictures are suggested—trees, lovers, strolling figures. All is dark and muted.

The ballet is no longer presented with its original second movement, *Hallowe'en.* Balanchine later substituted a movement named *Arguments;* still later, on November 29, 1955, he presented *Ivesiana* with *Barn Dance* (from *Washington's Birthday*) as the second movement. *Washington's Birthday,* composed in 1909, was rescored by Ives in 1913 and is an orchestral oddity in that jew's-harps are included in the instrumentation. *Barn Dance* has been excerpted from the score, and once was recorded. It is very complicated, and as presented by the New York City Ballet it uses two conductors in the pit.

Barn Dance, in its choreography by Balanchine, presents a girl and her partner against a group of three girls. The dancing echoes the folk-like flavor of the music. The three girls are in tights; the man wears blue denims and a shirt; the girl is in a short skirt and sweater. All of the dancing is simple and easily understood, though there is one fairly eccentric moment when the girl sits on one of the other girls, who is on her hands and knees. Toward the end of *Barn Dance* occurs a duet, almost a classical adagio with satiric undertones. The three girls tiptoe off; the boy and girl slowly waltz into the wings. At its *première* the movement was danced by Jacques d'Amboise, Patricia Wilde, Edith Brozak, Barbara Fallis, and Barbara Walczak.

The third movement is *The Unanswered Question* (one of Ives's most magical pieces of music). This is a *tour de force* in which four men keep a girl off the floor. She does not touch it once during the entire movement. A man constantly tries to reach her but never is able to put a finger on her. She is ingeniously maneuvered by the four men, and the effect borders on the sensational. For sheer invention this is the most interesting movement. Allegra Kent and Todd Bolender were the principal dancers here. Tanaquil LeClercq later took the girl's part.

Over the Pavements, danced at the *première* by Diana Adams and Herbert Bliss with a group of four men, brings an urban atmosphere to the ballet. The girl is in a sweater and short tights;

161

the leading male dancer wears city clothes. They dance against the evolutions of the boys; she is carried through them and above them. The three boys finally run off; then the partner runs off; then the girl. The general feeling is of a prank by youngsters. *In the Inn,* danced by Tanaquil LeClercq and Todd Bolender, is a jazzy duet featuring sinuous, exaggerated motions. Elements of burlesque are here. At the end the two dancers nonchalantly shake hands and walk off in opposite directions. The finale, *In the Night,* is short (about one minute and a half in length), and contains the knee-crawling episode and its rejection of classic ballet. Perhaps Balanchine, the arch-classicist of our time, was determined to show the world that he could be as experimental as the next innovator; or perhaps he was merely out to *épater le bourgeois.* But one wonders if it is in his blood.

Jinx
_____

Dance Players was a small company founded by Eugene Loring in November 1941. Prominent dancers in the group were Janet Reed, Joan MacCracken, Lew Christensen, Loring, and Michael Kidd. It lasted only one year, giving its last performance at Trenton, New Jersey, on November 12, 1942. Its repertoire consisted largely of ballets by Loring, but Lew Christensen created *Jinx* for the company, and the work received its *première* at the Erie Theater, Schenectady, New York, on April 9, 1942, with Janet Reed, Lew Christensen, and Conrad Linden in leading roles. The scenery was by James Stewart Morcom; costumes were by Felipe Fiocca.

It was Loring's idea to gather a nucleus of dancers who excelled in acting as well as dancing. He did not want any uncooperative ballet virtuosos, preferring all-around dancers who could project a mood

163

and had a working knowledge of modern dance in addition to good ballet technique. Most of the ballets produced during the short life of Dance Players stressed the dramatic side of dancing. As George Amberg says in his *Ballet in America,* Dance Players went one step farther than Ballet Caravan "by calling their ballets 'dance plays' " and presenting them frankly as danced and mimed drama. Although the physical and structural basis of their technique was the *danse d'école,* they also made free use of the modern expressional idiom. It was neither modern dance nor pantomime, but essentially ballet as lyrical drama.

Jinx uses a score by Benjamin Britten, the early *Variations on a Theme by Frank Bridge.* The ballet "is based on the atmosphere of theatrical superstition in a circus troupe, the element of chance in all spectacular performance." According to the official synopsis of 1942, the plot is as follows: "The Jinx, because he interrupts the romance between the Boy and the Girl, becomes the object of suspicion and distrust. The performers, with the exception of the Bearded Lady, believe him to be an evil influence in the circus. An accident to the girl is attributed to the evil-working Jinx. The Equestrian is angered and, determined to subdue fear and superstition, borrows the Ringmaster's whip and beats Jinx to death. The end of Jinx banishes superstitious fear and the performer and the performers are happy again. In sympathy for the Bearded Lady, who has lost her only romantic interest, they give Jinx a funeral. But Jinx returns to life and now the performers, more fearful than ever, surrender completely to the spell his presence creates."

A revival of *Jinx* was presented by the New York City Ballet Company at the New York City Center of Music and Drama on November 24, 1949, with Janet Reed, Francisco Moncion, and Herbert Bliss in the leading roles. Those with accurate memories detected many changes in the revised version. As originally performed by Dance Players, *Jinx* had been positively eerie. The performers had had such a sense of characterization as to seem alive and real; and the *Petrouchka*-like ending, with the spectre of the Jinx coming back to haunt the company, was a gripping piece of theater. The Bearded Lady emerged as a universal symbol of hidden love (for the Jinx); and one touching moment, when the other freaks—the Tattooed Lady and the Strong Lady—tried to console her, was done with subtlety and pity. Other similar moments, portrayed in dance pantomime, approached a quality that has not been otherwise achieved in contemporary ballet except in the works of Antony Tudor.

In the New York City Ballet revival, the eerie mood of the piece was missing. Janet Reed again danced the leading role, but the other members of the cast, trained in an entirely different school, lacked the dramatic ability to put their points across. Members of the New York City Ballet tend to be one-dimensional. The girls have been trained in the Balanchine style—a style demanding classic precision and a powerful ballet technique rather than acting ability and "program" delineation. *Jinx* is so superior when well done that it should find a place in a company that has the type of dancers to do it justice.

Judgment of Paris

 Greek mythology tells the story of how Paris chose among the three godly maidens, and the consequences thereof. Antony Tudor has recast the legend for our own day in a cynical little ballet named *Judgment of Paris*. The scene is a sleazy Paris *boîte de nuit*. Business is bad for the waiter and the three girls employed to please the customers. One customer finally wanders in and orders a bottle of wine. Already three sheets to the wind, he looks about him with a glazed eye. Juno is the first to dance for him. She goes through her amateurish capers, hopefully ogling him. The dance of Venus, who follows, is more frankly a *danse du ventre*. She is dressed in a vulgar fashion, and becomes quite self-satisfied as she goes through some convolutions involving a couple of large hoops. The customer, drinking steadily, approves, and has a drink sent to her table. Minerva, middle-aged and

166

beaten down with depravity, goes through an entertainment with a feather boa. She goes into a split, but the customer is not even looking at her. Her artistry affronted, she engages his attention and tries to make up to him. He will have none of it. He orders more wine and chooses Venus as his lady-love. But before she reaches him, he passes out, stone cold. In a moment the waiter and the three goddesses are swarming over his body, relieving him of his wallet and jewelry.

Judgment of Paris was first produced at the Westminster Theatre, London, in 1938. It was commissioned by Agnes de Mille and performed as a curtain-raiser for a play by Gogol. It was danced by Agnes de Mille, Charlotte Bidmead, Therese Langfield, Hugh Laing, and Antony Tudor. At the American *première,* by Ballet Theatre at the Center Theatre, New York, on January 23, 1940, the cast consisted of Viola Essen (Juno), Agnes de Mille (Venus), Lucia Chase (Minerva), Antony Tudor (the customer) and Hugh Laing (the waiter).

In a way, *Judgment of Paris* is a shocker, and it has not been a permanent part of the repertoire, though it is occasionally revived for special occasions. On April 28, 1955, to celebrate the fifteenth season of Ballet Theatre, the work was danced at the Metropolitan Opera by its original Ballet Theatre cast, to the accompaniment of cheers and yelps of laughter from the audience. But *Judgment of Paris,* whatever its satire on ballet and mythology, and whatever the humor of the creaky goddesses dancing their antiquated come-ons in horrid burlesque, is no laughing matter. It is bitter, sardonic, and highly sophisticated. It is strong meat for some; the ballet is not for children or for those who hold to the ideal of Sacred Womanhood and strong, clean men. It is hardly a ballet, in all truth, being more a series of pantomimes. In its way it is a masterpiece in the Toulouse-Lautrec tradition.

Part of the impact that *Judgment of Paris* makes is owing to the musical score. Tudor selected several of the arias from Kurt Weill's equally sardonic *Dreigroschenoper,* a musical testament of Germany in the throes of the anguish that followed the First World War. Weill's score, which had a tremendous vogue during the late twenties and early thirties, and is unquestionably the best thing he ever did, never had much of a vogue in America until it was revived in an English adaptation by Marc Blitzstein in 1954. (The audience at the 1955 performance of *Judgment of Paris* reacted violently when it heard the opening measures; an audible intake of recognition swept through the house.) Weill's score, with its use of ragtime and its desparing undertones, is one of the unique testaments of music. In juxtaposition to the action of *Judgment of Paris* it provides a perfect setting for Tudor's really vicious glimpse at life below the surface.

Lilac Garden

(Jardin aux Lilas)

 Originally done in England in 1936, *Lilac Garden* was the ballet that served to bring Antony Tudor to the serious attention of American audiences. Tudor had created several ballets previously, but, according to British critics who know his work, *Lilac Garden* was his first masterpiece, and in it his style emerged fully formed. Tudor wanted to compose a ballet cast in a certain mood and set in the Edwardian era. He was inspired to some extent by a short story by the Finnish author, Aino Kallas. A peasant couple is about to be married when the landowner announces his intention of exercising the *droit du seigneur*. The bride goes to fulfill the law, but armed with a dagger, *à la* Tosca. This situation was not suitable, so Tudor discussed allied themes with his friends. Finally he came up with a situation in which lovers about to be separated have a desperate longing to kiss each other before parting. This is the basic idea of *Jardin aux Lilas*. For music Tudor selected Chausson's *Poème*.

Chausson's score, for violin solo and orchestra, was composed in 1896, and thus does not truly belong to the Edwardian era, though it is close enough. It is rich, sensuous music that is a perfect complement to the period piece that Tudor created. (Practically speaking, it has one drawback: violinists engaged by ballet orchestras are not generally on the order of a Heifetz; and one has often had to sit in excruciating pain while the soloist was sawing away, a halftone separated from the correct pitch and miles away from the dancers.)

Like most of Tudor's psychological ballets, *Lilac Garden* has a plot, deals with the problems of people, faces a particular situation squarely, and by implication gives the situation a universal endowment. Cyril Beaumont sees something of a Maupassant in it; Fernau Hall, another British specialist, finds a strong suggestion of Proust. *Lilac Garden* does not cut as deeply as the later *Pillar of Fire;* it is less intense, more lyrical. But the undertone of frustration is ever-present as the girl is torn away from her lover, and a brooding quality runs through its elegiac atmosphere.

Tudor carried the theories of Fokine to a new development in *Lilac Garden*. By use of gesture—gesture not in the mime style of orthodox ballet, but everyday gestures used to heighten the impact of stylized ballet movements—he was able to point up his ballet in a manner that lent verisimilitude without destroying art. As Fernau Hall has pointed out in *World Dance,* he also telescoped time or expanded it at will to make clear the implication of certain gestures. *Lilac Garden* is not only a heart-rending ballet; it also is sheer technical virtuosity. On the surface it is relatively uncomplicated. The more one sees it, the more subtleties one unearths. It is not an objective, academic piece of work; it pulsates with life and has meaning, and its emotional impact (assuming, of course, a sympathetic performance) has not lessened since it first was seen. Of very few contemporary ballets can this be said. When an artist deals honestly with basic impulses, his message will not age.

The action of *Lilac Garden* concerns a girl named Caroline and her desire for a final meeting with the man she loves. For Caroline must marry a man she does not care for. She is giving a party for all of her friends. We see her and her fiancé engrossed in their own thoughts. Her lover enters; she secretly waves him away. When she is alone, she dances with her lover, but there is no joy in it; she does not wish anybody to see them, and she constantly looks around. A woman comes in, and Caroline introduces her lover to her. She does not know that this woman is her fiancé's mistress. Caroline then dances alone, miserable. Guests come in and go out. There is much byplay, including an impassioned sequence in which the fiancé and his mistress dance together, she supplicating, he nervous yet ardent. Caroline's distress and frustration are obvious, and two women offer their sympathy. More guests, more dancing. The two couples —Caroline and her lover, the fiancé and his mistress—are constantly mingling, separating, coming upon one another, each with his or her secret, each with his or her passion. As the ballet ends, the lover presents a bouquet of white lilacs to Caroline, kisses her hand, and goes out of her life forever. The fiancé brings her cloak and wraps it about her—a symbolic act by which his ownership is cemented. They walk out, leaving the lover alone in the garden.

Lilac Garden was first presented at the Mercury Theatre, London, by the Rambert Ballet Club on January 26, 1936. Maud Lloyd (Caroline), Hugh Laing (Her Lover), Peggy van Praagh (the Woman in His Past), and Antony Tudor (the Man She Must Marry) took the leading roles. Setting and costumes were by Hugh Stevenson. Ballet Theatre staged the first American performance at the Center Theatre, New York, on January 15, 1940. The cast, in the same order, consisted of Viola Essen, Hugh Laing, Karen Conrad, and Tudor. Sets and costumes were designed by Raymond Sovey after sketches by Hugh Stevenson. The occasion was the first Tudor ballet to be produced in this country. Tudor staged a new performance for the New York City Ballet Company on November 30, 1951. Given at the New York City Center of Music and Drama, the ballet was danced by Nora Kaye, Laing, Tanaquil LeClercq, and Tudor. Brooks Jackson later took Tudor's role. For this production Horace Armistead executed the sets and costumes.

It is not easy to dance *Lilac Garden.* A non-Tudor-trained dancer has as much trouble in the ballet as a non-Balanchine-trained dancer has in that choreographer's abstractions. Tudor often conveys his moods through gestures—a tilt of the hand, an inclination of the head, a characteristic walk. In a classical ballet—*Swan Lake,* say—the dancer must carry one phrase to another, never breaking a line. In Tudor's works the dancer must specifically break the line to accentuate an emotional situation. The problem is one of degree: how much to break, how much to accentuate? A dancer who has not been trained in the idiom finds the Tudor technique hard to master; and even Tudor-trained dancers fall into bad habits when he is not around to keep them on the mark.

As long as Tudor was associated with Ballet Theatre, there never was any question but that the dancers he used in his ballets were molded to his wishes. He always had a strong group from which to select, and even the most minor part in his ballets was choreographed with a particular dancer in mind. He took his leading dancers carefully in hand, and each one emerged true to the style. The proof lies in the fact that though his original Caroline and The Woman in His Past, Viola Essen and Karen Conrad, left nothing to be desired in their *Lilac Garden* performances, a stream of replacements (neither Essen nor Conrad stayed with the company very long) has been so convincing that one is hard put to recall the originals. Strangely enough, it has been the men, Laing and Tudor, who have been irreplaceable.

While the New York City Ballet production was handsomely mounted, and while three of the original principals—Kaye, Laing, and Tudor—were dancing in the City Center performance, there was a wide disparity in style between this trio and the rest of the company. Tanaquil LeClercq, as The Woman in His Past, was able to convey the subtleties of the role only after repeated performances. As for the ensemble, Tudor's language seemed utterly foreign to it; Jillana was the only one who seemed to have some understanding of what she was doing.

One other aspect of *Lilac Garden* is worth mention. For a decade or so in America (and elsewhere), choreographers were busily plundering the orchestral literature and making mincemeat of it. To those who liked music, the announcement that another "symphonic ballet" was on the way was a good reason to take to the hills. Tudor in 1936 was one of the first to take a piece of concert music, handle it with respect and sensitivity, and build a well-organized choreographic entity around it. Chausson's *Poème* could have been specifically commissioned for *Lilac Garden*. Here, told through movement, was a story that had a beginning, a middle, and an end, all cunningly fitted to music—and to music that did not wrench the credulity of those who heard it and saw the accompanying action.

Mam'zelle Angot

 Alexandre Charles Lecocq (1832–1918) was
a French composer who wrote failure after
failure until an opera named *Fleur de thé,*
which was produced at the Lyceum Theatre,
Paris, in 1871. After that he turned out an
incredible number of operas and light
operas, and assorted music in many genres.
His most enduring theater piece was *La
Fille de Mme Angot,* a three-act opera that
opened in Brussels on December 4, 1872,
and ran for 500 consecutive nights. It
achieved almost equal popularity in Paris
and London. "Lecocq," says Gustave Chouquet in the 1955 edition of *Grove's,* "realized that what the public really liked was
light, gay, sparkling melodies. His style, not
a very elevated one, made small demand
on the poetry or the intellect of the composer; but it required tact, ease, freedom
and, above all, animation."

Which is exactly what Leonide Massine

174

tried to achieve in his choreographic adaptation, *Mam'zelle Angot;* Chouquet's words would perfectly fit the ballet. Massine composed it for Ballet Theatre, and it was first performed by that group at the Metropolitan Opera House on October 10, 1943. Costumes and scenery were created by Mstislav Dobujinsky; music was "selected from the works of Alexandres [*sic*] Charles Lecocq." In the cast were Nora Kaye, Leonide Massine, Rosella Hightower, André Eglevsky, Simon Semenoff, and John Kriza.

The work is in three scenes: The Market, The House of the Aristocrat, and The Carnival. Following is the program supplied by Ballet Theatre:

SCENE 1. *The Market*

Mam'zelle Angot, betrothed against her will to a Barber, falls in love with a Caricaturist, who at first returns her affections. The artist has executed a drawing mocking a Government official and his Aristocratic Mistress, but the Caricaturist now becomes entranced with the Aristocrat, and forgets his first love. Mam'zelle Angot is jealous and insults the Aristocrat in public, realizing that the action will cause her arrest, and help her avoid her obligation to marry the Barber.

SCENE 2. *The House of the Aristocrat*

A reception is in progress, and the Caricaturist, fleeing from the soldiers sent to arrest him for his damaging caricatures, is discovered in the house. This scene is witnessed by the lovelorn Mam'zelle Angot, who has been sent for by the offended Aristocrat to explain her behavior, but the meeting reveals that they are old school friends. The unhappy Barber, in search of Mam'zelle Angot, is also present. The Government Official orders the Caricaturist to prison, and the latter chooses this exact moment to declare his love for the Aristocrat.

SCENE 3. *The Carnival*

Mam'zelle Angot has plotted a meeting between the Aristocrat and the Caricaturist at the Carnival. With the help of her market friends, she exposes the Aristocrat to the duped Government Official, who has arrived in disguise. All mock their victims unmercifully and Mam'zelle Angot decides, after all, that it is the Barber she loves.

Mam'zelle Angot never achieved the success of that other light Massine ballet, *Gaîté Parisienne*. Nor, in all truth, is it comparable. The action is a little cluttered; the Barber does not know whether to be tragic or comic; and the ballet as a whole lacks the spontaneity and organization of *Gaîté*. It has never been a permanent part of the Ballet Theatre repertoire. It has achieved more popularity in Europe, possibly because (in addition to whatever merit Massine's choreography may have) the musical idiom of Lecocq is closer to Continental than to American ears. Massine re-staged *Mam'zelle Angot* for Sadler's Wells on November 26, 1947, at Covent Garden, in London. He revised the choreography, and there were new settings and costumes by André Derain. Gordon Jacob re-orchestrated the music. The cast included Margot Fonteyn (in the title role), Alexander Grant (Barber), Moira Shearer (Aristocrat), and Michael Somes (Caricaturist). Mary Clarke, in her history of the Sadler's Wells Ballet, writes a sentence about this *première* which could be applied to the Ballet Theatre performance in 1943: "The first-night audience loved it, but the Press on the whole was grudging."

Ballet Theatre revived the work during its Fifteenth Anniversary Season at the Metropolitan Opera House, New York, in the spring of 1955. The cast included Lupe Serrano, John Kriza, Erik Bruhn, and Sonia Arova. The music was the Gordon Jacob orchestration. *Mam'zelle Angot* received a fine performance, but the lapse of about a dozen years had done nothing to enhance the intrinsic merit of the work.

Mother Goose Suite

 Ravel originally wrote his charming and delicate *Ma Mère l'Oye* ("Mother Goose") for piano, four hands, in 1910. Later he orchestrated it for a French ballet company organized by Jacques Rouché, the director of the Opéra, himself supplying the libretto. In its new form, *Mother Goose* was presented at the Théâtre des Arts on January 28, 1912. Neither the company nor Ravel's ballet ever took hold. The music, however, immediately entered the orchestral repertoire. It consists of five pieces—"Pavane of the Sleeping Beauty," "Hop o' My Thumb," "Laideronnette, Empress of the Pagodes," "Beauty and the Beast," and "The Enchanted Garden."

When Todd Bolender decided to use the score for a ballet, he devised a libretto in which a woman, by flashbacks, reminisces about events that happened to her as a young girl. He also rearranged the order of the music: "Pavane of the Sleeping Beauty," "The Enchanted Garden," "Hop o' My Thumb," "Laideronnette," and "Beauty and the Beast."

The ballet was first presented by the American Concert Ballet at the Central High School of Needle Trades Auditorium, New York, in October 1942. Mary Jane Shea and Francisco Moncion were the leading dancers. On November 1, 1948, the work was taken into the repertoire of the New York City Ballet Company, at the New York City Center of Music and Drama. In the cast were Marie-Jeanne, Francisco Moncion, Todd Bolender, and Beatrice Tompkins.

As the curtain rises on a dim stage, a girl surrounded by clouds is seen. She dances pensively. Another woman enters—the opposite half of the dancer, mature and experienced. She goes to one side of the stage to watch herself as the young girl.

The young girl dances with several others. Four couples enter and dance. None of the dancing couples pays any attention to the young girl. She is heartbroken. All leave, and she is left alone. In the next episode, Hop o' My Thumb enters, dropping crumbs, accompanied by a bird who dances around him. The bird leaves the stage, and Hop o' My Thumb dances with the young girl. But he really is in love with the bird, who returns to flit about the rear of the stage, and returns to her. Again the young girl feels terribly alone. She, too, leaves the stage.

Bolender has named the following section "Enchanted Princess," though of course the "Laideronnette" music is used. The Oriental theme is carried out in the dancing. A Chinese prince dances with four girls dressed in a rich crimson. When the young girl enters, the prince desires to dance with her. They dance happily together, but suddenly he disappears. The final section concerns beauty and the beast. The beast, with the head of a lion, approaches the young girl, terrifying her. She backs away in horror while he, conscious of his ugliness, falls to the ground. The young girl goes up to her older self, who has been quietly watching, and receives a ring. Clouds envelop the stage once again. When all is clear, the beast has become a handsome young man. The fairy godmother of the young girl blesses the couple as he carries her away. The girl's older self leaves, and the stage fills with clouds.

Mother Goose Suite was in the repertoire for several years, but it has not been done in recent seasons. It should be revived. In this work Bolender created one of the most sensitive pieces of choreography in the New York City Ballet's repertoire. The idiom is that of classic ballet, and the figure of the young girl has been sketched with a lyric, wistful quality rare in contemporary dance.

The basic idea and its treatment are reminiscent of Tudor. Bolender has worked not in imitation of Tudor, but rather with a recognition and respect for the other's style. He has sensibly avoided the psychological complexities and undercurrents in which Tudor glories. *Mother Goose Suite* is a slender work of real charm, well organized, with a thorough knowledge of ballet vocabulary and an artistic restraint that makes the figure of the young girl altogether appealing.

The ballet has been handsomely danced. Marie-Jeanne in the central role showed a versatility that was a pleasant surprise to those who had thought her solely the exponent of a sharp and brittle neo-classic style. Janet Reed, seen in the role after Marie-Jeanne left the company, provided a delicate characterization, exquisitely danced.

This was Bolender's first ballet in the repertoire: a highly talented, promising piece of work. Two ballets he has created since then, *The Miraculous Mandarin* and *The Filly,* were not successful. A great deal of interest had been centered around the former. The Béla Bartók work had been banned for reasons of immorality right after its *première* in Cologne in 1926, and it suffered the same fate at its second performance in Prague the next year. It did not turn up again in Europe until about twenty years later. There had been occasional orchestral performances in this country, but it had not been produced as a theater piece. Originally the work was conceived as a mimed play; naturally there was great speculation as to what kind of a ballet it would make. As Bolender saw it, it was a violent affair, obviously intended as a shocker (with a hanging sequence patterned after

Jean Babilée's in *Le Jeune Homme et la Mort*), full of obscure symbolism and *avant-garde* clichés. *The Filly* received only a few performances before it was permanently dropped. Bolender's most recent ballet, *Souvenirs,* is discussed elsewhere in this book.

The Nutcracker (Casse=Noisette)

 Because Marius Petipa choreographed *Sleeping Beauty* and most of *Swan Lake,* the impression has gotten around that he also was responsible for *The Nutcracker.* The fact is that Lev Ivanov, Petipa's associate, must take primary credit for the ballet. *The Nutcracker,* to be sure, originally was Petipa's assignment. He had worked with great thoroughness on the libretto of the ballet, had completed a musical cue book, and was in constant touch with Tchaikovsky about the music. As in the 1890 *Sleeping Beauty,* he badgered the unhappy composer with detailed instructions about melody, rhythm, and orchestration. He wanted four measures of this kind of music, five measures of that, and would send Tchaikovsky notes like this: "The stage is empty . . . Clara returns. Eight measures of mysterious but sweet music. Eight more measures of still more mysteri-

ous music for Clara's entrance. Two measures for her tremble
of fright, eight for fantastic and dance music. Rest. The clock
strikes midnight. After the chimes of the clock a short tremolo.
During the tremolo Clara sees how the owl turns into Drosselmeier with his cunning smile. She wants to run, but has no
strength. After the tremolo—five measures to hear the scratch-
ing of the rats and four measures for their whistling. After the
whistling—eight measures of accelerating music ending in a
chord." And so on, constantly. Tchaikovsky grew irked. On
June 25, 1891, he finished the *Nutcracker* sketches.

"No," he wrote, "the old man"—referring to himself—"is
breaking up. Not only does his hair drop out or turn as white
as snow; not only does he lose his teeth, which refuse their
service; not only do his eyes weaken and tire easily; not only
do his feet walk badly, or drag themselves along, but he loses
bit by bit the capacity to do anything at all. The ballet is infinitely worse than *Sleeping Beauty*—so much is certain; let's
see how the opera will turn out." The opera was *Iolanthe,* a
commission from the St. Petersburg Opera. Tchaikovsky was
working on his opera and his ballet at the same time, and was
more interested in the opera.

The thing that most interested Tchaikovsky about *The Nutcracker* was its scoring. In Paris, the previous March, he had
become familiar with Auguste Mustel's new instrument, the
celesta, and had greatly admired its "divinely beautiful tone."
He decided to use one for *The Nutcracker,* and ordered his
publisher, Jurgenson, to have one of Mustel's instruments secretly shipped from Paris to Moscow. All this was to be ultra-
confidential: Tchaikovsky confided to Jurgenson that if Rimsky-
Korsakov and Glazunov heard the instrument, they would use
it immediately and achieve the unusual sonority before *The
Nutcracker* was heard. "I expect," said Tchaikovsky, "that this
new instrument will produce a colossal sensation." He finished
his scoring in March 1892. During that month the Imperial
Music Society gave a preliminary performance of a concert suite
from the score, and no fewer than five numbers had to be en-
cored. Whether or not the celesta, used in the *"Dance of the*

Sugar-Plum Fairy," scored the colossal sensation that Tchaikovsky had anticipated, history does not report.

Rehearsal time for the *Nutcracker* production came in August 1892. Just about that time the seventy-year-old Petipa was taken seriously ill. Ivanov was assigned to compose the choreography, and was given Petipa's elaborate cue books and outlines to work from. The plot of *The Nutcracker* was based on E. T. A. Hoffmann's fairy tale, *Der Nussnacker und der Mauskönig* (*The Nutcracker and the Mouse King*), taken from a collection named *The Serapion Brothers*.

The ballet received its first performance on December 17, 1892, at the Maryinsky Theater, St. Petersburg. Sharing the bill was Tchaikovsky's new opera, *Iolanthe*. Alexandre Benois, at that time a young balletomane (he later was to be an important adviser to Diaghilev and the Ballets Russes), was present and filled his diary with an account of the two failures (*Iolanthe* also flopped). *"Casse* has not turned out a success," he wrote, and later reprinted those remarks in his *Reminiscences of the Russian Ballet.*

"And it was just on this ballet that I had placed all my hopes, knowing Tchaikovsky's talent for creating a fairy-tale atmopshere. But perhaps the chief cause of my disappointment lies not in the music, but in the hideous production. The overture (which I already knew on the piano) was hurried through at the tempo of a can-can gallop, and entirely lacked the salt that the orchestra should have given it. The *décor* of Scene 1, though by Ivanov, is both disgusting and profoundly shocking. Instead of having an elaborate chamber in rococo or Louis XVI style, lit up by chandeliers and sconces, but conveying at the same time an atmosphere of good-natured *bourgeoisie,* we were obliged to contemplate during a whole hour the salon of some rich parvenu banker in the Friedrichstrasse style. It was stupid, coarse, heavy, and dark. How absurd the kind of fresco portraits of Tchaikovsky, Petipa, and the rest of them on the walls! . . . I was indignant! . . . The second act is still worse. Levogt's decor is effective in a showy way, while at times the music reminds one of an open-air military band. (The serene unconcern of this judgment is owing to my having been twenty-two years old at that time.) Tchaikovsky has never written anything more banal than some of these numbers!"

Benois comes to the conclusion that Ivanov evidently did not understand certain sections of the ballet; and that what he did understand was undistinguished. "The ballerina's dances, though no worse than usual, have nothing remarkable about them, even when performed by a first-class virtuoso." Benois does not give the reaction of the audience, which was not favorable. It seems that the Russians neither took to the German story, nor welcomed the appearance of real children in a ballet. In addition, the dancer seen in the important role of the Sugar-Plum Fairy, Antoinetta Dell'Era, was not an attractive girl, though she was a fine technician. Modest Tchaikovsky, the composer's brother, describes her as downright ugly. At the second performance she was replaced. Paul Gerdt continued to dance the role of the Prince.

The ballet is in two acts and three scenes. Two of the scenes are in the first act. As the curtain rises, we see a Christmas party being given in a pleasant home. Clara and Fritz, the two children of the house, are excitedly watching the proceedings. The elders stand about, conversing; children are constantly coming in. (These, Clara included, are real children, not members of the *corps de ballet* in short dresses.) The children dance before their parents. Drosselmeier, Clara's godfather, enters and gives the children a present. Later on, when it is time for Clara to go to bed, he gives her a large nutcracker in the shape of a soldier. Fritz scuffles with her for it, and the nutcracker gets broken. The elders dance and retire, sending the children off to bed. The stage is dark and empty; some time has passed, and it is midnight. Clara sneaks into the room, looking for her nutcracker. She walks right into a battle in which the nutcracker is leading a group of toy soldiers against a regiment of mice led by the mouse king. The nutcracker and the mouse king personally engage at a moment when the battle is in doubt. Clara helps matters along by throwing her shoe at the mouse, killing him. The nutcracker turns into a young prince (also danced by a child). He wishes to reward her by taking her to the Palace of Confiturenbourg (the Palace of Sweets). Off they go, the little girl and her little prince.

The scene shifts to the journey to the palace. It is a wintry day; snow is falling. The Snow King and his Queen come forth to meet the little visitors. They dance, accompanied by snow-flakes. Clara and the prince resume their journey.

Act II takes place in the Kingdom of Sweets. The Sugar-Plum Fairy welcomes the young couple to the court. They are entertained by a series of divertissements. Most of these are named after dainties that children like to eat or drink. First comes Hot Chocolate, a Spanish dance. Then Coffee, a *Danse Arabe*. Then Tea, a Chinese dance, and a Russian dance (trepak). The Candy Canes are followed by the Marzipan Shepherdesses. The divertissements are topped off by the Waltz of the Flowers and the great duet between the Sugar-Plum Fairy and her cavalier. The finale immediately follows. All the dancers join the Sugar-Plum Fairy and her prince in a final tribute to Clara.

The first substantially complete performance of *The Nut-cracker* in America was given by the Ballet Russe de Monte Carlo at the Fifty-first Street Theater, New York, on October 17, 1940. It was revived with choreography by Alexandra Fedorova "after Petipa" (should be "after Ivanov"), with sets and costumes "after Benois." Alicia Markova and André Eglevsky were the Sugar-Plum Fairy and the prince. No children were in the cast. Clara was danced by Dorothy Etheridge, Fritz by Ian Gibson. In the Waltz of the Flowers, which on this occasion had original choreography by Fedorova, were Lubov Rostova, Milada Mladova, Tanya Grantzeva, Chris Volkoff, James Starbuck, and Ian Gibson. Nathalie Krassovaka was soloist in the Spanish Dance, Frederic Franklin in the trepak.

George Balanchine's revival was presented by the New York City Ballet Company at the City Center of Music and Drama, New York, on February 2, 1954, with scenery by Horace Armistead, costumes by Karinska. Thirty-nine children from the School of American Ballet participated in the production, among them Alberta Grant and Paul Nickel, who took the roles of Clara and The Little Prince. Among the grown-ups were Maria Tallchief (Sugar-Plum Fairy), Nicholas Magallanes (her Cavalier), Yvonne Mounsey (Spanish Dance), Francisco Moncion (Arabian Dance), Janet Reed (one of the Mirlitons in the Marzipan Shepherdesses dance), and Tanaquil LeClercq, Jillana, and Irene Larsson (in the Waltz of the Flowers). The production also used a chorus of forty boys' voices. André Eglevsky had been announced for the New York City Ballet *première* but an injured ankle prevented him from appearing. He later danced opposite Tallchief in the ballet.

Balanchine himself, it is interesting to note, has part of his roots in *The Nutcracker*. In 1919, when he was fifteen years old and a pupil in the Russian State Ballet School (formerly the Imperial Ballet School), he danced the role of the Nutcracker at the Maryinsky Theater. Still earlier, he had performed several of the children's parts in the ballet.

The New York City Ballet revival, an enormous success with the public, was less well-received by the critics. So successful was it that a long season of nothing but *The Nutcracker* was added to the regular season of the company. Every mother in New York, it seemed, took her children to see the tiny Miss Grant, Mr. Nickel, and the other homunculi who thronged the stage of the City Center. That the ballet children were cute there is no denying. That they could not dance on a professional level is also true. Those who went to the ballet to see dancing found precious little (*Nutcracker* occupied the entire bill), and despite the elaborate scenery, one left the theater feeling as though he had attended a dancing-school recital. The last *pas de deux* by the Sugar-Plum Fairy and her cavalier is, of course, ballet at its greatest; but there is a long, long wait for it to arrive. If, as one can safely assume, Balanchine's choreography is faithful to the original, the sad truth seems to be that *Nutcracker* is not, and never was, much of a ballet.

Orpheus

During the short, uneasy alliance between the Metropolitan Opera and the American Ballet, George Balanchine was called upon to create a ballet for Gluck's *Orpheus and Eurydice.* That was in 1936, and Balanchine's advanced ideas sat very poorly with the Metropolitan's board. About ten years later, in 1947, Balanchine and Lincoln Kirstein were discussing ideas for Ballet Society's season. (Ballet Society was the immediate predecessor of the New York City Ballet Company.) It was decided that Stravinsky should be commissioned to compose the score for a new ballet, and the composer gladly agreed. Balanchine told Stravinsky that he would like to do a new and modern *Orpheus.* It seemed to Balanchine that the myth was highly appropriate for ballet, particularly a ballet with music by a composer of neo-classical tendencies like Stravinsky. Balanchine also thought that the Orpheus legend was familiar enough not to be a mystery to most people, and that the public might like to see it danced.

Anatole Chujoy, in his *The New York City Ballet,* has some interesting stories about the formation of *Orpheus.* Balanchine made a visit to Los Angeles to work with Stravinsky on the details of the new work. "If there ever has been a closer collaboration between a composer and a choreographer during the process of composing the score of a ballet," writes Chujoy, "it has never been recorded. Marius Petipa's detailed instructions to Tchaikovsky during the creation of *The Sleeping Beauty* and *The Nutcracker* are well known. Their work was a collaboration to a degree, but it was rather mechanical." Chujoy goes on to explain that there was no direct communion between the two early giants. "The collaboration between Balanchine and Stravinsky, on the other hand, was basic and all-embracing. They discussed the production as a whole and every moment of it separately. Stravinsky demanded from Balanchine every detail the choreographer could give him, and in return asked Balanchine's opinion on every section of the score. Superb craftsmen and meticulous artisans as well as great artists, both men considered no detail small enough or unimportant enough to be left to chance. They actually worked with stopwatches on each scene, each movement.

"Balanchine delights in telling how Stravinsky asked him: 'George, how long do you think the *pas de deux* of Eurydice and Orpheus should run?'

"'Oh,' replied Balanchine, 'about two and a half minutes.'

"'Don't say "about," ' shouted Stravinsky. 'There is no such thing as "about." Is it two minutes, two minutes and fifteen seconds, two minutes and thirty seconds, or something in between? Give me the exact time and I'll try to come as close to it as I can.' "

Isamu Noguchi, who had done so much work for the modern dance, had been commissioned to do the *décor.* When Stravinsky arrived in New York about three weeks before the *première,* he visited Noguchi's studio to pass on the sets, and he attended nearly every rehearsal of the ballet. A few days before the *première,* it was discovered that Ballet Society lacked the money to buy the last piece of equipment for *Orpheus*— a front drop of silk. The material cost about one thousand dollars, and nobody had that much money. Balanchine was told about the situation. He went out and came back with the money. He has never revealed how he got it; his only comment was: "I did not steal it."

With Stravinsky conducting, *Orpheus* received its *première* at the New York City Center of Music and Drama on April 28, 1948. In the cast were Nicholas Magallanes (Orpheus), Maria Tallchief (Eurydice), Francisco Moncion (Dark Angel), Beatrice Tompkins (Leader of the Furies), Tanaquil LeClercq (Leader of the Bacchantes), and Herbert Bliss (Apollo).

Orpheus achieved a tremendous, unprecedented success. It also may have been the contributing factor of the emergence of the New York City Ballet Company from Ballet Society, for it created such a furor that the City Center decided to take the struggling company into its fold. Stravinsky's score was hailed as a masterpiece. Ingolf Dahl, a contributor to *Stravinsky in the Theatre,* pointed out the strong neo-classic elements of the score. "Never before has Stravinsky so consciously and so consistently applied himself to the creation of a one-levelled monochromatic music. He was aware of the responsibility that such a subjugation to the Apollonian principle would impose on him. But in rejecting the temptations which Dionysian dynamism constantly offers he accomplished a subtle variety of musical means of a much higher order. His insistence on unification produces no more monotony than one finds in the music of Bach or Buxtehude. For the shaping and profiling of melodic phrases, the life of the inner parts and of the harmonies, the vitality of the rhythm, all of these *in balance* supply a truly musical variety that seems inexhaustible."

There are three scenes in this one-act ballet. Scene 1 is The Grave of Eurydice. Orpheus stands mourning, his lyre discarded. Friends come in to console him; he pays no attention. Picking up his lyre, he gives vent to his sorrow. He puts the instrument on the grave and prepares to pull out its strings. A satyr and four wood sprites attempt to distract him, but he will not be consoled. The Angel of Death appears, and then there is stage business that has puzzled some audiences. The Angel of Death divests himself of a black coil and entwines it through the hands and arms of Orpheus. This coil represents the power of the Angel of Death in Hades; he is transferring it to Orpheus. Orpheus receives the coil and, accompanied by the Angel of Death, prepares for the trip to the underworld.

The Angel of Death also places over Orpheus's eyes a golden mask that must not be removed until he is back on earth. This is the crux of the entire Orpheus legend; he is not to look upon his wife until they have completed the homeward journey. The Angel of Death guides the masked Orpheus on his trip. One of the exciting touches in the staging occurs here: as the two figures begin their descent, a silk curtain comes down; and while they move, dim creatures stir behind it. As they descend still farther, the motion becomes violent, and the silk billows out in sheer menace. It is a brilliant and breathtaking effect.

Scene 2 is Hades. The Furies gather and prepare to attack Orpheus. The Angel of Death gives Orpheus his lyre and commands him to play. He lulls the Furies to sleep and continues playing. Pluto, God of the Underworld, comes forth, bringing Eurydice with him. Husband and wife are united. Orpheus pledges not to look at her until they reach earth. A blue stalactite descends; this is supposed to symbolize the reunion. The three figures start their return trip. On the way they dance together. Eurydice joyfully blows upon an imaginary pipe to express her happiness. Eventually, in sheer frustration because he cannot see his beloved, Orpheus tears off his mask. Immediately she dies. The Angel of Death disappears, and Orpheus realizes what he has done. He gets to earth in anguish, and encounters a band of bacchantes, who tear him to pieces.

Scene 3 is entitled "Apotheosis." Apollo comes to the grave of Orpheus and takes from behind a mound a golden mask symbolizing the minstrel's face. Apollo holds the mask high. He invokes the memory of Orpheus; from now on he will be deified as the God of Song. Apollo gently places the mask over the grave. As he raises his arm, the lyre of Orpheus ascends from the grave and mounts upward, another piece of symbolism: the spirit of Orpheus and his music will never die.

The symbolism and unity of Orpheus do not become clear at a first viewing. And despite its overwhelming success there have been a handful of critics who do not like the work. Their objections are, variously, to what they describe as a "pseudo-classical style," to a preponderance of story over dance, or to an excess of vague symbolism. All one can say is that the so-called "pseudo-classical style" seems entirely appropriate to the balletic treatment of the story; that after several viewings the symbolism becomes perfectly clear; and that, again after several viewings, one tends to forget about the story and regards the ballet purely in terms of movement. *Orpheus* is an *avant-garde* ballet, with many departures from tradition. No virtuoso solo work is present; the leading characters never once disregard the action. Even pantomime is down to a sheer minimum. The movements are all designed to tell the story. In the group dances—those of the Furies and Bacchantes—the dancing is of a somewhat more traditional nature, though the groups do not dance for the sake of dance, but move as adjuncts to the story. *Orpheus* is a complicated design, and it succeeds brilliantly in terms of what its creators set out to accomplish.

Petrouchka

 The music came first, the ballet later. Stravinsky was preparing himself for *Le Sacre du printemps,* but, as he says in his autobiography, he wanted to "refresh" himself by composing an orchestral piece with a prominent piano part. "In composing the music I had in mind a distinct picture of a puppet, suddenly endowed with life, exasperating the patience of the orchestra with diabolical cascades of arpeggios. The orchestra in turn retaliates with menacing trumpet blasts. The outcome is a terrific noise that reaches its climax and ends in the sorrowful and querulous collapse of the poor puppet. . . . I struggled for hours . . . to find a title that would express in a word the character of my music and, consequently, the personality of this creature. One day I leaped for joy. I had found my title—Petrouchka, the immortal and unhappy hero of every fair in all countries."

192

And so Stravinsky happily polished his score. This was in Switzerland; and when Diaghilev visited the composer to find out how *Le Sacre du printemps* was progressing, Stravinsky instead played him *Petrouchka*. Far from being annoyed, Diaghilev, who knew the ballet possibilities in any score he heard, was enchanted. Petrouchka is the Russian Punch (of Punch and Judy), or Guignol, or Harlequin; and, as the impresario listened to the music, all sorts of ideas entered his head. He discussed them with Stravinsky; and Stravinsky hastily sketched out a tentative plot. *Petrouchka* was on its way.

Stravinsky amplified the score (retaining the piano). Michel Fokine was appointed choreographer. Serge Grigoriev was placed in charge of the stage production, and Alexandre Benois was commissioned to paint the sets. Through the winter of 1910 and well into the following year, the principals constantly interchanged letters. The scenario of the ballet was thoroughly worked out, including a new finale that gave Stravinsky some trouble. "The finale did not come to Stravinsky at once," writes Benois, "and he had to search and use different combinations for it. He finished composing the music only a few weeks before the performance. We were staying at the same hotel in Rome for nearly a month, and every morning I used to hear from my room a confused tangle of sounds, interrupted from time to time by long pauses. . . . Those were indeed wonderful days for us!"

The first rehearsals took place in Rome in abnormally hot weather. Stravinsky himself was the rehearsal pianist; he alone was able to decipher his complicated manuscript. Fokine had some difficulty memorizing the melodies and rhythms. Rehearsals were moved to Paris, and everything went smoothly ahead —as smoothly, that is, as permitted by the chaos that accompanies the creation of a large-scale ballet. Benois was so helpful, and came up with so many ideas that eventually were adopted, that Stravinsky dedicated the score to him. He was especially responsible for the crowd scene. He wanted to reconstruct the fair as he remembered it from his youth (it had been discontinued in 1900), and insisted on "real people"—people of good

193

society with elegant manners, military men who looked like real soldiers and officers of the time of Nicholas I, street-hawkers, peasants who really looked like *muzhiks* and *babas*.

Fokine created the choreography with rapidity. Only once was he stuck. When he reached the third scene, where the Moor is left by himself, he could not think what to make him do. According to Grigoriev, who has some interesting things to say about *Petrouchka* in his *Diaghilev Ballet,* he "lost his temper, throwing the music on the floor and leaving the rehearsal. Next day, however, he appeared looking happier and said that he had thought of some 'business' for the accursed Moor: he would give him a coconut to play with—which would carry him at least through the first part of the scene." (Benois, in his autobiography takes credit for the coconut business, however: "I invented his [the Blackamoor's] monologue in all its absurd detail: the playing with the coconut, the coconut's resentment at being chopped open, etc.")

The *première* was scheduled for June 13, 1911, at the Théâtre du Châtelet, Paris. Pierre Monteux, who was to conduct the opening, noticed that his musicians had a bit of trouble with the score, one of the most difficult composed up to that time. He had to split his orchestra into groups and rehearse them individually. Fokine, at the same time, was trying to get some order into the crowd scenes, while patiently (and sometimes not so patiently) listening to dancers complaining that there was not enough room on the stage to move around. But the performance went off on June 13 as scheduled, with Tamara Karsavina as the Ballerina, Vaslav Nijinsky as Petrouchka, Alexandre Orlov as the Blackamoor, and Enrico Cecchetti as the Charlatan. "They enthralled the audience," writes Grigoriev. "The dramatic tension grew with each scene. Nijinsky was inexpressibly moving at the end. . . ." When Sarah Bernhardt saw Nijinsky's performance, she came away with this comment: *"J'ai peur, j'ai peur, car je vois l'acteur le plus grand du monde."* This, from Bernhardt—"I have seen the greatest actor in the world" —was really something. And Benois reports that "our ballet made a wonderful impression." Benois was no longer with the company at the *première:* he had resigned in a rage because Bakst had repainted his, Benois's, portrait of the Charlatan, which was to occupy a prominent place on the stage in one scene.

Nijinsky's success was particularly gratifying to the company because during rehearsal he had not been in good form. He had experienced trouble understanding the role, and Benois had had to explain it to him several times. "But in the end," Benois writes, "he amazed us. I was surprised at the courage Vaslav showed, after all his *jeune premier* successes, in appearing as a horrible half-doll, half-human grotesque. The great difficulty of Petrouchka's part is to express his pitiful oppression and his hopeless efforts to achieve personal dignity *without ceasing to be a puppet.* Both music and libretto are spasmodically interrupted by outbursts of illusive joy and frenzied despair. The artist is not given a single step or a display section to enable him to be attractive to the public, and one must remember that Nijinsky was then quite a young man and the temptation to 'be attractive to the public' must have appealed to him far more strongly than to an older artist."

Petrouchka has retained its place in the repertoire, and there are many who claim that it is the greatest ballet of all time. It also is a staple at symphony concerts, and many consider it Stravinsky's greatest score. Indeed, it is hard to overemphasize the impact that the score of *Petrouchka* made on listeners in 1911. To the Western world it was a barbaric evocation of Russia, painted with primary colors, orchestrated with infinite resource. Technically it contained the seeds of polytonality. So famous is one chord in the music that it has come to be known as the *"Petrouchka* chord." In it Stravinsky juxtaposed a pair of clashing tonalities—C major against F sharp major; and the sound made musicians and critics reel with joy or anguish, depending upon their progressiveness.

There were many other things to admire. Alexandre Tansman, in his study of the composer, *Igor Stravinsky: The Man and His Music,* exclaims over *Petrouchka's* "unprecedented rhythmic animation. . . . Stravinsky juggles with the bar like a virtuoso or an acrobat. Indeed, so inexhaustible does the composer's invention seem as he creates new meters, breaks rules to breathe new life into them, or introduces an irregular meter into a squared-off movement, that we seem to be faced with a truly new rhythmic language."

The younger musicians, you may be sure, studied *Petrouchka* until they knew every note and device in it; and for years, in the concert hall, you could hear echoes of that study. (Although, talking about polytonal chords, what about the one—B flat major against D minor—that opens the last movement of Beethoven's Ninth, which came almost one hundred years before *Petrouchka?*)

What *Aïda* and *Die Meistersinger* are to opera, *Petrouchka* is to ballet. *Aïda* and *Meistersinger* are "grand opera," using large casts and elaborate *décor;* and *Petrouchka* is "grand ballet," calling for the ultimate resources of dancers, *corps de ballet, décor,* and musicians. The ballet is in four scenes, the first of which takes place at the Shrovetide Fair, St. Petersburg, in 1830. "Butter Week" it is called: the days just before Lent, when the people feast and indulge themselves in revelry and great cheer. As the curtain rises, we see the folk—rich folk, peasants, beggars, soldiers, students—out for a good time at their festival. We see buildings and fair booths, flags and colorful costumes. The bustling noise of the orchestra accentuates the busy, festive atmosphere. It is cold, and the good-natured crowd stomps around to keep warm. An organ-grinder enters and a girl dances to his music; then another organ-grinder, with another girl who engages in a competitive dance. More crowd scenes. Then, from the big stage at the rear, come drummers, calling attention to the next attraction. The Charlatan, a pinched-looking man with a peaked hat, pokes his head through the curtains. He steps forth while the awed and now silent crowd watches. He blows his flute and signals. The curtains of the stage fly back and the three puppets are seen, unvitalized, just so much cloth and sawdust. There is the Ballerina, an insipid-looking doll, dainty and pretty in an empty way; there is the Blackamoor, in Oriental dress; and there is Petrouchka, in clown's costume (usually), head lolling to the side, his mouth a gash of anguish.

The Charlatan brings them to life. They step down and engage in a little skit—and not a very subtle one. Both of the male puppets are attracted to the Ballerina. She favors the Blackamoor. Petrouchka jealously assaults the Blackamoor. They are separated and continue dancing. Soon the Charlatan stops the show, the crowd wanders away, and the curtain falls.

In the second scene we are in Petrouchka's room. With a stroke of genius. Stravinsky used only a long, menacing drum roll to introduce the scene. Petrouchka is contemptuously tossed into his room by the Charlatan. From this point the action is heartbreaking. Petrouchka indicates by action and gesture his disgust with life, his hatred of the Charlatan, his utter despair. He tries to get out of the room, hysterically beating on the walls. Suddenly the Ballerina enters. Petrouchka, who loves her and yearns for her, wildly dances around her. She stands there disapprovingly, perhaps a little frightened, but finally leaves. Then Petrouchka goes into a frenzy of frustration. With superhuman strength he tears open a section of the wall and collapses.

As a contrast, the third scene brings us to the Blackamoor's room. He is a different sort of personality. Where Petrouchka is introverted, frustrated, has human feelings and aspirations, the Blackamoor is all animal, content with himself and the way things are. Where Petrouchka's room is little more than a bare cell, the Blackamoor's quarters are luxurious and colorful. Where Petrouchka has doubt, the Blackamoor is all confidence. There he lies, contentedly playing with a coconut. Finally he gets bored and hacks it with his scimitar. But it refuses to break, and the Blackamoor, astonished, obviously decides that as it is stronger than he a god must reside in it. He bends down and worships the coconut. The Ballerina comes in to him, just as she entered Petrouchka's quarters. But here, instead of feeling repelled, she gladly enters into dalliance with the Blackamoor. She dances for him, then with him, and finally allows herself to be taken into his arms. At this moment Petrouchka forces himself into the room through the wedge he had made in the wall. He advances upon the Blackamoor, who, recovering from his surprise, draws his scimitar and chases the unhappy puppet. A poor figure of a rescuing knight-errant Petrouchka makes! The Ballerina faints, Petrouchka manages to make an ignominious escape, and the Blackamoor returns to the Ballerina. With animal gestures he resumes his love-making.

Scene 4 brings us back to the carnival at the St. Petersburg Fair. A group of nursemaids dances to a Russian folk song. A trainer leads in a dancing bear, which clumsily performs. The nursemaids resume their dance; then everybody joins in. Snow begins to fall. Suddenly strange noises are heard from the curtained stage in which the puppet show reposes. All stop dancing to gaze in bewilderment as Petrouchka comes clumsily dashing into the open, followed by the Blackamoor brandishing a scimitar. The Ballerina tries to restrain the Blackamoor, but to no avail. He catches up with Petrouchka and, with wild thrusts, strikes him down. Petrouchka collapses and dies. A policeman enters, summoned by the horrified crowd. Out comes the Charlatan, who picks up the sawdust body of his puppet. He shows it to his audience: it is only a stuffed doll, after all, and how can a doll be murdered? Everybody leaves, and the Charlatan begins to lug the hacked puppet to his cell. Suddenly, fortissimo, the theme of Petrouchka is heard from the orchestra. As the frightened Charlatan gazes upwards, he sees an animated, jeering Petrouchka—the ghost of Petrouchka—who shakes a fist at him and the world. The Charlatan cowers and flees, and the curtain falls.

Small wonder that observers have seen all kinds of symbolism in *Petrouchka*. Charlie Chaplin has been brought into the picture: his delineation of the famous little tramp, always trodden upon, always the underdog, has reminded many of Petrouchka. Some have compared the *Petrouchka* scenario with the *commedia dell'arte*. Some have seen political implications: Petrouchka as the symbol of a downtrodden Russia, the Charlatan as a symbol of despotism. Some have seen in the figure of Petrouchka the dawn of intelligence and the struggle for self-expression; also, the birth of the imagination stimulated by love. *Petrouchka* has been described as universal drama, the tragedy of every man. Still another school of thought sees it as showing man as a toy in the hands of impenetrable, cruel, and amoral forces, life as a kind of mechanism of destiny wherein free will plays no part.

Petrouchka was first seen in America as performed by Diaghilev's Ballets Russes at the Century Theater, New York, on January 24, 1916. Lydia Lopokova, Leonide Massine, and Adolph Bolm were the principal dancers. In the surge of the ballet revival that America experienced in the thirties, *Petrouchka* made a reappearance at the St. James Theater, New York, on January 12, 1934. The company was the Colonel W. de Basil Ballet Russe, and the dancers were Tamara Toumanova, Leon Woizikowski, and David Lichine. Fokine himself restaged the ballet for the Original Ballet Russe; it was presented at the Fifty-first Street Theater, New York, on November 21, 1940, with Toumanova, Yura Lazowsky, and Alberto Alonso. Ballet Theatre added *Petrouchka* to its repertoire on October 8, 1942, at the Metropolitan Opera House, New York. Fokine also directed this production, which featured Irina Baronova, Lazowsky, and Richard Reed. (Ballet Theatre later had an all-American cast consisting of Lucia Chase, Jerome Robbins, and Richard Reed.)

America has seen brilliant dancers in the female role—Alexandra Danilova, Alicia Markova, and Nora Kaye, in addition to the ones already mentioned. A really convincing Petrouchka is a rarer phenomenon. Massine and Lazowsky were probably outstanding. André Eglevsky and Richard Reed have been among the convincing Blackamoors, and Eric Braun was an effective newcomer in the role during the fifteenth anniversary season of Ballet Theatre in 1955.

That *Petrouchka* is trotted out only on special occasions these days is not the fault of the ballet or of lack of audience appeal. The sad economic fact is that *Petrouchka* is expensive to mount, that most available sets and costumes are old and shabby, and that much rehearsal time is needed. The musical demands of

199

Petrouchka, too, are far in excess of the capabilities of most ballet orchestras heard these days on the American scene. It is safe to say that the *Petrouchka* performances we see today are a long way from the original. They look improvisatory and ragged, much like a performance of *Aïda* by a tenth-rate opera company in a blowsy theatre. Even in the twenties the process of deterioration had set in. Benois complained loudly when he saw some revivals of his masterpiece. "Many items have disappeared entirely, as, for instance, the merry-go-round on which children used to have rides." (This particular merry-go-round, a genuine antique of the time of Napoleon III, had been acquired by Diaghilev for the 1911 production. It fell into the Atlantic while being unloaded at Buenos Aires and was never recovered. *Petrouchka* went merry-go-roundless from then on.) "The gingerbread and sweetmeat stalls are gone too and the outside steps leading into the huge *balagan,* where the people crowded together, waiting for admission to the perform- ance. The small table with its enormous steaming samovar where tea was sold is hardly noticeable nowadays. All these things were there in 1911. . . . But I was still more grieved by the *disorder* which, in the later productions, reigned on the stage. . . . People wandered aimlessly from corner to 'empti- ness' by affected gesticulation." Benois sadly quotes the French saying about *des ans l'irreparable outrage.* Nobody, alas, has found a way to hold back the irreparable invasion of the years; and ballet, perhaps the most perishable of the arts, suffers from it most of all.

The Pied Piper

 We all know the story about the Pied Piper of Hamelin and what happened when he put pipe to mouth. Jerome Robbins, musing about this theme in *The Pied Piper*, has in effect come up with a contemporary take-off on the old legend. The ballet is what many Europeans think the essence of Americana—and, indeed, it *is* typically American in its brashness, good humor, and tongue-in-cheek attitude, and also in its irreverence toward the classic amenities.

A real piper is on stage—an honest-to-goodness clarinetist, dressed in ordinary business clothes, playing Aaron Copland's Clarinet Concerto. His music is mounted on a lectern at one side of a stage otherwise bare to the rear wall. Nor are the dancers costumed. They wear leotards, practice clothes—anything. This Pied Piper of a clarinetist begins to warm up, playing a few scales, loosening his lip and fingers.

Then he starts the Concerto. Dancers in the wings hear the music and are drawn forth. First a couple enters. The music at this point is quiet and lyrical, so the couple dances a tender *pas de deux*. Another couple enters and dances. One by one others enter. They look at the dancing couples; they regard the clarinetist with interest. Then everybody listens to the musician. They stand in fascination as he begins a perky-sounding melody. They have been captured. The music begins to take possession of them.

Their bodies do not even obey them. One dancer's hand begins to make twitching motions, and she regards it with amazement. Soon her entire body begins to shake uncontrollably. Other boys and girls are having the same trouble.

Now the music becomes rhythmic and jazzy. The dancers begin to sway; they break out into abandoned dances. They jitterbug, they play games, and the stage is in riotous upheaval. At one delirious moment the large group is flat on the floor, arms, legs, and bodies trembling to the music. Ballet has seen few stranger spectacles. They rise, there is more lively dancing, and the entire company finally dives across the stage to fall at the feet of the Pied Piper.

The Pied Piper received its *première* on December 4, 1951, by the New York City Ballet Company, at the New York City Center of Music and Drama. The cast was headed by Diana Adams, Nicholas Magallanes, Jillana, Roy Tobias, Janet Reed, Todd Bolender, Melissa Hayden, Herbert Bliss, Tanaquil Le-Clercq, and Jerome Robbins. Edmund Wall was the clarinetist.

This is an "abstract" ballet in that it has no specific plot. Nor has it costumes or *décor;* it relies entirely on the ingeniousness of the choreographer to hold the attention of the audience. And if Robbins is one thing, it is ingenious. He is as clever a choreographer as can be found today when working with straight dancing and humor devoid of a complicated message. Primarily a natural showman, he always keeps things moving.

In a way, *The Pied Piper* is a potpourri. Pure ballet is represented by a lyric *pas de deux,* beautifully danced by Adams and Magallanes at the *première*. This dance is in a very slow tempo and has a dreamy, soaring quality as the male dancer lifts the ballerina high into the air, constantly changing the positions by slow turns and broad assisted leaps. Jazz is represented by a melee of jitterbugging as the jazzy elements of the Copland score begin to hit the dancers. Comedy dance is often present. Robbins has conceived an extremely funny dance for LeClercq (he partnered her at the *première*). LeClercq is tall and thin, and has exceptionally long legs. She was dressed to accentuate those qualities, in tight-fitting striped top and dark tights, and her movements were what used to be described as eccentric jazz. Robbins was close to musical comedy here, and the audience was, as they say, paralyzed, though there was, in all truth, nothing particularly distinctive about the dance. Robbins also worked in a good deal of humorous "business" for Janet Reed, a clever comedian in her own right.

Even the purists were amused. Robbins has a nonchalance and a way with this sort of thing which can be most disarming. Musical comedy or not, *The Pied Piper* is a clever piece of work by the cleverest young choreographer active today on the American scene.

Pillar of Fire

The so-called "psychological ballet" came to full flower in *Pillar of Fire,* a work that many otherwise cautious critics will unhesitatingly call the greatest choreographic masterpiece of the generation. It was not an unexpected effort. Antony Tudor, its choreographer, had come to America from England and had staged several of his works for Ballet Theatre: the lovely *Lilac Garden, Judgment of Paris,* and *Gala Performance.* In addition he had created *Time Table,* now out of the repertoire, a small work for Kirstein's American Ballet, set to Aaron Copland's *Music for the Theater.*

On the evidence of these works, Tudor was a sensitive, imaginative choreographer who knew the theater inside out and who also had that rarest of traits—the ability to express humor in choreographic terms without degenerating into slapstick. The *première* of *Pillar of Fire* by Ballet Theatre at the Metropolitan Opera House on April 8, 1942, was one of the memorable evenings in contemporary ballet. Word had gotten around that *Pillar* was going to be something exceptional, and many doubters came armed with a show-me attitude. Just two days before, on April 6, Fokine's last ballet to be seen in this country had received its *première* and had fallen flat. This was *Russian Soldier,* set to Prokofiev's *Lt. Kije* suite. If a master like Fokine had failed to make an acceptable ballet from so lilting a score as *Lt. Kije,* skeptics were saying, how could Tudor succeed with such a long and (on the face of it) non-balletic work as Arnold Schoenberg's *Verklärte Nacht?*

But Tudor did succeed, as the audience realized shortly after the curtain went up. The ovation at the end lasted for twenty-six curtain calls. Overnight Nora Kaye became a star: her blazing performance as Hagar revealed an intensity almost frightening in its scope, just as *Pillar of Fire* revealed a new concept of ballet as a medium for dance drama.

Hence the term "psychological ballet." *Pillar of Fire,* like the earlier *Lilac Garden,* has a continuous plot line and deals with human beings in trouble—their frustrations and aspirations, their secret hopes and desires, the interplay of people in the world around them. And, most important, Tudor's people transcend themselves to become symbols of humanity and for humanity. Tudor, in a way, is an objectivist. He looks upon his characters with sympathy and understanding, but presents them as they are. He gives them no easy solutions; he does not gild the lily; and he is never guilty of sentimentalism. In short, he is an artist, a supreme artist in his field. And as such he is never responsible for a cheap effect. A supreme craftsman, he has expressed the inner world of his characters purely in choreographic terms, basically the terms that Noverre used. Naturally one encounters an extension of the Imperial Ballet vocabulary, and Tudor has not hesitated to call upon movements at times suggestive of the modern dance, even going as far as to place his dancers flat on the ground.

Tudor wrote his own libretto for the one-act *Pillar of Fire.* He undoubtedly got the idea from the program for Schoenberg's piece. *Verklärte Nacht* was composed as a string sextet (later amplified into a work for string orchestra) in 1899, and the score carries an extract from a poem by Richard Dehmel, *Weib und die Welt*. Henry Krehbiel's translation of the excerpt that Schoenberg cited is as follows:

Two mortals walk through a cold, barren grove. The moon sails over the tall oaks, which send their scrawny branches up through the unclouded moonlight. A woman speaks. She confesses a sin to the man at her side: she is with child, and he is not its father. She had lost belief in happiness and, longing for life's fullness, for motherhood and a mother's duty, she had surrendered herself, shuddering, to the embraces of a man she knew not. She had thought herself blessed, but now life had avenged itself on her, by giving her the love of him she walked with. She staggers onward, gazing with lack-luster eye at the moon which follows her. A man speaks. Let her not burden her soul with thoughts of guilt. See, the moon's sheen enwraps the universe. Together they are driving over chill waters, but a flame from each warms the other. It, too, will trans-figure the little stranger, and she will bear the child to him. For she has inspired the brilliant glow within him and made him too a child. They sink in each other's arms. Their breaths meet in kisses in the air. Two mortals wander through the wondrous moonlight.

With important modifications, this evokes the general mood of the Tudor ballet. The staging and costumes indicate a turn-of-the-century locale. The curtain rises to reveal an intense, tormented girl—Hagar—sitting on the steps of her house. She watches people pass by, and it is evident that she is suffering from a sense of frustration. Her two sisters, who come out of the house, are different. One is elderly, prim, puritanical; the other is young, beautiful, thoughtless, and selfish. A young man, with whom Hagar is in love, approaches them. Very polite and considerate, he pays attention to the two sisters. As Hagar watches, her younger sister makes a decided play for the young man, and he appears interested. He goes into the house with the two sisters, leaving Hagar to herself. In despair, she feels alone in the world. She looks with a mixture of desire and re-pulsion at a house across the street—a house where young men and women meet to make love. She is approaching the house tentatively when a young man comes out and boldly examines her. Hagar writhes under the inspection, and he scornfully re-enters.

When her beloved once more comes out of her house, accompanied by her younger sister, apparently smitten by her, Hagar loses control. She joins the man in the house across the street and passionately makes love to him. After the affair is over, Hagar finds herself in a worse state than before. Cold-blooded love-making is no substitute for affection, and she hates herself for having given her body in return for—nothing. The emotional experience she is undergoing shows in her face, and when the elder sister sees her, Hagar's guilt is apparent. And not only to her sister: the whole town knows about it. In the meantime, Hagar's younger sister has discovered some of the people in the house across the street, and is busy trying to cultivate them. They do not need much urging. Finally Hagar goes into her own house.

A change of scene takes place. Hagar is an outcast, shunned by her former friends. The young man—the one with whom she still is in love—comes to her, but she is ashamed and repels him. She even tries to attract her seducer, but he will have none of her. Instead, he is greatly interested in her younger sister, and the action of the ballet suggests that the youngster does not come through unscathed. Hagar does not know where to turn, but, persistently, her young man approaches her sympathetically and accepts her as she is. In a yearning, beautiful sequence, she gratefully accepts his love and the two of them wander into a forest bathed in moonlight.

Thus the plot. What Tudor does with it is uncanny. The more one sees *Pillar of Fire,* the more one realizes the unity of conception that went into it, the variety of characterization in which it abounds. Every gesture is meaningful. The sexual symbolism, of which there is considerable, is expressed with staggering force, but never is vulgar. The ballet abounds in fine details. The tight, clenched gestures of Hagar are those that a repressed girl would make. Tudor has paid especial attention to the younger sister, making her a malicious little monster who, in the eyes of the world, is a perfectly happy, normal child. The younger sister delights in twisting the knife in Hagar. She is possessive and sexually premature, and glories in the sufferings through which Hagar is passing. The young man across the street symbolizes sex pure and simple; he has nothing but a stud function in life, and thinks of nothing else. All of his movements show off his virility, as contrasted to the softer and more sensitive movements of the man Hagar loves.

During the years that *Pillar of Fire* has been before the public, Nora Kaye has continued to appear as Hagar. A performance without her would be unthinkable, so closely has she identified herself with the role. At the *première* performance for which Jo Mielziner designed the ingenious sets, Hugh Laing was The Young Man From the House Opposite; Lucia Chase danced the Eldest Sister; Annabelle Lyon the Youngest Sister, and Antony Tudor the Friend. Among the dancers in the lesser roles, Sono Osato was memorable as one of the Lovers in Experience. The ballet has been performed with replacements for Tudor and Laing, but not very successfully. Laing, indeed, was a perfect foil for Kaye, and no other dancer who has attempted the role has managed to project an equivalent amount of brute strength and sex.

And, having dwelt upon the psychological and dramatic import of *Pillar of Fire,* it remains to stress that the ballet is conceived first of all in terms of *dance,* as are all of Tudor's major works. His vocabulary is primarily classical, a functional classicism divorced from academic suggestions: meaning that Tudor has never found it necessary to fall back upon classroom formulae. He is very much a follower of the philosophy of dance represented by Fokine. The Russian choreographer maintained that every movement must bear relation to the mood and substance of the ballet in question. Tudor, however, has extended Fokine's theories. He has not hesitated to depart from classical movements when departure suits his purpose—but even his departures are generally recognizably classical. His use of gesture is particularly individual. Some of Tudor's characters use gestures that are entirely colloquial. A man will adjust his jacket, a woman will arrange her hair. This is a new type of naturalism in classic-derived ballet.

Tudor has made many departures in his technical concepts. When his ballerina is on toe, it is because he wants her on a different level rather than because she looks pretty on toe. He uses toe technique as a means of extension, to raise the body for a specific emotional meaning demanded at the moment. He makes extraordinary demands on his women dancers, much more than on the men. To get a dramatic idea across he will do anything, even to the point of having a ballerina dragged across the stage. And yet, despite this uninhibited quality and his penchant for breaking the rules, a strong sense of tradition is always present.

Pure pyrotechnics seldom play a part in the Tudor ballets. His roles can be extremely difficult, but often the difficulties will escape the audience. He will ask his ballerina to do a double turn and land in her partner's arms, or be ready for a quick lift almost without preparation ("preparation," in ballet, is the act of getting the body adjusted for a movement that is to follow immediately). He demands control and split-second timing from his dancers. Above all, he insists on a legato line; his dancers have to move with fluidity. Even in moments of stress, their movements are seldom sharp. The Tudor ballets have something Wagnerian about them: an endless flow of melody in which the solos and ensembles are subservient to an over-all conception.

The Prodigal Son (Le Fils Prodigue)

 The Prodigal Son was created in 1929 for Diaghilev's Ballets Russes. It was to be the last year of that great company, for Serge Diaghilev died on August 19, 1929. Serge Prokofiev had been commissioned to compose a ballet on the Biblical subject of the Prodigal Son, and early in the year Diaghilev went to Paris to see how the Russian composer was getting along. He seemed to like the new score, and hardly asked Prokofiev to alter anything, a fact that Serge Grigoriev received with some astonishment. Grigoriev was *régisseur* of the company.

George Balanchine was named the choreographer. In a letter to Vox Records he has explained the genesis of the ballet. "The first idea for the finale came from a primitive Russian popular wood-cut engraving showing in rather naïve terms the Biblical story. Boris Kochno suggested it. I think it is one of the best of all ballet libretti. It is simplicity itself, in the form of A-B and then A again. It is the story of some one who has everything, who throws it away to have nothing, and then has everything again. The famous painter, Georges Rouault, did two sketches for the backcloths which were magnificently executed by Prince Schervachidze. I think he deserved as much credit as the designer for the success of the *décor*. I was still a young man, and my choreography was considered too acrobatic, shocking, outrageously physical and against the classic dance. However, when I revived it for the New York City Ballet Company, in February, 1950, it was taken as an historic work, and it has remained in the repertoire ever since. I still think the adagio of the second scene is one of my most effective pieces of duo-composition."

The Prodigal Son was the third ballet that Prokofiev had composed for Diaghilev (*Chout—The Buffoon—*and *Pas d'acier* were its predecessors). Officials of the company were a little worried about the choice of Balanchine as choreographer; Grigoriev, for one, considered him over-intellectual. But when *The Prodigal Son* received its *première* at the Théâtre Sarah Bernhardt Paris, on May 21, 1929, it scored a success, and Diaghilev was highly praised for the production. The principal dancers were Serge Lifar (the Prodigal Son), Felia Dubrovska (Siren), Michael Fedorov (Father), and Leon Woizikowski and Anton Dolin (Servants to the Prodigal Son). Georges Rouault provided the sets and costumes.

The ballet, in one act, has three scenes. The first scene displays the Prodigal Son under the influence of two evil friends. He is going to leave home and make his way in the world. The Father enters, and we see that the Son resents him. Finally, the Son flaunts his independence and leaves with his friends, while the Father and his other children look on sorrowfully. The second scene takes place in a far country. Dissipated revelers amuse themselves. The Prodigal Son joins their party. He orders his friends to provide liquor for them, and is immediately accepted as a fellow spirit. Now the Siren enters, and the Prodigal Son, really a country boy, a little man trying to be big, is fascinated by her. She dances before him—a sensuous dance that inflames him. He is her slave. She dances with him, flatters him, and gets him drunk. While he is in a stupor, the Siren and his new friends rob him of everything he owns, including his clothes. When he recovers, he staggers off, heartbroken. The Siren returns with her companions and they dance in triumph, ending up with a sequence suggesting a ship sailing away.

The final scene is the same as the first—the home of the Prodigal Son. He enters, exhausted, emaciated, and poverty-stricken, collapsing as his Sisters come forth, joyfully. The Father comes out and stands motionless. Thinking that his Father refuses to admit him, the Son turns and prepares to leave. But the Father stretches out his arms in blessing and takes his Son close to him.

Balanchine says that the ending of his ballet was inspired by a story of Pushkin's, *The Stationmaster*. "In this story Pushkin described a wayside station at which travelers rested and changed horses. The walls of the waiting room were covered with lithographs of the story of the prodigal son. The last print showed the boy returning home on his knees."

Prokofiev's score was much admired. Israel V. Nestyev, in his biography of the composer, calls it a new departure in his music. Nestyev assails Stravinsky's "museum-like neo-classicism"—do we here detect a certain ideological bias?—and compares it unfavorably with Prokofiev's lyricism and melody as exemplified in *The Prodigal Son*. The music is an interesting link between the "age of steel" composer of the twenties and the immediately accessible works he wrote after his rturn to Russia in 1934. He decidedly was experimenting with a new style in this ballet score, discarding some of his harmonic acerbities in favor of a more direct, emotional approach. The latter can be heard in the theme that depicts the parting between the Prodigal Son and his parents, and also in the theme of the temptress. Compared to some earlier scores, such as the *Scythian Suite* or *Pas d'acier*, *The Prodigal Son* is uncomplicated and even ascetic.

Balanchine has not been the only choreographer to use the Prokofiev score. In 1939 the Original Ballet Russe presented

The Prodigal Son

The Prodigal Son in a version by David Lichine, who danced the title role. Sono Osato was the Siren. Lichine's version is no longer in the repertoire. In the revival by the New York City Ballet Company, at the New York City Center of Music and Drama on February 23, 1950, the cast included Jerome Robbins (the Prodigal Son), Maria Tallchief (the Siren), Michael Arshansky (the Father), Frank Hobi and Herbert Bliss (Servants to the Prodigal Son), and Jillana and Francesca Mosarra (the Sisters).

The scenery for this production was hastily scratched together. Some of the props had been constructed, but a backdrop for the first and last scenes was missing, and there was not enough money to remedy the situation. Balanchine, searching the property room for a makeshift of some sort, came up with Chagall's floor cloth for *The Firebird*. The color scheme was satisfactory, so up it went. *The Prodigal Son* has never been a permanent part of the repertoire, but it has an articulate body of admirers who consider it one of Balanchine's most important works.

Rodeo, or the Courting at Burnt Ranch

Until the *première* of *Rodeo,* Agnes de Mille was known as a conscientious dancer and a promising choreographer with one fair success to her credit: *Three Virgins and a Devil,* which Ballet Theatre had introduced in 1941. After *Rodeo,* de Mille was mistress of all she surveyed. The ballet was given its *première* by the Ballet Russe de Monte Carlo at the Metropolitan Opera, on October 16, 1942, and an equivalent hit has seldom graced Broadway. In her chatty autobiography, *Dance to the Piper,* de Mille has described that first night as though she still were living it: how the audience responded to every phrase, how there were some mishaps on stage, how she despaired. "Oh, Freddie," she whispered to Frederic Franklin, "what a lousy, stinking performance!" Then the final curtain, and a house gone mad. "We bowed and bowed. At the eighth bow, I looked into

214

the pit. The fiddlers were beating their bows on their instruments. The others were standing up yelling. No one gets the union boys to do this easily." It was not until then that de Mille realized that she had created a real hit. The principals received twenty-two curtain calls. Agnes de Mille says that Billy Rose was racing around the lobby demanding to know how such a talent could have been overlooked, and agents were already getting in line.

As with the Robbins *Fancy Free,* which arrived two years later, America was ripe for a ballet like *Rodeo.* We were at war; national feeling was running high; we wanted entertainment—American entertainment—that would be entertaining and not stretch minds too hard. *Rodeo* fit the bill. Its score, by Aaron Copland, employed the general treatment and musical philosophy that he had made so popular in another American cowboy ballet, *Billy the Kid.* These were tunes you could whistle, by golly. Unlike *Billy,* the ballet had no allegorical content. Instead it was a love story: cowgirl wants cowboy, cowgirl gets cowboy. It had as much corn as a Kansas granary, but it was corn that people were disposed in advance to love. The dances had something earthy about them; there was even a square dance, complete with caller. No tremendous degree of choreographic invention was present, but *Rodeo* was not the kind of ballet which needed abstruse patterns. It set commentators happily to inventing brand-new images about things being as American as apple pie, ham and eggs, corn on the cob. And to those who suggested that de Mille might have been influenced by some of the choreography in *Billy the Kid,* she had an answer in *Dance to the Piper* to the effect that *Rodeo* was an outgrowth of dances she had staged in England earlier.

The ballet, in one act and two scenes, has a straight story line. Cowboys are loafing around Burnt Ranch, gathered for the weekly rodeo, and the cowgirl is trying to show the men that she is as good as they are. Cowboys ride bucking horses (imitating the equine movements in stylized choreography). The cowgirl has a severe crush on the head wrangler. He tolerates her, but no more, and when she mixes into things too obstreperously,

215

he is annoyed. Girls in city clothes enter, among them the rancher's daughter, in whom the head wrangler is interested. In an effort to attract attention, the cowgirl tries to manage a bucking bronco and gets thrown for her troubles. Everybody, especially the city girls, laugh at her. The head wrangler tells her to leave, which she does, her heart breaking, but she tries to act in a nonchalant manner. The cowboys pair up with the girls and wander off. Returning to see the head wrangler go off with the rancher's daughter, the cowgirl stands in despair. Women and men have rejected her.

This ends the scene. In an interlude before the beginning of Scene 2, there is a square dance that goes faster and faster before it breaks up.

At the ranch house, in the second scene, the Saturday night dance is in full swing. The cowgirl sits quietly, watching the various couples dance. She is still dressed in the dusty man's clothes she had worn in the afternoon. The champion roper, an old friend of hers, asks her to dance, but she doesn't know how. Soon, however, she tries to get into a community dance, but nobody chooses her for a partner. The champion roper consoles her, even dances with her (she catches on remarkably fast). But when she sees the head wrangler dancing amorously with the rancher's daughter, she runs away. She is not missed, and everybody continues to dance.

When she returns, nobody recognizes her at first: she is no longer a cowgirl. She has put on a pretty dress and decorated her hair with a bow, and is determined to join the party. The men fall all over themselves: she is beautiful. The head wrangler and the champion roper compete for her attentions. She is tugged to and fro between them, until the champion roper, who always has liked her, and now is really in love with her, kisses her. She realizes that he is her man. Conclusion, amid general merriment.

Agnes de Mille danced the Cowgirl at the *première*. Others in the cast were Frederic Franklin (Champion Roper), Casimir Kokitch (Head Wrangler), Milada Mladova (Rancher's Daughter), and Anton Vlassoff (Square Dance Caller). The costumes were by Kermit Love. Oliver Smith's clever sets and scenery were very effective. *Rodeo* is now in the Ballet Theatre repertoire. It was revived by that company at the Rhine-am-Main Air Force Base in Frankfort, Germany, on August 14, 1950. Leading dancers on that occasion were Allyn McLerie, John Kriza, and James Mitchell.

As for Agnes de Mille, the next year found her busy staging the dances for a speculative Broadway venture known as *Oklahoma!* After the first night of that particular Rodgers and Hammerstein venture, *Oklahoma!* was the kind of speculation that bankers like to invest in, and ballet on Broadway had received a brand-new stimulus under which it is still coasting.

Romeo and Juliet

 Among its other distinctions, *Romeo and Juliet* is probably the only ballet to have been shown to the public before it was finished. Antony Tudor, a notoriously slow worker, was far behind on the day of the *première*, April 6, 1943. Sol Hurok, then managing Ballet Theatre, insisted that the ballet, having been announced, should be shown as it was. So *Romeo and Juliet* went on, but about fifteen minutes before the end, down came the curtain. Tudor then stepped before the audience, still dressed in his costume as Tybalt, and asked its indulgence. A few days later, on April 10, the ballet was given complete.

Himself a Briton, Tudor has Shakespeare in his blood. It is amazing how much of *Romeo and Juliet* has been retained in the choreographic version, and it is even more remarkable how the impressionistic music of another Englishman,

218

Frederick Delius, fits the action. Tudor selected four of Delius's pieces—*Over the Hills and Far Away, The Walk to the Paradise Garden, Eventyr,* and *Brigg Fair,* used uncut. All of this is intimate, exceedingly subjective music; but, despite its sophistication it does have its roots in the British *melos.* Often it is modal; its melodic content is strongly impregnated with folk flavor; and it has a plaintive, yearning, sensitive quality of which Tudor made full use.

The sets, designed by Eugene Berman, were strongly Renaissance in character, as was appropriate. Ingenious use was made of sets within sets for fast changes of scene (the ballet is in one long act). Salvador Dali originally had been asked to do the *décor,* but his ideas were perhaps a little too wild for Tudor. As Berman worked it out, the set for *Romeo and Juliet* consists of a three-sided colonnade, with curtains that are drawn or released when necessary by a pair of attendants. Berman obviously had been studying some of the Renaissance painters for his color schemes and composition. Juliet's costume is *à la Botticelli;* the style of architecture is fifteenth-century; often the groupings within the set have the exquisite quality of an early Italian painting. When all the curtains are drawn back, the locale is a square in Verona. The scene-changes are quickly and economically handled. It is amazing how quickly the observer accommodates himself to the staging: a hasty arrangement of curtains, and we *are* in Juliet's room; another quick shift, and the Capulets are battling the Montagues in the square. A very large cast is used; that, plus the colorful and elaborate scenery, makes *Romeo and Juliet* a theatrical spectacle.

As customary in his ballets, Tudor here compresses or expands time as he sees fit, halting the action completely to emphasize a certain point or speeding it along to further the plot. Hardly anything of the play is missing, but one thing has been added. In Shakespeare, there is no Rosaline—at least, she does not appear on stage. Tudor, wishing to accentuate the puppy love that Romeo has for Rosaline, actually presents her; and at the very opening of the ballet, Romeo is seen being spurned by her. He acts more irritated than broken-hearted. Next enter groups of Capulets and Montagues (*Two households, both alike in dignity,/In fair Verona, where we lay our scene . . .*). Mercutio and Tybalt, two hotheads, begin to duel, but the heads of the two clans stop them. The stage clears, leaving Romeo and Mercutio alone. They plan to attend a ball at the house of their arch-enemies, the Capulets, in the hope of seeing Rosaline. (In the play it is Benvolio rather than Mercutio with whom Romeo here speaks.) The next scene is the ball, where many dignified couples are dancing. Juliet enters and is introduced to Paris, to whom the Capulets intend to marry her. She dances with him. Romeo enters and sees Juliet (*O, she doth teach the torches to burn bright!/It seems she hangs upon the cheeks of night/ As a rich jewel in an Ethiop's ear . . .*). He waits until she is alone, then vows his eternal love. They dance. Mercutio and Tybalt come forth, Romeo is recognized, and hostility flares up. The two Montagues leave before there is trouble.

In the following scene Mercutio warns Romeo to keep away from Juliet, but he will not listen. He goes to the Capulet orchard (*But soft! what light through yonder window breaks?/ It is the east, and Juliet is the sun. . . .*). He asks for her hand and she accepts him. Friar Lawrence is seen in his cell, and an anxious Romeo enters. Soon Juliet appears, and they are married by the Friar (*So smile the heavens upon this act . . .*). She must get back to the Capulet castle before she is missed, and she hurries off, telling Romeo that he will receive a message from her. The friction between the houses erupts in the next scene. Tybalt and Mercutio battle, and the latter dies in Romeo's arms (*A plague o' both your houses . . .*). A furious Romeo makes an onslaught on Tybalt and kills him. Friar Lawrence takes the dagger from Romeo and tells him to flee. Juliet, horror-stricken, appears and sends her nurse after Romeo.

The lovers are reunited once more in Juliet's bedroom, where he has spent the night (*Wilt thou be gone? it is not yet near day./It was the nightingale, and not the lark,/That pierc'd the fearful hollow of thine ear . . .*). They dance together in one of the most intensely lyrical duets of the contemporary repertoire. He leaves, and Juliet, prostrated, falls upon her bed.

Maidens come in to prepare her for her wedding to Paris. She begs her father not to let the proceedings go any farther. He refuses to listen. Friar Lawrence secretly gives her a potion. She drinks it and faints, apparently lifeless (*Death lies on her like an untimely frost/Upon the sweetest flower of all the field . . .*). She is borne to the Capulet vault and placed on the bier. Romeo, who has not received Friar Lawrence's message, enters the tomb (*Here, here will I remain/with worms that are thy chambermaids. . . ./Thus with a kiss I die . . .*). He drinks a vial of poison. When Juliet comes out of her drugged stupor, Romeo, near death, staggers to her and falls. She grabs his dagger and kills herself (*O happy dagger! This is thy sheath . . .*).

As can be seen, a few liberties have been taken with the play, the chief one being that Romeo is still alive when Juliet comes to her senses in the tomb. On the legitimate stage such a situation would be intolerably drenched with sentimentality. Tudor, who handles the situation with restraint, gets away with it (one wishes that here he had stuck to the text, even though it would have meant a less effective curtain). Otherwise the choreography and the action are irreproachable. *Romeo and Juliet* has never proved a very successful ballet, even when Markova has appeared in it, and some connoisseurs frankly dislike it. Others, myself included, maintain that of this generation's ballets only *Pillar of Fire* is its superior for invention, lyricism, and passion.

Romeo and Juliet is by far the most stylized of Tudor's ballets. In an effort to achieve a Renaissance atmosphere, he has resorted to movements of an archaic nature suggested by paintings of the period and as described by early writers. Some of his choreographic patterns are purposely stilted. Much pantomime is employed, a notable instance illustrating Mercutio's "Queen Mab" speech. The entire ballet is *durchkomponiert*, to use a musical term: there are no set pieces to halt the flow of the action, and everything moves to the inexorable climax—expressed in purely choreographic terms.

The Metropolitan Opera House *première*, by Ballet Theatre, on April 6, 1943, presented the following cast: Hugh Laing (Romeo), Alicia Markova (Juliet), Borislav Runanine (Montague), John Taras (Capulet), Nicolas Orloff (Mercutio), Jerome Robbins (Benvolio), Antony Tudor (Tybalt), Dimitri Romanoff (Friar Lawrence), Richard Reed (Paris), Miriam Golden (Lady Montague), Galina Razoumova (Lady Capulet), and Sono Osato (Rosaline). In later performances Nora Kaye and Alicia Alonso were seen as Juliet, John Kriza and Igor Youskevitch as Romeo. With all deference to Mmes Kaye and Alonso, both brilliant dancers, Markova's characterization was beyond compare. She *looked* the part of the child "who had not seen the change of fourteen years" (yes; Shakespeare made Juliet very young; but it must not be forgotten that girls matured much faster in those days). In all cases within memory—all except Markova's—when an actress has been skilled enough to play Juliet she has looked much older than Juliet is supposed to look. Thus do the years treat us, but they touched Markova not at all. Hugh Laing's Romeo can be put in much the same category as Markova's Juliet; it was unique, impassioned, intense. John Kriza has given a good account of the role. Igor Youskevitch has also danced it, but his Slavic blood failed to respond to the Elizabethan mood.

Schéhérazade

 Most of the connoisseurs these days look condescendingly at *Schéhérazade;* and, in all truth, it has faded considerably, as has Rimsky-Korsakov's music. It was not always thus. *Schéhérazade* was the most exciting ballet Paris had ever seen when it was first produced there in 1910 by Diaghilev's Ballets Russes in its second season. To the Parisians it suggested barbaric Russia, the mysterious East. Such ink as was spilled over it! *Schéhérazade's* popularity lasted well into our own day, and for years it sustained the Ballet Russe de Monte Carlo on its American tours. It is still in that company's repertoire, though not as sought-for as it used to be; and no company would dare to show it in New York City. Of course, the current production is a very tired one; and were Diaghilev's original sets back, with a Nijinsky and a young Ida Rubinstein to dance the leading roles,

Schéhérazade might be another story, though one somehow doubts it.

The ballet was hatched in preparation for Diaghilev's 1910 season. Serge Grigoriev, *régisseur* of the company, tells us in his book about the Ballets Russes how *Schéhérazade* came into being. "The theme that had inspired Rimsky's symphonic poem was not really suitable as a ballet plot. Benois tried improvising an altered version; and we all joined in with various suggestions. I remember Bakst's jumping on to a chair, gesticulating, and showing how the Shah's retainers should cut everyone to pieces, '*everyone*: his wives and above all their Negro lovers!' But despite our contributions, the plot eventually used was the invention of Benois—and not of Bakst. Yet Diaghilev used to attribute it to Bakst—why I do not know; and this later led to a quarrel between him and Benois."

Benois amplifies the subject in his autobiography. "Both the idea of transforming Rimsky-Korsakov's symphonic poem into choreographic action and the entire stage version of the subject were mine. In arranging it I did not even keep to the author's own programme, but invented something quite different. According to Rimsky-Korsakov, his symphonic poem is meant to describe the adventures of Sinbad the Sailor; I preferred to represent the episode which forms, so to speak, the foreword to the *Thousand and One Nights,* in which the chief figure is Shahryar's unfaithful wife and not the righteous story-teller Schéhérazade." Benois describes the pains and trouble he took with the ballet.

And then he went to the opening performance at the Paris Opéra on June 4, 1910, and unfolded his program. "Ballet de L. Bakst," he read. When he went home, his heart "was filled with bitterness and indignation" in the best Russian style. He immediately wrote a letter to Diaghilev, breaking off relations. They were later reconciled.

Schéhérazade was a colossal success. The Parisians loved Bakst's *décor,* Rimsky's music, all the dances that Michel Fokine had created for it. "Spicy, sensuous aromas seem to be wafted from the stage," as Benois wrote. And Grigoriev recollects that the audience roared its applause with cries of delight. "It is impossible to describe the reception of this ballet. It took no little time for the audience even to calm down." The cast included Ida Rubinstein (Zobeide), Vaslav Nijinsky (Favorite Slave), Enrico Cecchetti (Chief Eunuch), Alexis Bulgakov (the Shah), Basil Kissilov (Zeman), and Sophie Fedorova (Odalisque).

Not all of Rimsky-Korsakov's music was used. The first movement was played as an overture (a practice now discontinued); the second and fourth movements were fused into one movement; the third movement was omitted (in occasional performances a section of it is inserted as a *pas de deux* for Zobeide and her lover). The action takes place in an enormous room in an Oriental palace, a room that is colorfully and even extravagantly decorated. The Shah, his harem, and his court are present, as is Zobeide, the Shah's favorite wife. Girls dance for their master. While they are dancing, the Shah's brother, Zeman, whispers to him his doubts about the fidelity of the Shah's wives. The Shah makes up his mind to go on a hunting trip. When all the men have gone, the women get ideas of their own. They bribe the chief eunuch—a portly gentleman cut out to be a bachelor—to release the Negro slaves. In they pour, and an orgy takes place. Zobeide further bribes the chief eunuch to release the Shah's favorite slave, who slinks forth and joins her. Now the scene is one of abandonment. The men and women dance together riotously and sensuously. All of a sudden the Shah darts in, scimitar raised high. His hunting expedition, of course, was only a ruse. The Shah personally kills his favorite slave; the soldiers despatch the other participants in the orgy. Only Zobeide is left. For an instant it appears that her beauty and repentance may restore her to the Shah's favors. But no. Before his soldiers can kill her, she stabs herself.

It did not take *Schéhérazade* much time to get to New York. The season after its *première* saw the production of a pirated version at the Winter Garden, on June 14, 1911. Gertrude Hoffman, the producer, also danced the role of Zobeide. In January 1916, the Ballets Russes presented *Schéhérazade* at the Century Theater; and on April 15, Nijinsky, who had been delayed in joining the company was seen as the Favorite Slave. The Catholic Theater Movement protested the production of so "obscene" a work, which helped attendance no end. A subsequent production by Leonide Massine was given in 1929. He was ballet master at Roxy's Theater in New York at the time, and he staged a *Schéhérazade* complete with elephants and Roxyettes. The de Basil Ballet Russe presented the ballet on October 9, 1935, at the Metropolitan Opera House, and it has remained in the repertoire since then. But *Schéhérazade* appears almost to have run its course.

Scotch Symphony

 A visit to Edinburgh in 1829 inspired Mendelssohn to compose his "Scotch" Symphony (No. 3 in A minor, Op. 56); and a visit to Edinburgh in 1952 led George Balanchine to compose a ballet using Mendelssohn's score. Mendelssohn had been directly inspired by the castle of Holyrood, where Mary, Queen of Scots, lived and loved. He went through the "broken and mouldering" building and pottered around. "I believe I found today in the old chapel the beginning of my 'Scotch' Symphony," he wrote to a friend on July 30, 1829.

Balanchine, on the other hand, found a different source of inspiration. He visited Edinburgh with the New York City Ballet Company, which was appearing at the Edinburgh Festival in August 1952. One of the things Balanchine found irresistible was the demonstration of parade units from various famous Scottish regiments in the evening military tattoo. Balanchine, like any other tourist, enjoyed the spectacle. Unlike other tourists, he was inspired to a ballet by the sight. It was not in his mind to create a new work based on the tattoo proper; rather, he wished to evoke the nature of Scotland.

When the company returned to New York, Balanchine set to work, keeping in mind that Scotland had been the scene of *La Sylphide,* the first great romantic ballet. A new ballet on Scottish themes, he thought, would do well to recollect that fact. Mendelssohn's "Scotch" Symphony, of course, came immediately to mind. Balanchine, however, decided to omit the first movement of the score as not suitable for dance.

The ballet is plotless. Boys and girls, some dressed in Scottish costumes, go through a series of typical Balanchinesque patterns, and there is a good deal of brilliant solo work. The first movement has an exceedingly brilliant and intricate solo for the ballerina, demanding much in the way of elevation and rapid beats—a sort of glorified Highland Fling. Patricia Wilde was magnificent here. In the slow movement, an adagio for a ballerina and her partner, Balanchine had in mind the romantic ballet of the *La Sylphide* period. As Maria Tallchief and André Eglevsky danced this *pas de deux,* it was lyric, beautifully designed and sustained, never forced. In a way, this duet is a period piece handled in the best of taste. The last movement presents much vigorous group and solo work, the patterns laid out in Balanchine's usual logical manner.

Scotch Symphony received its *première* by the New York City Ballet Company at the New York City Center of Music and Drama on November 11, 1952. Leading dancers were Maria Tallchief, André Eglevsky, Patricia Wilde, Frank Hobi, and Michael Maule. The scenery was by Horace Armistead; costumes were by Karinska and David Ffolkes.

The ballet is a pleasant work to watch, and has been composed with the fluency that one expects from Balanchine. It is not a probing work, nor does it pretend to exploit new resources. As for the "Scotch" in it, one finds no particular feeling of Scotland, though some of the dancers are attired in appropriate costume. Perhaps even the brilliant solo in the first scene is "Scotch" only through association; and had Balanchine called his work *Irish Symphony* one would undoubtedly be seeing Irish things in the dancing.

The amusing thing about this lack of Scotch in Balanchine's *Scotch Symphony* is that it is paralleled in Mendelssohn's score. Mendelssohn composed little that could be construed as truly Scotch. Some analysts find decided traces of Scotland in the second and fourth movements; but, one wonders, is that because of the clue given by the title of the symphony? It is not generally known, but no less astute a critic than Robert Schumann made the embarrassing error of thinking that Mendelssohn's "Scotch" Symphony was his "Italian." In one of his articles for the *Neue Zeitschrift* Schumann reviewed the A minor Symphony. Apparently someone had told him that it had resulted from Mendelssohn's Italian trip, and poor Schumann began reading things into the music, writing about its wonderful re-creation of Italy in tone—"a picture that for a while, like the picture of Italian travel in Jean Paul's *Titan,* causes us to forget the sorrow we feel at never having beheld that beautiful land." From which all kinds of interesting morals can be drawn.

Serenade

New Year's Day 1934 was auspicious for the future of American ballet: on that day the School of American Ballet opened. An instant success, the school was ready to present its first public program about five months later. George Balanchine, one of the founders of the school (the others were Lincoln Kirstein and Edward M. M. Warburg), readied three of his ballets for first American performances. These were *Serenade,* to Tchaikovsky's Serenade for String Orchestra; *Mozartiana,* to the Theme and Variations from Tchaikovsky's Fourth Suite; and *Dreams,* to a score by George Antheil.

The first performance was set for June 9 at Woodland, the estate of Felix Warburg, near White Plains, New York. *Mozartiana* went on as scheduled, but a heavy spring rain washed out the other works. "A more agonizing and inauspicious occasion could scarcely have been planned by the Devil himself," Lincoln Kirstein said. Everything got drenched, and the tears of the dancers added to the moistness. The entire program was given the following evening before a small but faithful audience.

Serenade was Balanchine's first ballet choreographed in this country. It was an outgrowth of classes in stage technique which he had inaugurated at the School of American Ballet. He chose the Tchaikovsky Serenade as music for a series of problems to be solved in the class—problems in spatial arrangements, in physical movements, in choreographic interpretation. As he worked with the music, the form of the ballet began to take shape in Balanchine's mind. Some of the problems must have been frustrating. The number of students in the class varied from session to session, and he had to work with those available. He eliminated the weaker dancers from the demanding parts, tailoring the choreography to whatever resources he had at his disposal.

In its final form the ballet is plotless, illustrating Balanchine's oft-repeated dictum that ballet is merely dancers in motion to a beautiful piece of music. The New York City Ballet program lists *Serenade* merely as "Classic Ballet." There are four movements, one for each movement of the Tchaikovsky score (Balanchine has reversed the order of the third and fourth movements). The only place where a suggestion of a story is implicit is the last movement, which is a *pas de trois* for one man and two ballerinas. The man must make up his mind to choose one of the girls, and when he does select one, the other collapses and is carried out by three boys. But all this is emotion rather than story, and the movement can be enjoyed as pure dance without any hint of a story. A similar theme—the relation of a man and a woman, expressed in lyric movements—occurs again and again in the abstract Balanchine ballets.

Serenade was one of the first in that line of creations in the strict classic tradition which has earned Balanchine the title of a "contemporary Petipa." Balanchine's background is the Imperial Russian ballet, and the idiom of Petipa is in his blood. In a lecture that he gave to the London Ballet Circle in 1950 he stated that a great deal of his choreography was based on passages from Petipa ballets that are unknown in the West, but which he remembers from his youth at the Maryinsky Theater. He has choreographed *Serenade* in broad, relatively free strokes. None of the detail is fussy, and there is an especially lovely adagio for the man and the two ballerinas in the last movement (this is one of the few Balanchine ballets that does not end with the stage full of people). Everything is clear, direct, and logical.

In the May 1945 issue of *Dance News,* Balanchine wrote some lines that completely underline his esthetic: "The important thing in ballet is the movement itself. . . . Choreographic movement is an end in itself, and its only purpose is to create the impression of intensity and beauty." *Serenade,* like the overwhelming majority of Balanchine's other ballets, adheres to this principle. He simply is not interested in story or dramatic ballets; any story he uses is extremely slight, more suggestion than plot. Even his few exceptions, like *Prodigal Son* or *Orpheus,* concentrate more on design than on characterization.

Serenade received its first professional performance by the producing company of the School of American Ballet at the Avery Memorial Theater, Hartford, Connecticut, on December 16, 1934. Principal roles were danced by Kathryn Mullowney, Heidi Voessler, and Charles Laskey. In rapid succession *Serenade* entered the repertoire of the American Ballet (1935), the Ballet Russe de Monte Carlo (1940), and Ballet Caravan (1941). It became part of the permanent repertoire of the New York City Ballet Company on October 18, 1948. The leading dancers on that occasion were Marie-Jeanne, Pat McBride, and Nicholas Magallanes.

Sleeping Beauty

(La Belle au bois dormant)

 The fairy tales of Charles Perrault (1628–1703) are almost as well known as those of Andersen or the brothers Grimm. One of Perrault's tales, *La Belle au bois dormant* (*The Sleeping Beauty*), especially struck the adult eye when it was published in 1697; and tales, fairy or otherwise, do not survive unless favored by the adult eye. *The Sleeping Beauty* made its way through Europe, enchanting everybody, including Marius Petipa, ballet master and choreographer of the Maryinsky Theater in St. Petersburg. In 1889, events *vis-à-vis* Petipa and Perrault came to a head, and Petipa decided to create a ballet on the fairy tale. He discussed it with Ivan Vsevolojsky, Director of the Imperial Theaters. They worked out a libretto and decided that Peter Ilyich Tchaikovsky was just the man for the music. Tchaikovsky, who seems to have been happy with the libretto, rapidly

233

set to work on the score, composing it bit by bit during a tour of Europe. Occasionally, however, he bogged down. An entry in his diary, dated at Hannover, Germany, on March 6, 1889, sounds like something out of Dostoyevsky: "Reading. Attempt at composing the ballet. Wrote something, but unwillingly and poorly. The weather is terrible, bleak, and misty. In my soul is gloom." And here is the entry for May 26; by then Tchaikovsky was back in Russia: "Finished the *composing* of the ballet, in spite of the headache and bad frame of mind. Decide to go down to Moscow."

The orchestration was finished in good time, and Petipa set to work on the choreography. The dress rehearsal of *Sleeping Beauty* took place at the Maryinsky Theater on January 13, 1890. It is only within recent times that the dress rehearsal has lost its glamour. Not long ago the dress rehearsal was *the* performance that counted. It was attended by the press and all of the bigwigs. At the dress rehearsal of *Sleeping Beauty*, Alexander III and important members of his court were present. The official *première* followed two days later, on January 15.

Despite the presence in the cast of such popular dancers as Carlotta Brianza (Princess Aurora), Paul Gerdt (the Prince), Enrico Cecchetti and Varvara Nikitina (the Bluebird and the Enchanted Princess)—Cecchetti also danced the role of Carabosse—and Marie Petipa (the Lilac Fairy), the ballet did not prove an outstanding success. His Majesty curtly remarked to the composer that the ballet was "very nice." Tchaikovsky, who considered *Sleeping Beauty* one of his finest scores, was keenly disappointed.

Perhaps the ballet was too subtle for those coming upon it for the first time. And Tchaikovsky's music, infinitely removed from the tum-ti-tum of hack court composers, may have been composed only too well. For *Sleeping Beauty* has in it a sensitivity and a correlation with the action that could hardly be found in any ballet music composed up to that time. It was not for nothing that Petipa would write to Tchaikovsky: "Suddenly Aurora notices the old woman who beats on her knitting needles a 2/4 measure. Gradually she changes to a very melodious waltz in 3/4, but then, suddenly, a rest. Aurora pricks her finger. Screams, pain. Blood streams. Give eight measures in 4/4, wide." And so forth. Connoisseurs argue whether *Sleeping Beauty* or *Swan Lake* is the greater score. One might as well argue about the relative merits of an emerald and a sapphire. Both are precious stones. *Sleeping Beauty* is as brilliant, as fluent and as colorful a score as Tchaikovsky ever composed; in some places, as in the first-act dance of the Fairy of the Songbirds, the orchestra actually throws off sparks.

Sleeping Beauty maintained a slim hold on the repertoire in Russia, but apparently never was enormously successful there. We turn now to London in 1921, where Serge Diaghilev, without a choreographer (he had severed relations with Leonide Massine), was considering a repertoire for the oncoming season of his Ballets Russes. Serge Leonidovich Grigoriev, *régisseur* of the company, tells, in his book about the Ballets Russes, how *Sleeping Beauty* got back into the repertoire: "It happened that a musical play called *Chu Chin Chow* was then running in its third year at His Majesty's Theatre. Diaghilev was amazed at the possibility of such an enormous run, and one day he said to me half jokingly how much he wished he could discover a ballet that would run forever—that would be happiness. I replied to him that not only was such a thing quite impossible, but it would bore him to death. 'Not at all,' he retorted. 'You'd run it and I'd do something else!'

" 'In that case, why not put on *Coppélia?*' said I. 'It's one of Petipa's best ballets and lasts a whole evening.' " (Grigoriev, of course, is referring to the Petipa adaptation of the famous ballet choreographed by Saint-Léon in 1870.) The conversation with Grigoriev set Diaghilev's mind working. "He kept returning to the subject," says Grigoriev, "till at last one day he said he had thought of the ideal solution. This was a production of another of the Petipa ballets, *La Belle au bois dormant.* . . . Once having made up his mind, Diaghilev went into action. By great good luck the Alhambra had had another failure and was available for the autumn. Mr. Wolheim, our agent, accordingly opened negotiations for it, and in a comparatively short time an agreement was duly drawn up."

Diaghilev prevailed upon Léon Bakst, with whom at the time he was not on particularly good terms, to do the sets and costumes. Then he began studying the Tchaikovsky score (Diaghilev was a good pianist), deleting material he considered dull and replacing it with other material from Tchaikovsky. He also asked Stravinsky to re-orchestrate the Prelude and Aurora's Variations in Act III. Another step was to engage Nicolas Sergeyev to restore Petipa's choreography. Sergeyev, former *régisseur* of the Maryinsky, was entirely familiar with the Petipa ballets. And instead of engaging one ballerina for the role of Princess Aurora, Diaghilev took on three—Vera Trefilova, Lubov Egorova, and Olga Spessivtzeva, each a famous soloist from the Maryinsky Theater. Carlotta Brianza—she who had created Aurora in 1890—was engaged for the role of Carabosse (a character role that can be danced by either man or woman). She also became the company's ballet mistress.

Strenuous rehearsals followed. Bronislava Nijinska, sister of the famous Vaslav, was in London at the time and arranged some of the choreography, including an invention of her own, the popular "Dance of the Three Ivans." Diaghilev met with some criticism for introducing a Russian dance into a ballet centering around the court of a French king. But Diaghilev replied that in a ballet anything was possible; and the dance turned out to be one of the most successful in the closing divertissements of the ballet.

The revival took place at the Alhambra Theatre, London, on November 2, 1921. Spessivtzeva danced the Princess; Pierre Vladimiroff the Prince; Lydia Lopokova the Lilac Fairy and Enchanted Princess; Carlotta Brianza the Fairy Carabosse; assorted fairies were Felia Dubrovska, Lydia Sokolova, Bronislava Nijinska, Lubov Egorova, and Vera Nemtchinova. Lopokova and Idikowski were the Bluebirds. Daily performances followed, with the three ballerinas alternating as Princess Aurora (a fourth, Vera Trefilova, later joined them). On January 5, 1922, a sentimental touch was provided by a performance in which Cecchetti, who had created the role, danced the Fairy Carabosse.

After 105 performances the production came to an end. Some commentators have held that Diaghilev's revival of *Sleeping Beauty* was a failure. It did not, in truth, earn enough to pay off the production costs. But surely 105 consecutive performances is an imposing run: it is doubtful that in this advanced and artistic day and age audiences could be obtained for anything near that number of consecutive *Sleeping Beauty* performances anywhere in the world.

Later in the year Diaghilev, determined to honor the centenary of Petipa's birth, got the idea of presenting some of the dances from *Sleeping Beauty* to a Paris audience. This he did, creating a brilliant divertissement that he named *Le Mariage de la belle au bois dormant,* and which is better known today as *Aurora's Wedding* or *Princess Aurora.* The first performance of *Le Mariage* took place at the Paris Opéra on May 18, 1922. Trefilova danced the title role.

Perrault's story of the sleeping princess is necessarily not as explicit as the action in the ballet, which takes place in the mythical kingdom of King Florestan XXIV. The curtain rises on the hall of the palace. It is the christening day of the King's daughter, Aurora. Cattalabutte (so spelled in the Sadler's Wells programs; other sources offer different spellings, such as Cantalbutte), the master of ceremonies, enters and sees to it that all is ready for the ceremonies. Fanfares; the King and Queen enter. When they are seated, the fairy godmothers enter. These are the Fairy of the Crystal Garden, the Fairy of the Enchanted Garden, the Fairy of the Woodland Glades, the Fairy of the Songbirds, the Fairy of the Golden Vine, and the Lilac Fairy. They bless Princess Aurora. Then they dance, first all together (a *pas de six*), then individually. Their cavaliers also dance. The King and Queen examine the gifts that the fairies have presented. Suddenly, ominous thunder. The King, in sudden awareness, grabs the guest list and looks at it. Sure enough, Cattalabutte has forgotten to invite the evil Fairy Carabosse. A coach drawn by large rats comes on stage. In it sits Carabosse, ugly and hunchbacked, in a towering rage. Carabosse tells the King, in mime (almost as explicit a language as speech), that Aurora will grow up to be a beautiful girl, but will prick her finger and die! And she curses the infant Aurora. Out comes the Lilac Fairy, before whom Carabosse quails. All the fairies surround the cradle, and Carabosse departs, cursing the whole court. The Lilac Fairy tells the horrified King and Queen that Aurora will indeed seem to die, but in reality will sleep for one hundred years. One day a Prince will come to her and kiss her. She will revive and live happily ever after.

All of the foregoing is the Prologue. In Act I, entitled *The Spell,* we find the court celebrating Aurora's sixteenth birthday. A bit of stage business reminds us that the King is strenuously enforcing an edict that no puncturing instruments be brought within the court. Three old women carrying spindles are seized by Cattalabutte and, when presented before the King, sentenced to death. But the Queen asks for mercy, reminding the King that it is Aurora's birthday. The King relents. Peasant girls dance. In the distance Princess Aurora appears. She comes forward, radiantly beautiful and radiantly dancing. She is joined by four foreign princes who have come to pay court to her. The *Rose Adagio* follows: Aurora dances with the princes, accepting a rose from each. More dancing. An old woman sidles up to the dancing Princess and offers her a gift. Aurora, never having seen anything like it before—it is a spindle—plays with it. The court rises in horror, but before they can take the spindle away, she pricks her finger and falls to the ground. She gets up, tries to reassure her mother, dances falteringly, and collapses, where-upon the old woman throws off her clothes. She is, of course, Carabosse, and she runs off stage screaming with delight. But the Lilac Fairy enters and tells the court that Aurora really is sleeping. Aurora is gently carried away and the stage clears. Darkness; and as the Lilac Fairy waves her magic wand, silence descends on the scene—a silence to last for one hundred years.

Act II is *The Vision*. Prince Florimund and his hunting party enter a deserted glade in the forest near the sleeping castle of King Florestan. They rest and play games. For some reason the

Prince is moody, despite (or, more likely, because of) the attentions that a personable young lady is paying to him. When his party leaves, he stays alone. It is now night. The Lilac Fairy enters and tells the Prince about the Sleeping Princess. She shows him a vision of Aurora in which the Princess dances while he pursues her. When she disappears, the Prince, deeply smitten, follows the Lilac Fairy, who promises to take him to Aurora.

The third act is divided into two scenes, "The Awakening" and "The Wedding." In Scene 1, the Prince is brought by the Lilac Fairy to the bedroom of Princess Aurora. He kisses her; she slowly awakes. The curse is broken. Then comes the second scene, the wedding. Enter the King and Queen, the guests, the musicians and entertainers. Many of the guests are fairy-tale characters taken from the stories of Perrault. An elaborate series of divertissements follow. There is a trio for Prince Florestan (he is Aurora's brother) and his two sisters. Then comes the dance of Puss-in-Boots and the White Cat to music that actually meows. After that, the most famous *pas de deux* of the ballet, and one of the great ones in all ballet history—the dance of the Bluebird and the Enchanted Princess. This is an unparalleled combination of lyricism, invention, and virtuosity. After the Bluebirds disappear, Red Riding Hood and the Wolf come on the scene (here the wolf captures the little miss). Another great *pas de deux* is the one now danced by Aurora and Florimund. This enchanting duet is followed by the Russian antics of the Three Ivans and a grand finale in which the entire court joins.

America had to wait until 1949 to see a definitive version of the complete ballet. Excerpts from it had been danced in this country earlier, of course. As early as 1916 Pavlova had done some sections at the Hippodrome in New York. These must have been something! Her troupe was called Pavlova's Hippodrome Company. The men were Alexandre Volinine, Warlau Zalewski, and Ivan Verginski; the female dancers were Stefa Plaskovietzka, Stazia Kuhn, and Hilda Butsova. For the *corps de ballet* there were the Hippodrome Ballet Girls. The *Sleeping Beauty première* took place on August 31, 1916, and the *Times* critic called it "a grievous disappointment." He described *Sleep-*

ing Beauty as "a charming, simple ballet . . . whose values are forfeited by bad staging. . . . The lighting is atrocious, the whole ballet sprawled without focus over an absurdly large area." Pavlova, of course, came in for praise. One wonders how complete this *Sleeping Beauty* was. It shared the evening with a dancing skeleton, a grand minstrel show, an ice pageant, the Six Musical Browns, and the Peerless Charlotte. No matter how short the production was, it soon became even shorter. According to the *Times,* not long after the *première,* "Hippodrome audiences evinced but the mildest interest in the ballet, and this, coupled with requests for some of the dances made famous by the artiste, led to the change."

A choreographic version by Catherine Littlefield for the Philadelphia Ballet was presented in 1937, but never held the stage. In 1935 the de Basil Ballet Russe introduced *Aurora's Wedding* to America on its first tour in this country; the first New York performance was given at the Majestic Theater on March 21, 1935. The leading dancers were Vera Zorina, Tatiana Riabouchinska, Irina Baronova, Lubov Rostova, Paul Petroff, David Lichine, and Roman Jasinsky. Tamara Toumanova alternated with Baronova as Princess Aurora in subsequent performances. Both were great ballerinas with completely different styles: Toumanova was brilliant, objective, flashing; Baronova was more lyric, softer in her movements, equally accomplished technically. The Bluebirds were Riabouchinska and Lichine.

Aurora's Wedding was popular, in one form or another, for years in America, and the Bluebird variation was constantly being offered as a short *pas de deux* divorced from *Aurora.* The Ballet Russe de Monte Carlo in 1939 featured Alicia Markova and Igor Youskevitch as the Bluebirds. For classic purity and elegance of phrasing their interpretation still stands unique, although two years later Ballet Theatre presented a brilliant young couple as the Bluebirds. They were Karen Conrad and Ian Gibson, and they appeared in a version of *Princess Aurora* staged by Anton Dolin. Karinska did the costumes, and the first performance took place at the Forty-fourth Street Theater, New York, on November 26, 1941. Leading dancers were Irina Baronova, Anton Dolin, Rosella Hightower, Karen Conrad, Lucia Chase, Sono Osato, Nora Kaye, Annabelle Lyon, Ian Gibson, and Charles Dickson. Baronova triumphed, but almost equal excitement was caused by the Bluebirds. Both Gibson and Conrad had spectacular elevation and seemed to spend most of their time flying around in the air. Unfortunately, both dancers had regrettably short careers with the company, leaving the stage for good not long thereafter. They could have developed into supreme artists.

Alicia Markova, Nora Kaye, and Tamara Toumanova also were seen as Princess Aurora in the Ballet Theatre version. Each brought a valid characterization to the role, though it is universally conceded that Markova in her prime added an extra dimension that nobody has been able to duplicate.

But it was Sadler's Wells that conquered America with the Tchaikovsky-Petipa masterpiece. This was not a new production by the company. It had come into the repertoire on February 2, 1939, at the Sadler's Wells Theatre, London. The revival had been staged by Nicholas Sergeyev (who had worked with Diaghilev on *his* revival in 1921), with scenery and costumes by Nadia Benois. Margot Fonteyn danced Aurora. The other leading members of the cast were Robert Helpmann (Prince Charming), June Brae (Lilac Fairy), Mary Honer and Harold Turner (Bluebirds), and John Greenwood (Carabosse). At the American *première,* which took place at the Metropolitan Opera House, New York, on October 9, 1949, Fonteyn and Helpmann danced the leading roles. Beryl Grey was the Lilac Fairy; Moira Shearer and Alexis Rassine were the Bluebirds, Frederick Ashton was the Carabosse. Local choreographic circles are still resounding from the excitement. When Fonteyn completed the "Rose Adagio," the audience surrendered. This dance, by the way, is a real test of a dancer's strength. She must stand on *pointe* in attitude position (a dancer in attitude is in a pose very much like the famous statue of Mercury) to greet the first prince. He holds her right hand and turns her while she remains in attitude. After she has made a complete turn, the prince releases her hand and she raises both hands over her

241

head to form a crown. This procedure is repeated with the three other princes in turn. When the last prince releases her hand, the dancer must extend her leg into an arabesque position and hold it as long as possible. This feat takes an inhuman amount of strength and balance. An inevitable concommitant is that the entire audience holds its breath with the dancer, releasing it with bravos when she is mistress of the situation.

Lovely as the "Rose Adagio" is, it is the Bluebird *pas de deux* that really whips an audience to a frenzy. The dance has a tense, nervous excitement about it, and the male dancer's part is exceptionally brilliant. He must give the impression of being suspended in soaring flight. Both dancers, indeed, should have extraordinary elevation and clear beats and know how to execute the quick, fluttering movements without appearing jerky. When two great dancers join in the series of *brisé-volé* variations diagonally across the stage, the effect is exhilarating—like Horowitz ending a Liszt rhapsody, or a brilliant coloratura soprano swarming over the high F's in the second "Queen of the Night" aria in *The Magic Flute*.

Alexander Benois, in his *Reminiscences of the Russian Ballet*, has beautifully summed up the impact that *The Sleeping Beauty* originally made and continues to make. According to him, the ballet was "a most significant turning point in the history of the theater because it put an end to the backwater slackness that had prevailed on the stage of the Maryinsky Theater." Benois continues with the observation that the chief reason for the success of *The Sleeping Beauty* lies in Tchaikovsky's music, which "really possesses so strong a power of suggestion that those who give themselves up to it are completely transported from reality into the magic world of fairy tale. Marius Petipa, himself inspired by the music, achieved in the composition of the dances a height of inspiration hitherto unsurpassed by him. It is enough to recall the variations of the fairies in the prologue, the grand *pas de deux* (the 'Rose Adagio') in the third scene and, the greatest masterpiece of all, the dance of the Bluebird and the Enchanted Princess. But what innumerable other gems of choreographic art are scattered by Petipa throughout *La Belle au bois dormant!"* And Benois cites some of the felicities, after a while achieving an almost hysterical note of rapture. But *The Sleeping Beauty* always arouses every balletomane to such a pitch that he becomes incoherent in praise.

Souvenirs

 As Samuel Barber conceived the music used in *Souvenirs,* it was a six-movement suite for two pianos using American dance forms that flourished around the turn of this century (waltz, tango, two-step, and others). The composer orchestrated it for the New York City Ballet, and the work, which retained its original title, was choreographed by Todd Bolender. It received its *première* on November 15, 1955, at the City Center of Music and Drama, New York. Scenery and costumes were provided by Rouben Ter-Arutunian.

The set for *Souvenirs* has been greatly admired. Simple, stylized, and suggestive, it evokes a grand hotel *circa* 1900, complete with potted palms and hydraulic elevator. The men wear clothes considered exceedingly sporting in those years. They have carnations in their buttonholes. Their hair is plastered flat.

Scene 1 takes place in the lobby of the Royal Palms Hotel. The year is 1914. Guests are arriving, or walking past, or conversing. Young couples openly flirt. Waltzing couples glide past. We see a pensive young girl in white. A siren enters, causing great consternation among the young bloods in the lobby. She throws a lucky man the key to her room and goes up in the elevator.

Scene 2 is a hallway on the third floor. A man about town does a smart dance with a cane. When a chambermaid passes by, he dances with her. His intentions are definitely not honorable. The elevator comes to the landing. Out come a bridal pair, who hastily disappear into a room. The man about town goes into another room with a woman. Her husband enters, and soon there is a Mack Sennett sort of chase, during which the inhabitants of four rooms pile out in a furious welter and end up in the elevator.

Scene 3 is a corner of the ballroom. Three wallflowers look anxiously around for any available unattached men. (Two of the girls deserve to be wallflowers; the third under no conditions ever could be.) A couple enters. They look at the girls, laugh, and go out. A dancing couple appears, and the wallflowers look on enviously. The stage is almost empty, and the forlorn trio quietly sits. Suddeny a man enters. He is attracted to the pretty girl and dances a lyrical duet with her. Another man cuts in; then still another. She dances, at the end, with four men, then resumes the duet with her original partner. As he goes off, she returns to her seat next to the other girls.

Scene 4 takes place in the tearoom of the palm court. A husband and wife are seen sitting across from each other at a table, engaged in a violent argument. He stalks off, and she drops her handkerchief in front of a passing man. Friendship rapidly develops. They dance a burlesque of old-fashioned ballroom steps. The husband appears and breaks up the courtship. But as he leads her away in great indignation, she winks at her new friend.

The next scene is named "A Bedroom Affair." We see the siren, *à la odalisque*, sultry as one could conceive, dressed in a

costume of outrageous doodads. She dances a sinuous solo. A
man about town enters the boudoir. He pursues her with an
intensity not seen in the entertainment world since Rudolph
Valentino was chasing assorted femininity on the silent screen.
She is forced to use a gun to protect herself. He takes it from her
and leaves with a sneer.

The ballet concludes with Scene 6, "The Next Afternoon."
It takes place on the beach. A lifeguard, bathing beauties wearing suits that come down to their knees, and men in similar
attire engage in horseplay. Everybody dances and has a fine time.
All leave except the lifeguard. But he is not to remain alone. A
girl comes out, and they fall into a clinch.

The ballet demands a large cast. Dancing in the world *pre-
mière* were Edith Brozak, Ann Crowell, and Carolyn George
(Three Young Girls), Arthur Mitchell (An Attendant), Roberta
Meier and Richard Thomas (Husband and Wife), Todd Bo-
lender (A Man About Town), Roy Tobias (Another Man About
Town), Jillana and Jonathan Watts (A Lady and Her Escort)
Wilma Curlet and Robert Barnett (A Bride and Groom), Irene
Larsson (The Woman), John Mandia (The Man), Jane Mason
(A Maid), Herbert Bliss (Man in Grey), Patricia Savoia, Dido
Sayers, Ronald Colton, Gene Gavin, and Walter Georgov (Hotel
Guests), and Eugene Tanner (An Attendant).

Souvenirs contains much frank slapstick, and its *première*
brought some reproving tut-tutting from the more staid members of press and audience. The ballet also had some antecend-
ents, which were promptly brought into light by the scholars.
Charles Weidman's *Flickers* had, in a way, anticipated *Souvenirs.* So had sections of choreography in Jerome Robbins's
dances for the musical comedy *High Button Shoes.* So had
Frederick Ashton's *Façade,* a repertory item of the Sadler's Wells
Ballet.

But *Souvenirs,* with all of its burlesque and musical-comedy
leanings, contains something individual. It took no mean degree
of choreographic organization to assemble so many disparate
elements into a cohesive whole. And while Bolender relies upon
slapstick, he gives it an air that removes his work from the

obvious kind of ballet humor that gets its laughs from pure situation of an elementary nature. For Bolender is not laughing only at his characters; he is also laughing at himself. And, indeed, there is even less laughter at the characters than at a certain period of American life, which those characters represent. *Souvenirs* contains more subtlety than one might gather from observing it merely as a humorous ballet. (It certainly contains more subtlety than the above bare description of the plot would suggest.) Bolender is an excellent craftsman and, despite the goings-on in *Souvenirs,* a choreographer of taste. To the sensitive observer, the ballet could easily bring a sigh as well as a laugh.

A Streetcar Named Desire

 Valerie Bettis had achieved a solid reputation as an exponent of the modern dance, both as soloist and choreographer, and many people were surprised when she made an entry into the ballet world. Her first endeavor was *Virginia Sampler* for the Ballet Russe de Monte Carlo in 1947. It did not remain long in the repertoire. *A Streetcar Named Desire,* however, which the Slavenska-Franklin Ballet introduced in 1952, drew much attention. Some observers admired it, some cordially detested it—but it was talked about.

Bettis based her libretto, of course, on the Tennessee Williams play. The action takes place in the flat of Stanley Kowalski in the French Quarter of New Orleans and also in the inner world of Blanche Du Bois.

The ballet has a detailed and explicit story line. Blanche is the last of a long line of Southern gentry. She comes to visit her

248

sister, Stella, as a final refuge from her past. Her husband has committed suicide, there has been a succession of family deaths, and the old plantation has been lost. Blanche, however, is far from blameless. An abnormal woman unable to cope with reality, she seeks escape in promiscuity. She has been unable to hold a job. Not only that, but she has been driven from the town in which she last lived. Her sister is her last hope.

Stanley, Stella's husband, does not like the idea of Blanche's arrival. The dislike is mutual. Stanley is too uncouth and animal-like for Blanche and her decayed gentility. Blanche is much too "uppity" for him. He also is greatly interested in knowing why, when the plantation was sold, Stella received no share. Trying to find more about the situation, he rifles Blanche's suitcase and comes across love letters from her dead husband. She is thrown into fear.

Stanley likes to invite his friends to the house for sessions of poker. At one of these sessions, Blanche meets Mitch. She is attracted to him and begins a flirtation, disrupting the game and bringing to a boil Stanley's hatred of her. Stella tries to soothe him and he strikes her. The two girls run from the house. Finally Stella returns to Stanley, leaving a trembling Blanche in the street.

She begins to become mentally unhinged and clings to Mitch in desperation. Mitch is interested until Stanley lets him know that Blanche is in the habit of spreading her favors indiscriminately. Blanche now retreats entirely within herself. She lives in a fantasy world, dressing herself in a replica of the past. While she is so attired one evening, Stanley exultantly comes home. His wife is expecting a child. Blanche shrinks from him, trying to flee through a series of doors that represent her past. Her grand manner and pretense at innocence infuriate Stanley. He attacks her. As a result she completely loses her reason. She is taken away, living her private dreams.

Alex North composed the music for *A Streetcar Named Desire*. The score was orchestrated by Rayburn Wright. The set was designed by Peter Larkin, and Saul Bolasni created the costumes. The ballet was first presented by the Slavenska-

Franklin Ballet at Her Majesty's Theatre, Montreal, Canada, on October 9, 1952. The leading dancers were Mia Slavenska (Blanche), Frederic Franklin (Stanley), and Lois Ellen (Stella). The same principals were seen in the first New York perform- ance at the Century Theater on December 8, 1952. Ballet Thea- tre took *A Streetcar Named Desire* into its repertoire at the Mc- Carter Theater, Princeton, New Jersey, on October 26, 1954. At that performance Valerie Bettis was seen as Blanche; Igor Youskevitch, sadly miscast, was Kowalski; and Christine Mayer danced Stella. The sight of the great Youskevitch, *danseur noble,* the most gallant and aristocratic of partners, loping around the stage like a Mickey Spillane character, was enough to sour milk.

Bettis quite apparently designed her ballet to be a shocker. It is heavily burdened with garish symbolism, deals with SEX in capital letters, and concentrates more on sex and the story than on dance interest. *A Streetcar Named Desire* lasts well over a half hour, but contains hardly one choreographic sequence that one can look forward to seeing. Bettis is a modern dancer with modern dance philosophy, a strong handicap when choreog- raphing for ballet. She almost necessarily must be eclectic, and here she draws upon Tudor, Martha Graham, and other sources without fusing them into a personal speech. There is, after all, no substitute for dancing in ballet.

Swan Lake

Peter Ilyitch Tchaikovsky, who had a nature that was up in the stratosphere one moment, down in the dumps the next, blew hot and cold about his first ballet score, a work in four acts named *Swan Lake*. Its first performance took place on March 4, 1877, at the Bolshoy Theater in Moscow. Shortly afterwards, Tchaikovsky happened to hear a ballet by Delibes. *"Swan Lake* is poor stuff compared with it," he wrote, discouraged, and decided to revise his score.

Part of Tchaikovsky's discouragement stemmed from the fact that *Swan Lake* in its original form was, if not exactly a dead failure, no howling success. He had put much time and effort into the composition of the music. In a letter to Rimsky-Korsakov dated September 10, 1875, he had written: "I accepted the work partly because I need the money and because I have long cherished a desire to try my hand at this type of music." The idea for the ballet had come from the director of the Bolshoy Theater, a man named Vladimir Begichev, who offered Tchaikovsky about $500 for the score. Tchaikovsky gladly accepted, suggesting that Begichev himself supply a libretto based on the age of chivalry. This Begichev did, in collaboration with Vasily Geltzer, the father of Catherine Geltzer, prima ballerina of the Bolshoy and later the first to dance a representative *Swan Lake* in America.

Although Tchaikovsky intended to rewrite *Swan Lake* after it was so flatly received, the fault of its reception was not his. The choreographer assigned to the ballet was Julius Reisinger, whose creative talent obviously was not on a par with Tchaikovsky's. Pauline Karpakova was the ballerina who danced the central role. She was past her prime, and she insisted on interpolating excerpts from other ballets with which she was familiar. Apparently Tchaikovsky's score did not mean much to her. And Reisinger gave in to all her demands. Under these circumstances, Tchaikovsky's great score failed to make an impression. After a few years the scenery was in shreds and very little of the original score remained, Tchaikovsky's music having gradually been replaced by that of other composers. When the scenery finally became impossible to use, *Swan Lake* was dropped from the repertoire.

The Moscow production was revised in 1901, but not in the version we know today as *Swan Lake*. What we are familiar with has descended from the St. Petersburg production of January 27, 1895—a date well over one year after Tchaikovsky's death on November 6, 1893. Tchaikovsky had never got around rewriting the music for *Swan Lake*. This is fortunate: he could not possibly have improved the score, and he very possibly might have weakened it.

What was *Swan Lake* doing away from the Bolshoy Theater? After Tchaikovsky's death there were many memorial performances of his music, and on March 1, 1894, the Maryinsky Theater in St. Petersburg gave a program honoring the dead master. On this program was Act II of *Swan Lake,* with Pierina Legnani as the Swan Queen, and with choreography by Lev Ivanov.

Ivanov was the assistant of the great Marius Petipa, choreographer of the Maryinsky Theater. Ivanov's revival created a stir, and Petipa, who knew a good thing when he saw it, decided to produce the entire ballet. Petipa and Ivanov worked together. It is interesting to note that the most popular section of *Swan Lake,* the second act, was choreographed by Ivanov, not Petipa (who usually gets the credit).

Legnani again was the ballerina in the January 27, 1895, presentation of the entire work. It was she who had turned Russia upside down when she became the first dancer to do thirty-two successive *fouettés* (a smart, stationary spin in which the leg whips out to the side while the body faces front—George Bernard Shaw once described it as a "teetotum spin"), one of the really exciting virtuoso tricks in the dancer's lexicon. At the first performance, *Swan Lake* received a tremendous reception. By the time the third act came along, Legnani was so flushed with success that she went into the thirty-two *fouettés* as a climax to the "Black Swan" *pas de deux*. They have remained there ever since.

Begichev's original story was retained, and this is the *Swan Lake* that we know today. The curtain rises on a festive scene. It is Prince Siegfried's twenty-first birthday. People have come to honor him. Wolfgang, the Prince's tutor, a venerable man with an affinity for the bottle, enters and goes like a homing pigeon to the liquid refreshment. Dances have been arranged to entertain the Prince. The Prince's mother enters and views the festive scene with disfavor. She tells him that he now is of age and must choose a wife. Tomorrow night, she continues, there will be a formal birthday ball, at which he must select the girl he will marry. She leaves. Wolfgang, tipsy by now, tries to console the Prince. He takes one of the girls, dances with her, gets dizzy, and falls to the ground. Festivities continue, but Prince Siegfried is unhappy. A flight of swans passes overhead. Benno, the Prince's closest friend, suggests that a swan-hunt be organized. Crossbows are brought, and the hunting party, headed by the Prince and Benno, goes off to the woods.

Act II takes place in the woods. The curtain rises on a foreboding landscape: a lake, trees, mountains, a craggy castle brooding in the distance. The hunters enter and, seeing the swans, disperse in order to get closer to them. As Prince Siegfried is about to leave the stage, he sees something and hides. A beautiful apparition enters: Odette, the Queen of the Swans. She preens herself. Prince Siegfried enters. She tries to escape; he assures her that he means no harm. Indeed, he loves her at first sight. Odette lets the Prince know that a magician, Von Rotbart, has placed her under an enchantment; she must remain a swan except between midnight and dawn unless a man will marry her and never love another.

Prince Siegfried vows to be that man. The magician enters. Odette gets between the two men, begging Von Rotbart to spare Siegfried and preventing Siegfried from firing an arrow at Von Rotbart. The latter disappears. The lovers go into the forest. As they go, he tells her to be at the ball so that he can choose her as his wife. She tells him that the spell will prevent her from attending, and that the wily Von Rotbart will do everything he can do to make him break his promise.

Immediately after Siegfried and Odette disappear, the swans come on stage. They dance. The hunters enter and prepare to fire on them. Siegfried and Odette rush forth and prevent the slaughter, explaining to the hunters that, like Odette, the swans are maidens under a spell. A series of dances follow, including the popular *pas de quatre* of the cygnets and the great *pas de deux* of Siegfried and Odette. Dawn approaches, and the swans prepare to leave. Von Rotbart again appears, all menace, and calls Odette. The swans disappear. As they fly overhead, Benno consoles Siegfried.

In Act III we are at the ball. Dances; merriment; presentations; pomp; but the Prince thinks only of his Odette. His mother orders him to dance; he does so with monumental lack of enthusiasm. The girls from among whom Siegfried is to choose a wife are dismayed, and Siegfried's mother is furious when he refuses to make a choice. Suddenly the heralds announce the arrival of a new couple. A man enters with his daughter Odile, who is dressed in black. To Siegfried, she is the very image of Odette; he looks upon her, entranced. She, of course, is not Odette, but the daughter of Von Rotbart, who has brought her to the ball. At the rear of the stage the figure of Odette is seen, far in the distance, pleading to Siegfried, trying to warn him; but nobody notices her. Odette fades away, and Odile and Siegfried come on stage to perform what is known to all ballet-lovers as the "Black Swan" *pas de deux*. She has Siegfried completely in her power. Odette again appears in the distance, and again tries to warn the hapless Prince. He sees nothing, for Von Rotbart and Odile, well aware of her presence, keep Siegfried occupied. Siegfried asks for her hand in marriage. Von Rotbart demands an oath from him: will he swear to love her forever? Siegfried hesitates and, for a fleeting moment, almost fights his way out of the spell. Then he swears eternal fidelity. A crash of thunder! Darkness, and the courtiers flee. Siegfried stands astounded. Suddenly, seeing the image of Odette, forlorn and wracked, he falls to the floor.

Act IV returns the swans to the forest. Odette appears, heartbroken. Siegfried enters, searching for her. When he finds her, he swears eternal love. Odette forgives Siegfried, but tells him that her death must follow, for her life was forfeited when she was betrayed. Von Rotbart comes forth and is cursed by Siegfried. Odette, longing for death, throws herself into the lake. Siegfried does not hesitate before following her. Von Rotbart again comes forth, but his powers are lost. He dies and the stage darkens. As it becomes light again, Odette and Siegfried appear, transfigured, and then disappear over the waters.

As originally conceived, the roles of Odette and Odile were intended for two dancers. But at the first St. Petersburg performance, Legnani danced the double role of Odette-Odile, thereby establishing a precedent that most great ballerinas have followed. Occasionally, however, as in a Russian film of the work, the ballet is produced with two female dancers in the leading parts. In the two-act Diaghilev production, two dancers were used. In 1940, when the San Francisco Opera Ballet presented a full-length version in America choreographed by William Christensen, there were two dancers, Jacqueline Martin

(Odette), and Janet Reed (Odile). This was not, however, the first full-length version that America had seen. New York newspapers in 1911 had carried big advertisements about the "Entire Imperial Russian Ballet," with its "fourteen solo dancers and entire corps de ballet." On December 20, 1911, the first New York production of *Swan Lake* was given at the Metropolitan Opera House, with scenery painted by James Fox of the Metropolitan. Carl Van Vechten reported for *The New York Times* that a good deal of the four acts was cut. He had fine things to say about Catherine (or "Katrina," as she was billed) Geltzer's dancing, especially in the third act. Michael Mordkin was the Prince. After *Swan Lake* a series of divertissements was danced by members of the company.

Most American-based companies have, at one time or another, presented *Swan Lake* in a one-act version—the second act, virtually a ballet in itself, and certainly the crown of the four acts. Revivals go back to 1930, when Act II, with choreography by Laurent Novikoff, was presented at the Chicago Civic Opera House. Next on the scene was Col. W. de Basil and his Ballet Russe. This company's one-act *Swan Lake* was first seen in America at the St. James Theater, New York, on March 9, 1934. Alexandra Danilova and David Lichine were the leading dancers; scenery was by Prince A. Schervachidze. The Ballet Russe de Monte Carlo offered *Swan Lake* at the Metropolitan Opera House on October 15, 1938. Danilova and Michel Panaieff were Odette and the Prince; scenery was by Emile Bertin, costumes by Karensky [*sic*]. A novelty that did not stay long in the repertoire was *The Magic Swan* as presented by the Ballet Russe de Monte Carlo in 1941—the third act of *Swan Lake* as staged by Alexandra Fedorova.

The 1940–50 decade saw a rash of one-act *Swan Lakes*. Anton Dolin re-staged the ballet "after choreography by Petipa" for Ballet Theatre at the Center Theater, New York, on January 16, 1940. Scenery was by Augustus Vincent Tack, costumes by Lucinda Ballard. The leading dancers were Patricia Bowman and Anton Dolin. Vera Nemtchinova and Michel Panaieff were the leading dancers in the version staged by the Original Ballet

Russe on November 23, 1940, at the Fifty-First Street Theater, New York, with scenery and costumes by C. Korovine.

Dolin's re-staging for Ballet Theatre came back in a refurbished version at the Metropolitan Opera House on October 6, 1942, with new scenery by Lee Simonson, new men's costumes by Karinska. Irina Baronova and Anton Dolin were the principals. At the International Theater, New York, on October 31, 1944, the Ballet International presented Viola Essen and André Eglevsky as the leading dancers. This production, supervised by Anatole Vilzak, offered a version of Tchaikovsky's score orchestrated by Giuseppe Creatore. Eugene Dunkel designed the scenery. Still another one-act version, given at the Century Theater on November 8, 1950, had *décor* by Natalie Gontcharova and was danced by Rosella Hightower and André Eglevsky. The most recent version of Act II before the American public was introduced by the New York City Ballet Company at the New York City Center of Music and Drama on November 20, 1951. George Balanchine re-staged this production, which had scenery and costumes by Cecil Beaton. Only the central adagio and the *pas de quatre* of the cygnets were traditional; the rest was newly choreographed by Balanchine. Maria Tallchief and André Eglevsky were the leading dancers.

Many American audiences have had a chance to see *Swan Lake* in its entirety as danced by Sadler's Wells, the only company seen in America that has the complete ballet in its repertoire. Its *Swan Lake* was first performed at the Sadler's Wells Theatre, London, on November 20, 1934, and has gone through several changes since then. The version first presented in this country, at the Metropolitan Opera House on October 20, 1949, was produced by Nicholas Sergeyev, with scenery and costumes by Leslie Hurry. At the American *première*, Margot Fonteyn and Michael Somes danced the principal roles.

The ballerina in *Swan Lake* has probably the most difficult assignment in the repertoire. Not only is it technically demanding, but it calls for transcendent acting ability. Odette should be danced with plastic quality, with infinite poetry and lyricism. Odile's dances in the third act feature sharp brilliance and great technical aplomb. A further difficulty in the Odile characterization is that of projection. The audience must know at once the kind of vicious mind and soul she has, but she must be close enough to Odette's tenderness and femininity to deceive Siegfried. The dividing line between subtlety and obviousness is of a hair's breadth, and very few living ballerinas are able to dance and mime both roles convincingly. Naming great Swan Queens is invariably part of the agenda when ballet-lovers get together of an evening. You may be sure that at least four names will be discussed reverently: Markova, Alonso, Fonteyn, and Maria Tallchief—Markova for her incredible lightness, her introspection and sheer lyricism; Alonso for her more decided quality, her elegance and strong technique; Tallchief for her brilliant, clear, almost brittle approach and technical nonchalance; Fonteyn for her dramatic synthesis of the role, her appealing femininity, perfect *port de bras,* and exquisite phrasing.

Fonteyn is especially successful in the adagio movements of the Swan Queen. For these sections a ballerina must have exceptional control. In ballet, as in music, it often is easier to move fast. Slow, lyric sections show up whatever defects a dancer may have in her line (just as a long, slow bow can often tell more about a violinist than any number of running passages).

The dancer who takes the part of Prince Siegfried must be a finished artist in the true classical tradition. He must be handsome, have dignity, know how to act without emoting all over the stage, and be the most gallant of partners. His is not an easy part technically, either; it calls for considerable brilliance. One of the great moments in the ballet occurs when the Prince makes his entrance in the third-act "Black Swan" *pas de deux* with a series of soaring *grands jetés* which starts in the wings and continues in a bounding circle around the entire stage. When done with virtuosity, this pulls the audience right out of its seats. Often this *pas de deux* is performed as a divertissement on a ballet program. When so taken out of context, it loses somewhat in dramatic force (those *jetés* represent Siegfried's uncontrollable excitement at finding what he thinks is his lady love, just as Odile's following *fouettés* represent her exultation at having deceived him) and becomes a brilliant, athletic *tour de force,* perhaps the greatest applause-getter in the entire repertoire. It should no more be danced by second-class dancers than a Liszt operatic paraphrase should be played by second-class pianists. When either is well done, the effect is electrifying.

One of the most popular dances in *Swan Lake* is performed by the four cygnets in Act II. This is executed with the hands crossed in front, each dancer's hand clasping a partner's, and is what is called precision work. Albertina Rasch, in the late twenties and early thirties, made virtually a whole career out of this one dance. Nearly every Broadway show, every vaudeville theater and, later, movie houses, had a line of sixteen girls doing very much the same thing. Rasch's theory, based on simple mathematics, must have run something like this: if the dance of the cygnets, for four girls, is so effective, it will be four times as effective with sixteen girls.

A note about the music of *Swan Lake.* It is not only a great score; it also is a functional score. Concert-goers who know their *Swan Lake* only from a symphonic performance or from records cannot begin to realize the extent to which every phrase dovetails with a specific movement or a specific emotion on the stage. Its rich melodic content, its inventive harmonies, its brilliant orchestration—these come through immediately, and have helped establish *Swan Lake* as a concert favorite. But it is safe to say that those who have missed seeing the ballet can never appreciate the genius of the score; what may seem merely a pretty interlude when divorced from the action suddenly assumes tremendous significance when allied to the physical movements for which it was intended.

Les Sylphides

It probably was Théophile Gautier who coined the expression *ballet blanc*. Marie Taglioni, the most popular ballerina of the 1830s, had popularized a costume of white, gauzy material in which the dress reached midway between ankle and knee. Most other ballerinas hastened to follow suit, especially after Taglioni's great success in *La Sylphide* (1830). By the middle 1840s, Gautier was heartily sick of the phenomenon, and he remonstrated in print (in rather mild language, to be sure, for the man who once described a dancer—Mlle Louise Fitzjames—as being "as thin as a lizard, as thin as a silkworm").

Had Gautier lived for several more decades, he would have seen the virtual disappearance of the *ballet blanc*. Ballet pursued a different course, heavily costumed, detailed in plot, sumptuous in stage settings. All of this was culminated in the great ballets of Tchaikovsky, choreographed by Petipa and his assistants.

Fokine restored the *ballet blanc,* and *Les Sylphides* is probably the greatest specimen of its kind in the active repertoire. It is also one of the most beautiful ballets ever conceived, and has easily survived all changes of choreographic fashion. It is pure dance; and, even more, pure ensemble dance. It is plotless; and while it affords beautiful solo opportunities, it depends upon much more than solo dancing. It demands pure quality of movement, and every member of the *corps de ballet* must be able to sustain a classical line and the most elegant of legato phrasing. A great performance of *Les Sylphides* breathes an airiness and a floating quality that completely transport the spectator from this world. For if it lacks a magical quality the choreographer's purpose is lost, and the ballet takes on the aspect of a series of classroom exercises. *Les Sylphides* is probably the most sensitive and delicate ballet in the repertoire.

This perfect ballet was not originally named *Les Sylphides.* The idea of arranging a ballet to Chopin's music came to Fokine when he found a suite named *Chopiniana* orchestrated by Glazunov. It consisted of four pieces—a polonaise, a nocturne, a mazurka and the *Tarantelle.* (None of these four ended up in the final version.) To these Fokine decided to add a waltz, which Glazunov orchestrated at his request. The work received its *première* on March 21, 1908, in St. Petersburg, where Fokine was a teacher at the Imperial School of Ballet. It was called *Chopiniana,* and at least one of the dances had a plot revolving about an incident in the life of Chopin (an apocryphal incident, it might be added). Less than one month later, on April 6, a new version of *Chopiniana* was danced at the annual students' performance of Imperial School members. Now it was a purely classical ballet, with the dancers dressed in white. It also had a new score orchestrated by Maurice Keller.

It did not take long for *Chopiniana* to enter the Ballet Russe's repertoire. When Diaghilev met Fokine to discuss ballets for the 1909 season in Paris, Fokine mentioned *Chopiniana.* Diaghilev agreed, but said that he did not like the name, and would like to call it *Les Sylphides*. Fokine was not happy about the change, but in the end gave in. There also was discussion about the overture. At the previous performances a Chopin polonaise had been used. Diaghilev considered this stylistically unsuitable, and suggested that one of Chopin's preludes instead be used. He further complained about the orchestration, demanded that it be redone, and decided to engage Alexandre Benois for the scenery and costumes.

Diaghilev had his way, and Fokine's *Chopiniana* was touched up a bit. It was the 1830 *La Sylphide,* of course, that had given Diaghilev the idea for the new name. Four composers were called in to tinker with the score—Stravinsky (his first Diaghilev commission), Tcherepnin, Lyadov, and Glazunov. (Arranging *Les Sylphides* has become an indoor sport for many subsequent composers, among them Taneyev, Caillet, Britten, Rieti, Boutnikov, Anderson, and Bodge.)

The *première* of *Les Sylphides* took place at the Théâtre du Châtelet, Paris, on June 2, 1909. The leading dancers were Tamara Karsavina, Anna Pavlova, Alexandra Baldina, and Vaslav Nijinsky. Serge Grigoriev, in his book about the Ballets Russes, has described the first performance: "The female dancers taking part were all dressed alike in long skirts *à la Taglioni*. . . . Anna Pavlova was at her best in this ballet. She was the very essence of the romantic, ethereal and unearthly, a Sylphide incarnate; and if Nijinsky was compared to Vestris, Pavlova in the opinion of all who saw her was a second Taglioni. The second Sylphide was Tamara Karsavina, tender and poetic, dancing with exquisite charm and enchanting the audience. Alexandra Baldina was delightfully graceful, young and attractive. Nijinsky created an unforgettable image as the youthful poet. His dancing was faultless, and the rendering of the waltz by him and Pavlova truly incomparable. . . . *Les Sylphides* was a renaissance of the romantic ballet in all its charm. The public were genuinely moved and enchanted."

And Benois, who had designed the costumes, was quite pleased with the results. "All the artistes," he has written in his memoirs, "had white tutus *à la Taglioni*. As relics of what seemed, at the time, a forgotten age, they had a particular charm." Benois speaks of the music, and how the arrangers strove to achieve sounds that "should be softened, wrapped, so to speak, in a haze, in order to convey the impression given on the stage—the languid vision of spirits and of dead maidens, dancing their dreamy dances among the moonlit ruins and mausoleums. This was the atmosphere that my *décor* was calculated to evoke and it was enhanced by Fokine's dances, wonderfully performed by our artistes." As creator of the original backdrop, Benois takes exception to later innovations. "How absurd was the novelty introduced in our creation by de Basil when he used the copy of a well-known Corot as back-cloth for *Sylphides*." But, as a matter of fact, it is this inspiration from a Corot painting that many spectators these days will see; and, in all truth, it is not as inappropriate as Benois suggests.

The separate dances of *Les Sylphides* are not always done in the order in which the Diaghilev company presented them. Different companies vary the sequence. Usually, however, the ballet is done according to the following plan:

Overture (Prelude in A, Op. 28, No. 7). The curtain rises on moonlit ruins (or, depending upon the backdrop, a wooded glen; in any event it's all quiet, mysterious and romantic). The lighting is a diffused glow giving the impression of moonlight. The girls, in white, are grouped in a tableau around one man in the center. As the Nocturne in A flat (Op. 32, No. 2) begins, the girls dance to the sentimental, long-phrased melody. They are joined by the principal dancers. The Waltz in G flat (Op. 70, No. 1) calls for a solo variation from one of the ballerinas. Next follows the solo variation for the man, the Mazurka in C (Op. 67, No. 3); this has the reputation of being one of the most ungrateful male solos in the repertoire. The movement is slow, demands iron control, and must achieve a sustained quality of line and phrasing. It is like a Mozart piano piece that in itself has few technical difficulties, but poses more problems for the pianist than any number of Liszt potpourris. Similarly, the mazurka demands more from the dancer than the most amazing *tour de force* of beats and turns in air. Few in our day have been really successful in it.

Another Mazurka (Op. 33, No. 2 in D, wrongly described in many standard ballet guides as Op. 33, No. 3) is danced by one of the ballerinas. This dance opens with *grands jetés* diagonally across the stage from the wings, repeated several times. When the soloist has a good natural elevation and knows how to handle herself correctly, she seems to be soaring across the stage. The Overture (Prelude in A) is repeated while the sylphs form new groups. Another soloist enters softly, pauses, then moves among the posed groups, winding in and out. Like the male solo, this takes control, lightness, and balance that make for the ultimate in artistry when performed well.

A *pas de deux,* to the familiar Waltz in C sharp minor (Op. 64, No. 2), starts with the male dancer lifting the soloist across the stage, starting from the back of the wings so as to give the effect of the ballerina floating in air. Then comes the finale, the Waltz in E flat (Op. 18), in which the entire company fills the stage and one of the soloists has rapid *bourrées* back and forth across the stage, with bent back and arms stretched overhead—tremendously effective when brilliantly danced. The curtain falls on the tableau on which it rose.

America first saw *Les Sylphides* at the Century Theater, New York on January 20, 1916, during the first United States tour of the Diaghilev company. The principals were Lydia Lopokova, Lubov Tchernicheva, Xenia Maclezova, and Adolph Bolm. Nijinsky danced the male solo in New York for the first time on April 14. In 1939, Benois designed a revival for Sadler's Wells, in England; it superseded a version that had been in the company's repertoire since 1932. The following year, 1940, Fokine himself staged a version for Ballet Theatre. (He had previously staged the work for René Blum's Ballet Russe de Monte Carlo in 1936 and for the Royal Danish Ballet in 1925.) Benjamin Britten's musical arrangement was used, and Eugene Dunkel painted the scenery, using certain paintings of Corot as inspiration. Karen Conrad, Nina Stroganova, Lucia Chase, and William Dollar were the leading dancers at the *première,* at the Center Theater, New York, on January 11, 1940. It has been Ballet Theatre's custom ever since to open its season with *Les Sylphides.*

Fokine's career was long and active, but it is doubtful that any of his other ballets has the unity, grace, and sheer loveliness of *Les Sylphides.* It does not date; it has the timelessness of a Greek frieze, the formal perfection of a Mozart symphony. Fokine once stated his principles of ballet in a letter to the London *Times.* This was in 1910, and he said, among other things, that a choreographer must "invent in each case a new form of movement, corresponding to the subject and character of the music, instead of merely giving combinations of ready-made steps. Dancing and gesture in ballet have no meaning unless they serve as an expression of dramatic action. Man can and should be expressive from head to foot. The group is not merely an ornament. The new ballet advances from the expressiveness of the face or the hands to that of the whole body, and from that of the individual body to groups of bodies and the expressiveness of the combined dancing of a crowd." All of which is taken for granted today, but was revolutionary in 1910. In *Les Sylphides* Fokine carried his esthetic to a point that he himself never again reached.

Symphony in C

 Originally named *Le Palais de Cristal,* *Symphony in C* was created in 1947 by George Balanchine for the Paris Opéra. He had been invited there as guest choreographer and had staged several revivals of his ballets—*Apollon Musagète, Le Baiser de la Fée, Serenade.* He also decided to stage a new work for the principal dancers of the Opéra and, as seemed appropriate, settled on the Symphony in C by Georges Bizet. This symphony, composed by Bizet in 1855 at the age of seventeen, is a remarkable work, written in less than a month. Haydn, Beethoven, and Rossini play their parts in it, but its craftsmanship, *joie de vivre,* and bubbling melodic flow mark it as the product of a young genius.

In the Paris production on July 28, 1947, the leading roles were danced by Lysette Darsonval, Tamara Toumanova, Micheline Bardin, Madeleine Lafon, Alexandre Ka-

266

lioujny, Roger Ritz, Michel Renault, and Max Bozzoni. Scenery and costumes were by Léonor Fini. Under the title *Symphony in C,* it was presented by Ballet Society at the New York City Center of Music and Drama on March 22, 1948.

The leading dancers at the American *première* were Maria Tallchief, Tanaquil LeClercq, Beatrice Tompkins, Elise Reiman, Nicholas Magallanes, Francisco Moncion, Herbert Bliss, and Lew Christensen. The ballet has remained in the permanent repertoire of the New York City Ballet Company. It is an example of Balanchine at his best as the creator of a plotless ballet full of virtuosity, in which huge numbers of dancers are confidently spotted over the stage.

Symphony in C is not easy to do. It demands not only strong dancers, but dancers well versed in the Balanchine idiom; and the obvious necessity for careful and detailed rehearsal, so that the dancers will not be treading on each other's toes, must create a problem of considerable proportions. At the climaxes, forty-eight dancers are used.

The ballet has four movements. Not only is there no plot; scenery also is missing. A blue background is used, and the dancers are dressed in classical ballet costumes. Balanchine has named the movements after Bizet's tempo indications. The first is Allegro vivo. Two groups dance in opposed patterns until the entrance of the ballerina at the second subject. She is joined by two girls who have been the leaders of the opposed groups. During the development section of the music, the ballerina returns with her partner. The other two girls also have partners, and the six soloists, together with the *corps de ballet,* engage in complicated ensemble.

The second movement, Adagio, is a romantic *pas de deux* between another ballerina (each movement has its own female dancer, and they all appear together only toward the end of the ballet) and her partner. Balanchine has designed many elaborate lifts here; the impression is that of the ballerina constantly turning and soaring in the air, an effect emphasized by the placement of the ballerina's legs, which describe tremendous arcs as she is lifted by her partner. Tanaquil LeClercq has been the ballerina in this dance since the *première,* and it could be accomplished successfully only by a woman of her physical characteristics. Anybody with shorter legs and arms would find it impossible to convey the type of sweep Balanchine had in mind. In many of the Balanchine ballets, one dance appears to have been created with a specific dancer in mind. This one *is* LeClercq.

An entirely different sort of mood is encountered in the lively third movement, Allegro vivace. As in the first movement, the patterns are extremely rapid and complicated. A *corps de ballet* of six girls, two couples, and a ballerina with partner provide one of the most kinetic movements in contemporary ballet. The last movement, also Allegro vivace, resembles the previous ones in that it has its own soloists and *corps de ballet.* Toward the end, Balanchine brings all of the dancers together. Much eye-filling virtuosity ensues; the dances of the four ballerinas have almost the aspect of a competition. Just as all of the solo dancers are brought together at the finale, so are the four *corps de ballet.* A whirling finish provides a brilliant curtain; and just as the curtain drops, all of the dancers assume poses, the men supporting the women.

Unless memory is faulty, *Symphony in C* is the longest stretch of pure dance in the repertoire today: a choreographic setting of a full four-movement symphony (Balanchine's *Scotch Symphony* uses only three of the movements). Balanchine's inspiration scarcely flags through the immense length of *Symphony in C.* The variation of steps he has conceived is nothing short of remarkable, just as the endurance of the dancers, faced with the virtuoso feats Balanchine has demanded, must be equally remarkable. Of all the soloists who have danced any one of the allegro sections, only a few have had both the technique and stamina to come through successfully. Among those few are Maria Tallchief, Marie-Jeanne, Patricia Wilde, and Melissa Hayden.

Theme and Variations

 The only Balanchine ballet currently in the repertoire of Ballet Theatre (now that *Waltz Academy* seems to have been dropped) is *Theme and Variations,* which was brought to the public at the New York City Center of Music and Drama on November 26, 1947. Like most of Balanchine's ballets, it is plotless. It resembles *Ballet Imperial* in being an evocation of the Russian Imperial Ballet, and the sumptuous sets and costumes by Woodman Thompson lend a lavish quality to the production. The Theme and Variations from Tchaikovsky's Third Suite for Orchestra was the music Balanchine chose; it was conducted at the *première* by Max Goberman. Since then, the ballet has never been absent from Ballet Theatre's repertoire.

Balanchine did not create anything especially novel or daring in *Theme and Variations,* but he mixed the ingredients

269

of the classic dance into a beautifully integrated unit. Most of the familiar Balanchine patterns are present—the carefully calculated geometrical architecture, the spotting of one group to balance another, the long diagonals, the under-and-over interweavings. The final parade sequence, in which the whole company comes down a long diagonal to a proud and blood-tingling climax by Tchaikovsky, is pure theater, as the ballet itself is pure dance.

The curtain rises on a set that suggests an ornate ballroom—crystal chandeliers, draperies, galleries, a garden in the background. The ballerina wears a tutu; the man's costume is blue. The *corps de ballet* of twelve girls surrounds the principals. As the orchestra states the theme, so do all of the dancers echo the music, simply and sympathetically. In the first variation, the members of the *corps de ballet* dance in ensemble. Variation 2 brings back the ballerina, who has a difficult and virtuosic dance with many *fouettés*. Variation 3 splits the *corps de ballet* into three groups, which dance in contrasting patterns. The fourth variation, for the male dancer, is another exhibition of solo virtuosity, demanding great elevation. (Into this variation Tchaikovsky, for no apparent reason, introduces the *Dies irae* melody that so many composers have used in their scores.) A fugal variation is then danced by the *corps de ballet,* after which, in Variation 6, the male dancer returns. Balanchine has created another very difficult and very effective solo for him, involving *jetés* and *entrechats*. An ensemble variation, Number 7, sets off the ballerina as she dances an adagio movement to the accompaniment of four girls. Variation 8 presents the ballerina in a fast dance. She is joined by the male dancer in Variation 9. This *pas de deux* according to Balanchine, opens in a quiet and lyric manner; but as a new variation (Number 10) begins, the dancing becomes grave and intense. The ballerina and her partner are given a type of movement that is slow and controlled. The last two variations are consecutive. Eight boys join the *corps de ballet,* and the two principals dance a polonaise followed by a series of quick variations. At the extraordinarily effective climax, the two principals lead the entire company in a sweeping circle around the stage. The ballet as a whole gives a sense of perfect design and balance. *Theme and Variations* is, despite the effective solo work Balanchine has inserted, primarily an ensemble ballet. It might be described as neo-Petipa, a reincarnation of classic ballet at its most traditional.

At the first performance of *Theme and Variations,* Alicia Alonso and Igor Youskevitch headed the large cast. Since then Youskevitch has had a virtual monopoly on the male role, though several dancers—among them Diana Adams, Nora Kaye, Mary Ellen Moylan, Maria Tallchief, and Melissa Hayden— have been seen as the ballerina. After Youskevitch left the company, Erik Bruhn replaced him.

La Valse

One of the funniest events in the history
of music, though Maurice Ravel probably
did not think so at the time, took place at
the *première* performance of his piano
piece known as *Valses nobles et sentimentales*. In 1911, the Société Musicale Indépendente, of which Ravel was a founder,
decided to give an unusual concert. Believing that too much attention was paid to the
composer and not enough to the music, and
believing that there was too much preju-
diced criticism around, the Société Musicale Indépendente announced that the
names of the composers would not be given
on its program. Only the committee members knew the music selected. One of the
pieces on that May 9th program was a new
Ravel work played by Louis Aubert.

Ravel sat in a box surrounded by friends.
When Aubert began to play, these connoisseurs, looking at Ravel for approval, began

to rip the music apart. Nor were they the only ones in the audience who ridiculed the composition. Some wild guesses were made about the identity of the composer: Kodály, Satie, and others were mentioned. History does not relate the reaction of Ravel's companions when they learned that the music was his. About three per cent of the audience, however (according to the French critics' records), made correct guesses.

Ravel is quoted in Victor Seroff's biography of him as saying: "The title *Les Valses nobles et sentimentales* sufficiently indicates that I was intent on writing a set of Schubertian waltzes." Among Schubert's piano works is a group of simple, delicious *Valses nobles,* very (despite their title) *Ländler*-like and unsophisticated. Ravel's waltzes, eight in number, are anything but simple and unsophisticated. Where Schubert evoked the peasant, Ravel evoked the aristocratic salon. But, compared with a finger-breaker like the earlier *Gaspard de la Nuit,* the writing here is relatively simple.

Ravel later orchestrated the music and reintroduced it to the French public as a ballet named *Adélaïde ou le langage des fleurs.* Four performances were given in April 1912 by a Parisian company, but the ballet (and the ballet company) failed to take hold.

The composer's other famous work in waltz form is *La Valse.* For many years Ravel had toyed with the idea. In 1906 he had written to a friend: "It is not subtle—what I am undertaking at the moment. It is a Grande Valse, a sort of *hommage* to the memory of the Great Strauss, not Richard, the other—Johann. You know my intense sympathy for this admirable rhythm and that I hold *la joie de vivre* as expressed by the dance in far higher esteem than the Franckist puritanism." Ravel never got beyond sketches for *Wien,* as he had tentatively named the work. But in 1919 he finally finished the score, renaming it *La Valse,* and subtitling it "a choreographic poem for orchestra." Serge Diaghilev asked to see it, then turned it down as a ballet; and Ravel (says Seroff) was mortally offended. Ravel had imagined a ballet in which "drifting clouds give glimpses, through rifts, of couples dancing. The clouds gradually scatter, and an immense hall can be seen, filled with a whirling light. The scene gradually becomes illuminated. The light of chandeliers bursts forth. An Imperial Court about 1855."

Bronislava Nijinska choreographed *La Valse* for Ida Rubin-stein in 1929 in a version that has vanished from the repertoire.

As a postscript it might be mentioned that in 1925, in Monte Carlo, Diaghilev met Ravel and offered him his hand. Ravel refused, whereupon Diaghilev became insulted and challenged the composer to a duel. Friends intervened, and the matter was hushed up. They never met again.

In 1951 George Balanchine put both scores—*Valses nobles et sentimentales* and *La Valse*—together to form a ballet named, simply, *La Valse*. The New York City Ballet Company gave the *première* on February 20, 1951, at the New York City Center of Music and Drama. The leading dancers were Tanaquil Le-Clercq, Nicholas Magallanes, and Francisco Moncion. Of the eight *Valses nobles et sentimentales,* the first was used as an overture. Vida Brown, Edwina Fontaine, and Jillana danced Number 2; Patricia Wilde and Frank Hobi, Number 3; Yvonne Mounsey and Michael Maule, Number 4; Diana Adams and Herbert Bliss, Number 5; Diana Adams, Number 6; Herbert Bliss, Vida Brown, Edwina Fontaine, and Jillana, Number 7; Tanaquil LeClercq and Nicholas Magallanes, Number 8. Ra-vel's choreographic poem immediately followed, with LeClercq, Magallanes, and Moncion in addition to a large *corps de ballet*. Karinska designed the costumes, and the lighting was brilliantly handled by Jean Rosenthal.

Balanchine's *La Valse* is really two ballets in one. The *Valses nobles et sentimentales* is little more than a series of elegantly choreographed, plotless divertissements. Balanchine has matched the music in sophistication, and his entire approach is less aca-demic and objective than in most of his other plotless ballets. The dancing throughout the first section is graceful and varied, but always in the spirit of the waltz. Especially interesting is the final dance before *La Valse* proper. In Ravel's music one hears a summing up, with reminiscences of earlier themes. Balanchine counterpoints this idea by introducing the two dancers who are

274

to play such an important part in the following section of the ballet. They dance an exceptionally lyric *pas de deux* before leaving the stage.

Then begins the music to *La Valse*—low, throbbing, even threatening. Dancers flit by, crossing the stage and streaking into the wings. As the scene lights up, eight couples dance to the abandoned waltz rhythm. An ominous note, however, is lent by chandeliers hung with black crepe. New dancers enter, pair off, swing across the stage. Ravel's music becomes more nervous and sinuous. The ballerina, in white, dances happily with her partner.

Suddenly a black figure emerges from the rear of the stage. All look at him in awe and horror. Wearing a black medal on a black necklace, he somberly approaches the ballerina, followed by a page bearing a mirror and a black dress. The ballerina is frightened, but a mysterious force pulls her to the spectre. He gives her the necklace and bades her look into the mirror. She recoils. He next offers her a pair of long, black gloves into which she inserts her hands. The page presents her with the black gown, and she gets into that also, slipping it over her white costume. Now the spectre is ready to waltz with her. As they dance faster and faster, she begins to fail. She wants to escape, but cannot. Clutched fast by the mysterious stranger, she dies. He disappears, and her former partner removes her body. Again the dance resumes. As a final macabre touch, her partner returns, bearing the body in his arms. Other dancers remove his burden and lift it high, turning her round and round to the music as the ballet comes to an end.

The theme of Death coming to a party is hardly new in literature. Poe, whom Ravel idolized, had handled the theme in one of his finest stories, "The Masque of the Red Death." As Balanchine has conceived it, the ballet is full of symbolism. Nothing in the gaiety of the preceding *Valses nobles et sentimentales* prepares the audience for the grim horrors of *La Valse*. The music, however, calls for it. Even in Ravel's own day *La Valse* was adjudged by sensitive critics to be a grim work with an inner theme that far transcended its surface prettiness. Lawrence

The New Borzoi Book of Ballets

Gilman called *La Valse* "essentially a work of tragic irony . . . as perturbing and ominous as a mobilization order." Gilman also cited the French critic, Raymond Schwab, on the sinister undertone of the music, and in addition quoted the famous line of Prud'homme: "We dance on a volcano."

Balanchine has fully captured this morbid undercurrent, and has done it entirely in choreographic terms. Avoiding literalism, relying mostly on mood and movement, he has created one of the most successful works in the repertoire of the New York City Ballet Company. Many see in the work an allegory of our own day, which it may or may not be. History being what it is, the allegory would seem pertinent to all eras.

Western Symphony

 The latest entry in the cowboy sweepstakes (as typified by ballets like *Rodeo* and *Billy the Kid*) has been *Western Symphony*, which received its *première* on September 7, 1954. George Balanchine was the choreographer, and he used a commissioned score by Hershy Kay, the composer who had created such a success in *Cakewalk*, a lively potpourri of Gottschalk melodies.

Kay had a few words to say about *Western Symphony* in the program notes. "A number of ballets," he wrote, "have been derived from American folk themes (*Fall River Legend, Billy the Kid, Appalachian Spring, Rodeo*) and a good many of these have been derived from cowboy lore. But, I think without exception, these have been narrative ballet—melodrama, romance, slapstick—which employed at least in part the dance idiom of their sources. Balanchine's idea, on the contrary, was to mount a formal ballet, which would derive its flavor from the West, but which would always move within the framework of the classic school and be no more a 'Western' than *Scotch Symphony* is *Lorna Doone* on points.

"Having agreed on this project, I set about determining a suitable format for the music. Classic ballet is straightforward, uncomplicated, and I wished to supply music having those same virtues. But classic ballet is also disciplined, almost mathematically rational beneath the play of fancy, and I felt the music should support that rigor. So the form I chose is what the ballet is now called—a symphony, with the formal pattern of an introduction and four movements (allegro, adagio, scherzo, and rondo.)"

Western Symphony was introduced by the New York City Ballet at the New York City Center of Music and Drama on September 7, 1954. The dancers were Diana Adams, Herbert Bliss, Janet Reed, Nicholas Magallanes, Patricia Wilde, André Eglevsky, Tanaquil LeClercq, and Jacques d'Amboise. Costumes by Karinska had been announced, but the new ballet was performed in practice clothes and without scenery until February 25, 1955, when the company had enough money to employ the Karinska costumes and a set by John Boyt.

Western Symphony is a ballet without a plot, and, as Kay suggested, the movements bear as much real relationship to the West as the movements of Balanchine's *Scotch Symphony* bear to Scotland—very little. The score, to be sure, uses actual cowboy tunes, catchily dressed in an orchestral coat of many colors. *Western Symphony*'s choreography, however, is almost a charade *sur les pointes,* in which certain American elements—hoedowns, square dances, and other such manifestations—are dimly seen through the classical *port de bras.* An American mind hardly could have conceived the choreography, which is essentially that of a cosmopolitan pleasantly kidding around and having a fine time.

Which is not to be construed as negative criticism of *Western Symphony per se.* The ballet, which does not set out to make artistic history, is a clever piece of work, and audiences have found it immensely enjoyable. The first movement has an easy-going quality, with many carefully judged patterns and some effective solo and duet work. The second movement uses a ballerina and her partner against a small *corps* of four dancers. It is very sentimental, oozing with young, clumsy romance. The third movement, a scherzo, is a technical *tour de force* that somehow misses: it lacks character, and one has the feeling of having seen it all before in other Balanchine ballets. An amusing last movement, with steps that intentionally verge on the burlesque, was conceived specifically for Tanaquil LeClercq, and her antics with Jacques d'Amboise have never failed to bring down the house. The movement is brought to a whirling finish in which the entire large ensemble takes part.

Balanchine often makes changes and revisions in his ballets from season to season, and *Western Symphony* has been no exception. In the fall of 1955, ballet-goers noticed a slight revision and shift in emphasis in at least two movements. Melissa Hayden had replaced Janet Reed in the second movement, and the accent now was much more on broad comedy than on sentimental humor. And in the finale, in which Arthur Mitchell danced Jacques d'Amboise's role, the entire burlesque mood was much toned down. Plenty of vigorous athletics were in evidence, but not the purposeful exaggerations that had delighted many beholders during the first season of *Western Symphony's* life.

Appendix

A comprehensive list of ballets presented in
the United States by the Ballet Russe
de Monte Carlo, Ballet Theatre,
the New York City Ballet, the Marquis de
Cuevas Grand Ballet, and their predecessor
companies—with information on book,
music, choreography, scenery, costumes,
places, and dates of *premières*.

 The following is an attempt to list all of
the ballets ever presented in America by
the four major American-based companies
that have been active here since 1933. They
are the Ballet Russe (in one or another of
its manifestations—Ballets Russes de
Monte Carlo; Col. W. de Basil's Ballet
Russe de Monte Carlo; Original Ballet
Russe; Ballet Russe de Monte Carlo), Ballet
Theatre, the New York City Ballet, and
the Marquis de Cuevas Grand Ballet de
Monte Carlo, which originally appeared in
America in 1944 as Ballet International.
The Marquis de Cuevas group operates
under a charter from Albany, New York,
and thus can be considered American-
based. What is now known as the Ballet
Russe de Monte Carlo used to be European-
based, but it has made its headquarters
here since the war.

When I originally compiled this listing,

it ran to several hundred typed pages and aroused consternation in the Knopf editorial office. A system of abbreviations had to be devised, and all of the information was greatly condensed. None of the material has been dropped, however, and the listing, I believe, is the most complete and accurate that has been attempted up to this time. If it is not all-encompassing, that is because of the sorry state of records kept by many ballet companies. Some information, especially concerning the Russian ballet, has been impossible to track down. Apparently no records are available about the repertoire in the thirties and even later; and dates of European *premières* are lost in the depths of antiquity—an antiquity measuring only about one generation, true; but in this case it could just as well extend back to Greek mythology.

Thanks to the marvelous files that John Martin keeps in his office at *The New York Times,* I have had the opportunity to examine every program given by the four companies in New York since they first appeared here. Thus I can vouch for the accuracy of the dates of the New York *premières* (which very often were world *premières*). But the information on the programs themselves is often frustrating. Names of the musical scores, scenic designers, and costumers are frequently omitted. The entries abound in misspellings. I have not hesitated to add information when possible; and I have tried to bring the spellings of proper names into some degree of conformity.

In the following lists, the names of the ballets are given as they appeared on the programs. When the same ballet has been given under different names (*L'Après-midi d'un faune* or *Afternoon of a Faun*), I have cross-indexed the material. The abbreviation *w.p.* (world *première*) is self-explanatory. The abbreviation *p.* (*première*) should not be confused with *w.p.* or *a.p.* It refers to the first time the ballet was given at the place cited. Each indented paragraph under specific ballets refers to a different production. Taking *Apollo* as an example, the material directly following the title refers to the world *première* in Washington, D.C. The first indented entry refers to a new version with choreography by Balanchine. In the second indented entry, the fact that no choreographer is given means that Balanchine remains the choreographer; but this new production by the American Ballet had new sets and costumes, both of which are identified, together with the date of the American *première* by the American Ballet. Because Ballet Theatre used the same choreography, sets, and costumes, the date of its first production of *Apollo* follows directly, in the same entry, after that of the American Ballet. But as the New York City Ballet's program for the production of *Apollo* gives no credit for sets or costumes, it gets an indented entry to itself. (Whenever there is a change in any of the participants in the production of a ballet, that production gets an indented entry.)

Many ballets currently in the repertoire of one or another of the four companies were originally introduced by previous organizations. For instance, some of the Monte Carlo productions had their genesis with the Diaghilev Ballets Russes, while some works now in the New York City Ballet repertoire were originally presented by the American Ballet or Ballet Society. In all cases, I have given information about these earlier world *premières*.

Some mistakes and some gaps in information are bound to occur in a compilation of this sort. If any reader cares to point out any errors or omissions to me, I will be most happy to take note of them and make a correction in any future editions.

Abbreviations of Ballet Companies

BI—Ballet International
BRMC—Ballet Russe de Monte Carlo
BS—Ballet Society
BT—Ballet Theatre
DB—Col. W. de Basil's Ballet Russe de Monte Carlo
DBR—Diaghilev's Ballets Russes
MCGB—Marquis de Cuevas's Grand Ballet
NYCB—New York City Ballet
OBR—Original Ballet Russe

Abbreviations of Theaters

BYT—Broadway Theater, New York
CG—Royal Opera House, Covent Garden, London
CT—Center Theater, New York
CYT—Century Theater, New York
FF—Forty-fourth Street Theater, New York
FFT—Fifty-first Street Theater, New York
IT—International Theater, New York
M—Majestic Theater, New York
MOH—Metropolitan Opera House, New York
NYCC—New York City Center of Music and Drama
SJT—St. James Theater, New York
TCE—Théâtre des Champs-Elysées, Paris
TDC—Théâtre du Châtelet, Paris
TMC—Théâtre de Monte Carlo, Monte Carlo

Other Abbreviations

a.p.—United States *première*
bk.—book (libretto)
ch.—choreographer
co.—costumes
mu.—music

p.—*première*
s.—set
sc.—score
s. & c.—set and costumes
w.p.—world *première*

Ballet Listings

THE AFTERNOON OF A FAUN
(L'APRÈS-MIDI D'UN FAUNE)
  bk. Nijinsky; *mu.* Debussy; *sc.* Prélude à
  L'Après-midi d'un faune; *ch.* Nijinsky; *s.*
  Prince A. Schervachidze; *co.* Bakst; *p.* N.Y.
  Nov. 27, 1940, FFT; OBR
  —*ch.* Robbins; *co.* Irene Sharaff; *p.* N.Y.
  May 14, 1953, NYCC; NYCB

THE AFTERNOON OF A FAUN
  see also *L'Après-midi d'un faune*

THE AGE OF ANXIETY
  bk. based on poem by Auden; *mu.* Bernstein; *sc.* Symphony No. 2; *ch.* Robbins; *s.*
  Oliver Smith; *co.* Irene Sharaff; *w.p.* N.Y.
  Feb. 26, 1950, NYCC; NYCB

ALEKO
  bk. based on Pushkin's *Gypsies,* adapted by
  Massine; *mu.* Tchaikovsky; *sc.* Trio in A
  minor, orch. by Erno Rapee; *ch.* Massine;
  s. & co. Chagall; *w.p.* Mexico City, Sept. 8,
  1942, Palacio de Bellas Artes; BT; *a.p.* N.Y.
  Oct. 6, 1942, MOH; BT

L'AMOUR ET SON AMOUR (CUPID AND HIS LOVE)

bk. Jean Babilée; *mu.* Franck; *sc. Psyché; ch.* Babilée; *s. & co.* Cocteau; *w.p.* Paris, Dec. 13, 1948, TCE; Les Ballets des Champs-Elysées
—*a.p.* N.Y. Apr. 17, 1951, MOH; BT

ANCIENT RUSSIA

bk. Bronislava Nijinska; *mu.* Tchaikovsky; *sc.* Piano Concerto No. 1; *ch.* Nijinska; *s. & co.* Natalie Gontcharova; *w.p.* Cleveland, Ohio, Oct. 11, 1943, Music Hall; BRMC

APOLLO, LEADER OF THE MUSES (APOLLON MUSAGÈTE)

bk. Stravinsky; *mu.* Stravinsky; *ch.* Bolm; *s. & co.* Nicolas Remisoff; *w.p.* Washington, D.C., Apr. 27, 1928, Library of Congress Auditorium; Chamber Music Society
—*ch.* Balanchine; *s. & co.* André Bauchant; *w.p.* Paris, June 12, 1928, Théâtre Sarah Bernhardt; DBR
—*s.* Eugene Dunkel; *co.* Karinska; *a.p.* N.Y., Apr. 27, 1937, MOH; American Ballet; *p.* N.Y., Apr. 25, 1943, MOH; BT
—*p.* N.Y., Nov. 15, 1951, NYCC; NYCB

L'APRÈS-MIDI D'UN FAUNE (THE AFTERNOON OF A FAUN)

bk. Nijinsky; *mu.* Debussy; *sc. Prélude à L'Après-midi d'un faune; ch.* Nijinsky; *s. & co.* Bakst; *w.p.* Paris, May 29, 1912, TDC; DBR; *a.p.* N.Y., Jan. 18, 1916, CYT; DBR
—*s.* Prince A. Schervachidze; *co.* Bakst; *p.* N.Y., Nov. 1, 1936, MOH; DB
—*ch.* after Nijinsky; *s. & co.* after Bakst; *p.* Mexico City, Nov. 2, 1941, Palacio de Bellas Artes; BT; *p.* N.Y., Nov. 1, 1942, MOH; BT

L'APRÈS-MIDI D'UN FAUNE

see also *Afternoon of a Faun*

AURORA'S WEDDING
(LE MARIAGE D'AURORE) (PRINCESS AURORA)

mu. Tchaikovsky; *sc.* excerpts from *Sleeping Beauty; ch.* Nicholas Sergeyev, after Marius Petipa; *s. & co.* Bakst; *w.p.* Paris, May 18, 1922, Opéra; DBR
—*ch.* Marius Petipa; *s.* Bakst; *co.* Benois; *a.p.* N.Y., Mar. 21, 1935, M; DB
—*ch.* after M. Petipa; choreography for first variation and Three Ivans by Bronislava Nijinska; *s.* Bakst; *co.* Benois; *p.*

N.Y., Nov. 6, 1940, FFT; OBR
—*ch.* Anton Dolin, after Marius Petipa; *s. & co.* after Bakst;
p. Mexico City, Oct. 23, 1941, Palacio de Bellas Artes; BT;
p. N.Y., Nov. 26, 1941, FF BT

BACCHANALE
    bk. Dali; *mu.* Wagner; *sc.* Bacchanale from *Tannhäuser; ch.*
Massine; *s. & co.* Dali; *w.p.* N.Y., Nov. 9, 1939, MOH; BRMC

LE BAISER DE LA FÉE (THE FAIRY'S KISS)
    bk. Stravinsky, after Andersen; *mu.* Stravinsky; *ch.* Bronislava
Nijinska; *s. & co.* Benois; *w.p.* Paris, Nov. 27, 1928, Opéra; Ida
Rubinstein Ballet
    —*ch.* Balanchine; *s. & co.* Alice Halicka; *w.p.* N.Y., Apr. 27,
1937, MOH; American Ballet; *p.* N.Y., Apr. 10, 1940, MOH;
BRMC; *p.* N.Y., Nov. 28, 1950, NYCC; NYCB

THE BALL (LE BAL)
    bk. Massine and Boris Kochno; *mu.* Rieti; *ch.* Massine; *s. & co.*
Giorgio di Chirico; *w.p.* Monte Carlo, May 9, 1929, TMC;
DBR; *a.p.* N.Y. Mar. 20, 1935, M; DB

BALLADE
    mu. Debussy; *sc. Six épigraphes antiques; ch.* Robbins; *s. & co.*
Boris Aronson; *w.p.* N.Y., Feb. 14, 1952, NYCC; NYCB

BALLET IMPERIAL
    mu. Tchaikovsky; *sc.* Piano Concerto No. 2; *ch.* Balanchine;
s. & co. Mstislav Dobujinsky; *w.p.* N.Y., May 27, 1941, Hunter
College Playhouse; American Ballet; *p.* N.Y., Feb. 20, 1945,
NYCC; BRMC

BALLET SCHOOL (SCUOLA DI BALLO)
    bk. Massine, after Goldoni; *mu.* Boccherini; orch. by Françaix;
ch. Massine; *s. & co.* Count Étienne de Beaumont; *w.p.* Monte
Carlo, Apr. 25, 1933, TMC; DB; *a.p.* N.Y., Nov. 14, 1940, FFT;
OBR

BALLET SCHOOL
    see also *Scuola di Ballo*

BALUSTRADE
    mu. Stravinsky; *sc.* Concerto for Violin and Orchestra; *ch.*
Balanchine; *s. & co.* Tchelitchev; *w.p.* N.Y., Jan. 22, 1941, FFT;
OBR

BARN DANCE
>*bk*. Catherine Littlefield; *mu*. David Guion, John Powell, and Louis M. Gottschalk; *ch*. Littlefield; *s*. Angelo Pinto; *co*. Salvatore Pinto; *w.p*. Philadelphia, Apr. 23, 1937, Fox Theatre; Philadelphia Ballet
>—*s. & co*. Salvatore Pinto; *p*. N.Y., May 9, 1944, MOH; BT

BAYOU
>*mu*. Virgil Thomson; *sc. Acadian Songs and Dances; ch.* Balanchine; *s. & co*. Dorothea Tanning; *w.p*. N.Y., Feb. 21, 1952, NYCC; NYCB

BEACH
>*bk*. René Kerdyk; *mu*. Françaix; *ch*. Massine; *s. & co*. Raoul Dufy; *w.p*. Monte Carlo, 1933, TMC; DB; *a.p*. Jan. 2 1934, SJT; DB

LE BEAU DANUBE
>*bk*. Massine; *mu*. Johann Strauss; *sc*. arr. and orch. by Roger Désormière; *ch*. Massine; *s. & co*. Vladimir Polunin, after Constantin Guys; *w.p*. Monte Carlo, Apr. 15, 1933, TMC; DB; *a.p*. N.Y., Dec. 22, 1933, SJT; DB
>—*s. & co*. after Constantin Guys; *p*. Paris, Jan. 19, 1949; MCGB; *p*. N.Y., Nov. 8, 1950, CYT; MCGB

THE BELLS
>*bk*. Ruth Page, after Poe; *mu*. Milhaud; *ch*. Page; *s. & co*. Noguchi; *w.p*. Chicago, Ill., Apr. 26, 1946; Ruth Page-Bentley Stone Ballet; *p*. N.Y., Sept. 6, 1946, NYCC; BRMC

BELOVED
>*bk*. Benois; *mu*. selections from Schubert and Liszt; *sc*. arr. by Milhaud; *ch*. Bronislava Nijinska; *s. & co*. Benois; *w.p*. Paris, Nov. 22, 1928, Opéra; Ida Rubinstein Ballet
>—*bk*. Bronislava Nijinska; *s. & co*. Nicolas de Molas; *a.p*. N.Y., Nov. 13, 1941, FF; BT

LES BICHES
>*mu*. Poulenc; *ch*. Bronislava Nijinska; *s. & co*. Marie Laurencin; *w.p*. Monte Carlo, Jan. 6, 1924, TMC; DBR; *p*. Paris, Nov. 17, 1947; MCGB; *a.p*. N.Y., Nov. 13, 1950, CYT; MCGB

288

BILLY SUNDAY, OR GIVING THE DEVIL HIS DUE
> *bk.* Ruth Page, Remy Gassman, and J. Ray Hunt; *mu.* Gassman; *ch.* Pages; *s.* Herbert Andrews; *co.* Paul DuPont; *w.p.* Chicago, Dec. 13, 1946, Mandel Hall; Ruth Page Company; *p.* N.Y., Mar. 2, 1948, NYCC; BRMC

BILLY THE KID
> *bk.* Lincoln Kirstein; *mu.* Copland; *ch.* Eugene Loring; *s. & co.* Jared French; *w.p.* Chicago, Oct. 16, 1938, Chicago Civic Opera House; Ballet Caravan; *p.* Chicago, Dec. 8, 1940, Chicago Civic Opera House; BT

BIRTHDAY
> *bk.* Tatiana Chamie; *mu.* Rossini; *ch.* Chamie; *s.* Mstislav Dobujinsky; *co.* Karinska; *w.p.* N.Y. Sept. 27, 1949, MOH; BRMC

BLACK RITUAL
> *bk.* Agnes de Mille; *mu.* Milhaud; *sc. La Création du monde;* *ch.* de Mille; *s. & co.* Nicolas de Molas; *w.p.* N.Y. Jan. 22, 1940, CT; BT

BLUEBEARD
> *bk.* Fokine; *mu.* Offenbach; *sc.* arr. by Dorati; *ch.* Fokine; *s. & co.* Vertès; *w.p.* Mexico City, Oct. 27, 1941, Palacio de Bellas Artes; BT; *a.p.* N.Y., Nov. 12, 1941, FF; BT

THE BLUE DANUBE
> *mu.* Johann Strauss; *sc.* arr. and orch. by Eugene Fuerst; *ch.* Lifar; *s. & co.* Count Étienne de Beaumont, after Constantin Guys; *a.p.* N.Y., Oct. 4, 1946, MOH; OBR

BOGATYRI
> *bk.* Massine; *mu.* Borodin; *sc.* Symphony No. 2; *ch.* Massine; *s. & co.* Gontcharova; *w.p.* N.Y., Oct. 20, 1938, MOH; BRMC

BOLERO
> *mu.* Ravel; *ch.* Argentinita and Pilar López; *co.* Federico Rey; *w.p.* N.Y., Oct. 22, 1944, MOH; BT
> —*ch.* Bronislava Nijinska; *s.* Enrico Donati; *co.* Ignatiev; *a.p.* N.Y., Oct. 30, 1944, IT; BI

289

LE BOURGEOIS GENTILHOMME

mu. Richard Strauss; *ch.* Balanchine; *s. & co.* Eugene Berman; *w.p.* N.Y., Sept. 23, 1944, NYCC; BRMC

BOURRÉE FANTASQUE

mu. Chabrier; *sc. Marche joyeuse, Bourrée fantasque, Fête Polonaise,* Interlude from *Gwendolyn; ch.* Balanchine; *co.* Karinska; *w.p.* N.Y., Dec. 1, 1949, NYCC; NYCB

LA BOUTIQUE FANTASQUE (THE FANTASTIC TOY SHOP)

bk. André Derain; *mu.* Rossini; *sc.* arr. and orch. by Respighi; *ch.* Massine; *s. & co.* Derain; *w.p.* London, June 5, 1919, Alhambra Theatre; DBR; *a.p.* N.Y., Mar. 20, 1935, M; DB; *p.* Omaha, Jan. 4, 1943, Central High School Auditorium; BT

BRAHMS VARIATIONS

bk. Bronislava Nijinska; *mu.* Brahms; *sc. Handel* and *Paganini Variations,* orch. by Ivan Boutnikov; *ch.* Nijinska; *s. & co.* Vertès; *w.p.* N.Y., Oct. 30, 1944, IT; BI

THE CAGE

mu. Stravinsky; *sc.* Concerto in D for String Orchestra; *ch.* Robbins; *s.,* Jean Rosenthal; *co.* Ruth Sobotka; *w.p.* N.Y., June 14, 1951, NYCC; NYCB

CAIN AND ABEL

bk. Lichine; *mu.* Wagner; *sc.* arr. by William McDermott; *ch.* Lichine; *s. & co.* Miguel Prieto; *w.p.* Mexico City, Feb., 1946, Palacio de Bellas Artes, *p.* N.Y., Oct. 2, 1946, MOH; OBR

CAKEWALK

mu. Louis Moreau Gottschalk; *sc.* arr. and orch. by Hershy Kay; *ch.* Ruthanna Boris; *s. & co.* Robert Drew; *w.p.* N.Y., June 12, 1951, NYCC; NYCB

CAMILLE

bk. John Taras, after Alexandre Dumas, fils; *mu.* Schubert; *sc.* orch. by Rieti; *ch.* John Taras; *s. & co.* Cecil Beaton; *w.p.* N.Y., Oct. 1, 1946, MOH; OBR

CAPITAL OF THE WORLD

bk. Eugene Loring and A. D. Hotchner, based on story by Hemingway; *mu.* Antheil; *ch.* Loring; *s. & co.* Esteban Francés; *w.p.* N.Y., Dec. 27, 1953, MOH; BT

CAPRICCIO BRILLANT
mu. Mendelssohn; *ch.* Balanchine; *co.* Karinska; *w.p.* N.Y., June 7, 1951, NYCC; NYCB

CAPRICCIO ESPAGNOL
bk. Massine; *mu.* Rimsky-Korsakov; *ch.* Massine; *s. & co.* Mariano Andreù; *w.p.* Monte Carlo, May 4, 1939, TMC; BRMC; *a.p.* N.Y., Oct. 27, 1939, MOH; BRMC
—*ch.* Massine, in collaboration with Argentinita; *p.* San Francisco, Jan. 28, 1943, War Memorial Opera House; BT

CAPRICCIOSO
mu. Cimarosa; *sc.* orch. by Malpiero and Rieti; later by Paul Bowles; *ch.* Dolin; *s. & co.* Nicolas de Molas; *w.p.* Chicago, Nov. 3, 1940, Chicago Civic Opera House; BT

CAPRICHOS
bk. based on Goya's commentaries to *Caprichos* etchings; *mu.* Bartók; *sc.* Contrasts for Piano, Violin and Clarinet; *ch.* Herbert Ross; *co.* Helene Pons; *w.p.* N.Y., Jan. 29, 1950, Hunter College Playhouse; Choreographer's Workshop; *p.* N.Y., Apr. 26, 1950, CT; BT

CARACOLE
mu. Mozart; *sc.* Divertimento No. 15 in B flat Major, K. 287; *ch.* Balanchine; *co.* Bérard; *w.p.* N.Y., Feb. 19, 1952, NYCC; NYCB

CARD PARTY (JEU DE CARTES) (POKER GAME)
bk. Stravinsky and M. Malaieff; *mu.* Stravinsky; *ch.* Balanchine; *s. & co.* Irene Sharaff; *w.p.* N.Y., Apr. 27, 1937, MOH; American Ballet; *p.* N.Y., Feb. 15, 1951, NYCC; NYCB

CARD PARTY
see also *Poker Game*

CARNAVAL
bk. Fokine; *mu.* Schumann; *sc.* orch. by Rimsky-Korsakov, Glazunov, Lyadov, and Tcherepnin; *ch.* Fokine; *s. & co.* Bakst; *w.p.* St. Petersburg, 1910, Pavlova Hall; *a.p.* N.Y., Jan. 19, 1916, CYT; DBR
—*ch.* after Fokine; *s. & co.* Bakst; *p.* N.Y., Mar. 16, 1934, SJT; DB; *p.* N.Y., Nov. 28, 1940, FFT; OBR

The New Borzoi Book of Ballets

—*sc.* orch. by Konstantinov; *ch.* Fokine; *co.* traditional, after Bakst; *p.* N.Y., Jan. 13, 1940, CT; BT

LES CENT BAISERS see *The Hundred Kisses*

CHILDREN'S GAMES
> *bk.* Boris Kochno; *mu.* Bizet; *sc. Jeux d'enfants; ch.* Massine; *s. & co.* Joan Miró; *p.* N.Y., Jan. 4, 1941, FFT; OBR

CHILDREN'S GAMES see also *Jeux d'enfants*

CHOPIN CONCERTO
> *mu.* Chopin; *sc.* Concerto for Piano and Orchesta No. 1; *ch.* Bronislava Nijinska; *s. & co.* Ignatiev; *w.p.* World's Fair Grounds, N.Y., June 6, 1939, Hall of Music; Dancers From Poland (the ballet on this occasion was named Concerto in E minor); *p.* N.Y., Oct. 12, 1942, MOH; BRMC

CHOREARTEUM
> *mu.* Brahms; *sc.* Symphony No. 4; *ch.* Massine; *s. & co.* Constantine Terechkovich and Eugene Lourie; *w.p.* London, Oct. 24, 1933, Alhambra Theatre; DB; *a.p.* N.Y., Oct. 16, 1935, MOH; DB; *p.* N.Y., Nov. 28, 1940, FFT; OBR

CIMAROSIANA
> *mu.* Cimarosa; *ch.* Massine; *s. & co.* José María Sert; *w.p.* London, 1920, CG; DBR; *a.p.* N.Y., Nov. 4, 1936, MOH; DB; *p.* N.Y., Nov. 27, 1940, FFT; OBR

CINDERELLA
> *bk.* after Perrault's fairy tale; *mu.* Frédéric d'Erlanger; *ch.* Fokine; *s. & co.* Natalie Gontcharova; *w.p.* London, July 19, 1938, CG; OBR; *a.p.* Los Angeles, Oct. 16, 1940, Philharmonic Auditorium; OBR

CIRCO DE ESPAÑA (SPANISH CIRCUS)
> *bk.* Carmelita Maracci; *mu.* Falla, Albanese, Turina, and Granados; *ch.* Maracci; *s. & co.* Rico Lebrun; *w.p.* N.Y., Apr. 18, 1951, MOH; BT

CIRQUE DE DEUX
> *bk.* Ruthanna Boris; *mu.* Gounod; *sc. Valpurgisnacht* from *Faust; s. & co.* Robert Davison; *w.p.* N.Y., Sept. 10, 1947, NYCC; BRMC

THE COMBAT
> *bk.* based on the tale of Clorinda and Tancred from Book XII

of Tasso's *Gerusalemme liberata; mu.* Raffaello de Banfield; *ch.* William Dollar; *s. & co.* Georges Wakhevitch; *w.p.* London, July 23, 1953; CG; BT; *a.p.* Plainfield, N.J., Dec. 30, 1953, Oxford Theatre; BT

COMEDIA BALLETICA (MUSICAL CHAIRS)

mu. Stravinsky; *sc.* Suite from *Pulcinella; ch.* Todd Bolender; *s. & co.* Robert Davison; *w.p.* N.Y., Sept. 17, 1945, NYCC; BRMC

CON AMORE

bk. James Graham-Luhan; *mu.* Rossini; *ch.* Lew Christensen; *s. & co.* James Bodrero; *w.p.* San Francisco, Mar. 10, 1953, War Memorial Opera House; San Francisco Ballet; *p.* N.Y., June 9, 1953, NYCC; NYCB
—*co.* Esteban Francés; *p.* N.Y., Mar. 9, 1954, NYCC; NYCB

CONCERTINO

mu. Françaix; *ch.* Balanchine; *co.* Karinska; *w.p.* N.Y., Dec. 30, 1952, NYCC; NYCB

CONCERTO BAROCCO

mu. Johann Sebastian Bach; *sc.* Concerto for Two Violins in D minor; *ch.* Balanchine; *s. & co.* Eugene Berman; *w.p.* N.Y., May 29, 1941, Hunter College Playhouse; American Ballet
—*p.* N.Y., Sept. 9, 1945, NYCC; BRMC
—*s. & co.* after sketches by Eugene Berman (present production does not use sets or costumes); *p.* N.Y., Oct. 11, 1948, NYCC; NYCB
—*p.* London, Aug. 5, 1948, CG; MCGB; *p.* N.Y., Nov. 2, 1950, CYT; MCGB

CONCERTO IN E MINOR see *Chopin Concerto*

LA CONCURRENCE (COMPETITION)

bk. André Derain; *mu.* Auric; *ch.* Balanchine; *s. & co.* Derain; *w.p.* Monte Carlo, 1932, TMC; DB; *a.p.* N.Y., Dec. 22, 1933, SJT; DB

CONSTANTIA

mu. Chopin; *sc.* Concerto for Piano and Orchestra No. 2; *ch.* William Dollar; *s.* Horace Armistead; *co.* Grace Houston;

w.p. N.Y., Oct. 31, 1944, IT; BI; *p.* N.Y., Oct. 16, 1946, MOH; OBR
> —*s. & co.* Robert Davison; *p.* N.Y., Apr. 9, 1951, MOH; BT

COPPÉLIA

bk. Arthur Saint-Léon and Charles Nuitter, after a story by E. T. A. Hoffmann; *mu.* Delibes; *ch.* Arthur Saint-Léon; *s.* Cambon, Desplechin and Lavastre; *w.p.* Paris, May 25, 1870, Opéra
> —*a.p.* N.Y., Mar. 11, 1877, MOH
> —*ch.* Nicholas Sergeyev, after Petipa; *s. & co.* Pierre Roy; *p.* N.Y., Oct. 17, 1938, MOH; BRMC
> —*ch.* Simon Semenoff, after Louis François Merante; *s. & co.* Roberto Montenegro; *p.* Mexico City, Sept. 1, 1942, Palacio de Bellas Artes; BT; *p.* N.Y., Oct. 22, 1942, MOH; BT

LE COQ D'OR (OPERA BALLET)

bk. Bielsky, revised by Benois; *mu.* Rimsky-Korsakov; *ch.* Fokine; *s. & co.* Natalie Gontcharova; *w.p.* Paris, May 21, 1914, Opéra; DBR
> —*bk.* Fokine; *w.p.* London, 1937, CG; DB; *a.p.* N.Y., Oct. 23, 1937, MOH; DB
> —*bk.* after Bielsky and Pushkin; *p.* N.Y., Nov. 6, 1940, FFT; OBR

COTILLON

bk. Boris Kochno; *mu.* Chabrier; *sc.* orch. by Chabrier, Mottl, and Rieti; *ch.* Balanchine; *s. & co.* Bérard; *w.p.* Monte Carlo, Apr. 12, 1932, TMC; DB; *a.p.* N.Y., Mar. 16, 1934, SJT; DB; *p.* N.Y., Nov. 15, 1940, FFT; OBR

THE CUCKOLD'S FAIR

bk. Garcia Lorca and Rivas-Cherif; *mu* Gustavo Pittaluga; *ch.* Pilar Lopez; *s. & co.* Joan Junyer; *w.p.* Cleveland, Oct. 9, 1943; BRMC

LA DAME ET LA LICORNE

bk. Cocteau; *mu.* 15th and 16th Century songs; *sc.* arr. by Jacques Chailly; *ch.* Heinz Rosen; *s. & co.* Cocteau; *w.p.* Munich, May 1953
> —*p.* Toronto, Oct. 14, 1955, Royal Alexandra Theatre; BRMC; *a.p.* Baltimore, Oct. 19, 1955, Lyric Theatre; BRMC

DANSES CONCERTANTES
   mu. Stravinsky; *ch.* Balanchine; *s. & co.* Eugene Berman; *w.p.*
   N.Y., Sept. 10, 1944, NYCC; BRMC

DANSES SLAVES ET TZIGANES
   mu. Alexander Dargomijsky; *sc.* from *Russalka; ch.* Bronislava
   Nijinska; *s.* S. Soudeikine; *co.* C. Korovine; *a.p.* N.Y., Apr. 17,
   1936, MOH; DB

DARK ELEGIES
   bk. Tudor; *mu.* Mahler; *sc.* *Kindertotenlieder; ch.* Tudor;
   s. & co. Raymond Sovey, after sketches by Nadia Benois; *w.p.*
   London, Feb. 19, 1937, Dutchess Theatre; Ballet Rambert;
   a.p. N.Y., Jan. 24, 1940, CT; BT

DEATH AND THE MAIDEN
   bk. Andrée Howard; *mu.* Schubert; *ch.* Howard; *w.p.* London,
   Feb. 23, 1937, Dutchess Theatre; Ballet Rambert; *a.p.* N.Y.,
   Jan. 18, 1940, CT; BT

DEL AMOR Y DE LA MUERTE (OF LOVE AND DEATH)
   bk. adapted from a story by Alijambro del Campo Finistere;
   mu. Granados; *sc.* excerpts from *Goyescas,* arr. by Ernest Schel-
   ling; *ch.* Ana Ricarda; *s. & co.* Celia Hubbard; *w.p.* Monte
   Carlo, Apr. 28, 1949, TMC; MCGB; *a.p.* N.Y., Nov. 1, 1950,
   CYT; MCGB

LES DEMOISELLES DE LA NUIT
   bk. Roland Petit, from a scenario by Jean Anouilh; *mu.*
   Françaix; *ch.* Petit; *s. & co.* Léonor Fini; *w.p.* Paris, May 21,
   1948, Théâtre Marigny; Les Ballets de Paris; *a.p.* N.Y., Apr. 13,
   1951, MOH; BT

DESIGNS WITH STRINGS
   mu. Tchaikovsky; *sc.* second movement of Trio in A minor arr.
   for piano and strings; *ch.* John Taras; *w.p.* Wimbledon, England, Feb. 6, 1948; Metropolitan Ballet
      —*co.* Irene Sharaff; *a.p.* N.Y., Apr. 25, 1950, CT; BT
      —*co.* Jean Robier; *p.* Monte Carlo, Jan. 18, 1949, TMC;
   MCGB; *p.* N.Y., Nov. 1, 1950, CYT; MCGB

DESTINY
   bk. Massine; *mu.* Tchaikovsky; *sc.* Symphony No. 5; *ch.* Massine; *s. & co.* André Masson; *p.* N.Y., Nov. 30, 1940, FFT; OBR

DESTINY

see also *Les Présages*

DEVIL'S HOLIDAY

bk. Vincenzo Tommasini; *mu*. Tommasini; *sc*. based on themes by Paganini; *ch*. Frederick Ashton; *s. & co*. Eugene Berman; *w.p*. N.Y., Oct. 26, 1939, MOH; BRMC

LES DIEUX MENDIANTS (*THE GODS GO A-BEGGING*)

bk. Sobeka; *mu*. Handel; *sc*. selected and orch. by Beecham; *ch*. Balanchine; *s*. Bakst; *co*. Juan Gris; *w.p*. London, July 16, 1928, His Majesty's Theatre; DBR; *a.p*. N.Y., Oct. 28, 1937, MOH; DB

DIM LUSTRE

bk. Tudor; *mu* Richard Strauss; *sc. Burleske* for Piano and Orchestra; *ch*. Tudor; *s. & co*. Motley; *w.p*. N.Y., Oct. 20, 1943, MOH; BT

DIVERTIMENTO

mu. Alexei Haieff; *ch*. Balanchine; *w.p*. N.Y., Jan. 13, 1947, Hunter College Auditorium; Ballet Society; *p*. N.Y., Nov. 2, 1948, NYCC; NYCB

DIVERTISSEMENT

mu. Tchaikovsky; *sc*. Eight excerpts from *The Sleeping Beauty;* *ch*. John Taras, after Petipa; Dance of the Three Ivans by Bronislava Nijinska; *s. & co*. André Delfau; *w.p*. Monte Carlo, Apr. 11, 1950, TMC; MCGB; *a.p*. N.Y., Oct. 30, 1950, CYT; MCGB

DON DOMINGO

bk. Alfonso Reyes; *mu*. Silvestre Revueltas; *ch*. Massine; *s. & co*. Julio Castellanos; *w.p*. Mexico City, Sept. 16, 1942, Palacio de Bellas Artes; BT; *a.p*. N.Y., Oct. 9, 1942, MOH; BT

DON JUAN

bk. Eric Allatini and Fokine, after G. Angiolini; *mu*. Gluck; *ch*. Fokine; *s. & co*. Mariano Andreù; *w.p*. London, June 25, 1936, Alhambra Theatre; René Blum's Ballet Russe; *a.p*. N.Y., Oct. 22, 1938; MOH; BRMC

THE DUEL

bk. based on the tale of Clorinda and Tancred from Book XII of Tasso's *Gerusalemme liberata; mu*. Raffaello de Banfield;

296

ch. William Dollar; *co*. Robert Stevenson; *w.p*. N.Y., Feb. 24, 1950, NYCC; NYCB

LES ELFES (THE ELVES)
bk. Fokine; *mu*. Mendelssohn; *sc*. excerpts from *A Midsummer Night's Dream,* and Andante and Allegro from Concerto for Violin; *ch*. Fokine; *s. & co*. Bérard; *w.p*. N.Y., Feb. 26, 1924, MOH; Fokine Ballet; *p*. N.Y., Mar. 22, 1939, MOH; BRMC

THE ENCHANTED MILL
bk. Leandre Vaillet and Lichine; *mu*. Schubert; *sc*. arr. by Gustave Cloez; *ch*. Lichine; *s. & co*. Benois; *w.p*. July 14, 1949, CG; MCGB; *a.p*. N.Y., Nov. 14, 1950, CYT; MCGB

ENSAYO SINFONICO
mu. Brahms; *sc*. *Variations on a Theme by Haydn; ch*. Alicia Alonso; *co*. Irene Sharaff; *w.p*. N.Y., Apr. 19, 1951, MOH; BT

L'EPREUVE D'AMOUR,
OR CHUNG-YANG AND THE MANDARIN
bk. André Derain and Fokine; *mu* attributed to Mozart; *ch*. Fokine; *s. & co*. Derain; *w.p*. Monte Carlo, Apr. 4, 1936, TMC; BRMC; *ap*. N.Y., Oct. 14, 1938, MOH; BRMC

ETERNAL STRUGGLE (LUTTE ETERNELLE)
bk. Igor Schwezoff; *mu*. Schumann; *sc*. *Études Symphoniques,* orch. by Dorati; *ch*. Schwezoff; *s. & co*. Kathleen and Florence Martin; *w.p*. Sydney, Australia, July 29, 1940, Theatre Royal, OBR; *a.p*. Los Angeles, Oct. 15, 1940, Philharmonic Auditorium; OBR

ÉTUDE
mu. Johann Sebastian Bach; *ch*. Bronislava Nijinska; *s. & co*. Boris Belinsky; *w.p*. Cleveland, Ohio, Oct. 9, 1943, Music Hall; BRMC

FACSIMILE
mu. Bernstein; *ch*. Robbins; *s*. Oliver Smith; *co*. Irene Sharaff; *w.p*. N.Y., Oct. 24, 1946, BYT; BT

THE FAIR AT SOROCHINSK
bk. Lichine, after Gogol; *mu*. Mussorgsky; *sc*. *A Night On Bald Mountain; ch*. Lichine; *s. & co*. Nicolas Remisoff; *w.p*. N.Y., Oct. 14, 1943, MOH; BT

THE FAIRY'S KISS
see *Le Baiser de la fée*

FALL RIVER LEGEND
bk. Agnes de Mille; *mu.* Morton Gould; *ch.* de Mille; *s.* Oliver Smith; *co.* Miles White; *w.p.* N.Y., Apr. 22, 1948, MOH; BT

FANCY FREE
bk. Robbins; *mu.* Bernstein; *ch.* Robbins; *s.* Oliver Smith; *co.* Kermit Love; *w.p.* N.Y., Apr. 18, 1944, MOH; BT

FANFARE
mu. Benjamin Britten; *sc. The Young Person's Guide to the Orchestra; ch.* Robbins; *co.* Irene Sharaff; *w.p.* N.Y., June 2, 1953, NYCC; NYCB

LES FEMMES DE BONNE-HUMEUR
bk. after Goldoni; *mu.* Domenico Scarlatti; *sc.* arr. by Vincenzo Tommasini; *ch.* Massine; *s. & co.* Bakst; *w.p.* Rome, Apr. 12, 1917, Teatro Constanza; DBR; *a.p.* N.Y., Oct. 15, 1935, MOH; DB

LES FEMMES DE BONNE-HUMEUR
see also *The Good-Humored Ladies*

LA FILLE MAL GARDÉE
bk. Dauberval; *mu.* Wilhelm Hertel; *ch.* Dauberval; *w.p.* Bordeaux, 1786; *a.p.* N.Y., July 6, 1839, Park Theatre
—*bk.* Dauberval and Bronislava Nijinska; *ch.* Nijinska; *s. & co.* Sergei Soudeikine; *w.p.* N.Y., Jan. 19, 1940, CT; BT

FILLING STATION
bk. Lincoln Kirstein; *mu.* Virgil Thomson; *ch.* Lew Christensen; *s. & co.* Paul Cadmus; *w.p.* Hartford, Conn., Jan. 6, 1938, Avery Memorial Theatre; Ballet Caravan; *p.* N.Y., May 12, 1953, NYCC; NYCB

THE FILLY (OR A STABLEBOY'S DREAM)
mu. John Colman; *ch.* Todd Bolender; *s. & co.* Peter Larkin; *w.p.* N.Y., May 19, 1953, NYCC; NYCB

LE FILS PRODIGUE
see *The Prodigal Son*

THE FIREBIRD
> *bk.* Fokine; *mu.* Stravinsky; *ch.* Fokine; *s. & co.* Natalie Gontcharova; *p.* N.Y., Dec. 6, 1940, FFT; OBR
>> —*ch.* Bolm; *s. & co.* Chagall; *p.* N.Y., Oct. 24, 1945, MOH; BT
>> —*bk.* Balanchine and Stravinsky; *ch.* Balanchine; *s. & co.* Chagall; *p.* N.Y., Nov. 27, 1949, NYCC; NYCB

THE FIREBIRD
> see also *L'Oiseau de feu*

THE FIVE GIFTS, OR FIVE BOONS OF LIFE
> *bk.* based on Mark Twain's fable; *mu.* Dohnányi; *sc. Variations on a Nursery Theme; ch.* William Dollar; *co.* Esteban Francés; *w.p.* N.Y., Nov. 14, 1943, Kaufmann Auditorium; American Concert Ballet; *p.* N.Y., Jan. 20, 1953, NYCC; NYCB

THE FOUR TEMPERAMENTS
> *mu.* Hindemith; *sc.* Theme and Four Variations for String Orchestra and Piano; *ch.* Balanchine; *s. & co.* Kurt Seligmann (present production does not use sets or costumes); *w.p.* N.Y., Nov. 20, 1946, Central High School of Needle Trades Auditorium; Ballet Society; *p.* N.Y., Oct. 25, 1948, NYCC; NYCB

À LA FRANÇAIX
> *mu.* Françaix; *sc.* Serenade for Small Orchestra; *ch.* Balanchine; *w.p.* N.Y., Sept. 11, 1951, NYCC; NYCB

FRANCESCA DA RIMINI
> *bk.* Lichine and Henry Clifford; *mu.* Tchaikovsky; *ch.* Lichine; *s. & co.* Oliver Messel; *w.p.* London, July 15, 1937, CG; DB; *a.p.* N.Y., Oct. 24, 1937, MOH; DB; *p.* N.Y., Jan. 4, 1941, FFT; OBR

FRANKIE AND JOHNNY
> *bk.* Michael Blandford and Jerome Moross; *mu.* Moross; *ch.* Ruth Page and Bentley Stone; *s. & co.* Paul DuPont; *w.p.* Chicago, June 19, 1938, Great Northern Theatre; Ruth Page and Bentley Stone Company
>> —*s.* Clive Rickabaugh; *co.* after designs by Paul DuPont; *p.* N.Y., Feb. 28, 1945, NYCC; BRMC

GAÎTÉ PARISIENNE
> *bk.* Count Étienne de Beaumont; *mu.* Offenbach; *sc.* arr. and orch. by Manuel Rosenthal; *ch.* Massine; *s. & co.* de Beaumont;

w.p. Monte Carlo, Apr. 5, 1938, TMC; BRMC; *a.p.* N.Y., Oct. 12, 1938, MOH; BRMC

GALA PERFORMANCE

bk. Tudor; *mu.* Prokofiev; *sc.* First movement of Concerto for Piano and Orchestra No. 3, and *Classical Symphony; ch.* Tudor; *s. & co.* Hugh Stevenson; *w.p.* London, Dec. 5, 1938, Toynbee Hall Theatre; London Ballet

—*s. & co.* Nicolas de Molas; *a.p.* N.Y., Feb. 11, 1941, M; BT

GHOST TOWN

bk. Marc Platoff and Richard Rodgers, based on historical research by Gerald Murphy; *mu.* Rodgers; *ch.* Platoff; *s. & co.* Raoul Pène du Bois; *w.p.* N.Y., Nov. 12, 1939, MOH; BRMC

GIFT OF THE MAGI

bk. Simon Semenoff, based on the story by O. Henry; *mu.* Lukas Foss; *ch.* Semenoff; *s. & co.* Raoul Pène du Bois; *w.p.* Boston, Oct. 5, 1945, Boston Opera House; BT

GISELLE

bk. Saint-Georges and Théophile Gautier; *mu.* Adolphe Adam; *ch.* Jean Coralli and Jules Perrot; *s.* Pierre Cicéri; *co.* Paul Lormier; *w.p.* Paris, June 28, 1841, Théâtre de l'Academie Royale de Musique; *a.p.* Boston, Jan. 1, 1846, Howard Athenaeum

—*ch.* re-staged by Serge Lifar; *s. & co.* after Benois; *p.* N.Y., Oct. 12, 1938, MOH; BRMC

—*sc.* orch. by Eugene Fuerst; *ch.* Anton Dolin, after Jean Coralli; *s. & co.* Lucinda Ballard; *p.* N.Y., Jan. 12, 1940, CT; BT

—*bk.* Saint-Georges, Théophile Gautier, and Coralli; *ch.* after Marius Petipa; *s.* after Benois; *co.* Jean Robier; *p.* N.Y., Nov. 3, 1950, CYT; MCGB

LA GLOIRE

mu. Beethoven; *sc. Egmont, Coriolanus, Leonore III* Overtures; *ch.* Tudor; *s.* Gaston Longchamp; *co.* Robert Fletcher; *w.p.* N.Y., Feb. 26, 1952, NYCC; NYCB

THE GODS GO A-BEGGING

see *Les Dieux mendiants*

THE GOOD-HUMORED LADIES

    bk. after Goldoni; *mu.* Domenico Scarlatti; *sc.* arr. by Vincenzo Tommasini; *ch.* Massine; *s. & co.* Bakst; *a.p.* N.Y., Dec. 9, 1940, FFT; OBR

        —*s. & co.* Derain; *p.* London, July 17, 1949, CG; MCGB; *p.* N.Y., Nov. 9, 1950, CYT; MCGB

THE GOOD-HUMORED LADIES

    see also *Les Femmes de bonne-humeur*

GOYESCAS

    bk. Alden Jenkins; *mu.* Granados; *sc. Prélude, Añoranza, Ecos, Fandango, Intermezzo,* and *Zapateado* from a set of piano pieces, later a three-act opera; *ch.* José Fernández; *s. & co.* Nicolas de Molas; *w.p.* N.Y., Jan. 15, 1940, CT; BT

        —*bk.* Nicolas de Molas; *sc.* orch. by Harold Byrns; *ch.* Tudor; *p.* N.Y., Feb. 13, 1941, M; BT

        —*ch.* Argentinita; *p.* Mexico City, Nov. 2, 1941, Palacio de Bellas Artes; BT

GRADUATION BALL

    bk. Lichine; *mu.* Johann Strauss; *sc.* arr. and orch. by Antal Dorati; *ch.* Lichine; *s. & co.* Benois; *w.p.* Sydney, Australia, Feb. 28, 1940, Royal Theatre; OBR; *a.p.* Los Angeles, Oct. 10, 1940, Philharmonic Auditorium; OBR

        —*s. & co.* Mstislav Dobujinsky; *p.* Montreal, Sept. 26, 1944, His Majesty's Theatre; BT; *p.* N.Y., Oct. 8, 1944, MOH; BT

GRAZIANA

    mu. Mozart; *sc.* Violin Concerto in G (K. 216); *ch.* John Taras; *co.* Alvin Colt; *w.p.* N.Y., Oct. 25, 1945, MOH; BT

THE GREAT AMERICAN GOOF

    bk. William Saroyan; *mu.* Henry Brant; *ch.* Eugene Loring; *s. & co.* Boris Aronson; *w.p.* N.Y., Jan. 11, 1940, CT; BT

THE GUESTS

    mu. Marc Blitzstein; *ch.* Robbins; *w.p.* N.Y., Jan. 20, 1949, NYCC; NYCB

HARLEQUINADE PAS DE DEUX

    mu. Richard Drigo; *ch.* Balanchine; *co.* Karinska; *w.p.* N.Y., Dec. 6, 1952, NYCC; NYCB

HAROLD IN ITALY

mu. Berlioz; *sc.* orch. and arr. by Ivan Boutnikov; *ch.* Massine; *s. & co.* Bernard Lamotte; *w.p.* Boston, Oct. 14, 1954, Boston Opera House; BRMC

THE HARVEST ACCORDING

bk. Agnes de Mille; *mu.* Virgil Thomson; *sc.* excerpts from *Symphony on a Hymn Tune, Mother of Us All,* and Cello Concerto; *ch.* de Mille; *s. & co.* Lemuel Ayers; *w.p.* N.Y., Oct. 1, 1952, MOH; BT

HARVEST TIME

bk. Bronislava Nijinska; *mu.* Wieniawski; *sc.* arr. by Dorati; *ch.* Nijinska; *co.* Enid Gilbert; *w.p.* N.Y., Apr. 5, 1945, MOH; BT

HELEN OF TROY

bk. Fokine; *mu.* Offenbach; *sc.* arr. and orch. by Dorati; *ch.* Fokine; *s. & co.* Vertès; *w.p.* Mexico City, Sept. 10, 1942, Palacio de Bellas Artes; BT

    —*bk.* Lichine and Dorati; *ch.* Lichine; *s. & co.* Vertès; *w.p.* Detroit, Nov. 29, 1942, Masonic Auditorium; BT

THE HUNDRED KISSES (LES CENT BAISERS)

bk. Boris Kochno, after fairy tale by Andersen; *mu.* Frédéric d'Erlanger; *ch.* Bronislava Nijinska; *s. & co.* Jean Hugo; *w.p.* London, July 18, 1935, CG; DB; *a.p.* N.Y., Oct. 18, 1935, MOH; DB; *p.* N.Y., Nov. 8, 1940, FFT; OBR

ICARE

bk. Lifar; *mu.* Lifar; *sc.* percussion arr. of Lifar rhythms by J. E. Szyfer; *ch.* Lifar; *s. & co.* Paul-René Larthe; *w.p.* Paris, July 9, 1935, Opéra; Paris Opéra Ballet

    —*s. & co.* Berman; *a.p.* N.Y., Oct. 21, 1938, MOH; BRMC

IGROUCHKA (THE RUSSIAN TOY)

bk. Fokine; *mu* Rimsky-Korsakov; *sc. Fantasy on Russian Themes,* Op. 33; *ch.* Fokine; *s. & co.* Natalie Gontcharova; *a.p.* N.Y., Oct. 31, 1939, MOH; BRMC

ILLUMINATIONS

bk. based on a poem by Arthur Rimbaud; *mu.* Benjamin Britten; *sc. Les Illuminations* for Tenor and Strings; *ch.* Frederick Ashton; *s. & co.* Cecil Beaton; *w.p.* N.Y., Mar. 2, 1950, NYCC; NYCB

INTERPLAY
> *mu.* Morton Gould; *sc. American Concertette; ch.* Robbins; *w.p.* N.Y., June 1, 1945, Ziegfeld Theatre; Billy Rose's Concert Varieties
> —*s.* Oliver Smith; *co.* Irene Sharaff; *p.* N.Y., Oct. 17, 1945, MOH; BT
> —*p.* N.Y., Dec. 23, 1952, NYCC; NYCB

ITALIAN SUITE
> *mu.* Cimarosa; *ch.* Anton Dolin; *co.* Nicolas de Molas; *w.p.* Philadelphia, July 15, 1940, Robin Hood Dell; BT

IVESIANA
> *mu.* Charles Ives; *sc. Central Park in the Dark; Hallowe'en; The Unanswered Question; Over the Pavements; In the Inn,* and *In the Night; ch.* Balanchine; *w.p.* N.Y., Sept. 14, 1954, NYCC; NYCB. Note: *Barn Dance* has replaced *Hallowe'en* as second movement of current production.

JARDIN AUX LILAS
> *bk.* Tudor; *mu.* Chausson; *sc. Poème; ch.* Tudor; *s. & co.* Raymond Sovey; *w.p.* London, Jan. 26, 1936, Mercury Theatre; Ballet Rambert; *a.p.* N.Y., Jan. 15, 1940, CT; BT

JARDIN AUX LILAS
> see also *Lilac Garden*

JARDIN PUBLIC
> *bk.* Vladimir Dukelsky and Massine, based on a fragment from André Gide's *The Counterfeiters; mu.* Dukelsky; *ch.* Massine; *s.* Gaston Longchamp; *co.* Jean Lurcat; *w.p.* Chicago, Mar. 1935, DB

JEU DE CARTES
> see *Card Party*

LE JEUNE HOMME ET LA MORT
> *bk.* Cocteau; *mu.* Johann Sebastian Bach; *sc.* Passacaglia in C minor, orch. by A. Goedicke; *ch.* Roland Petit; *s. & co.* Georges Wakhevitch; *w.p.* Paris, June 25, 1946, TCE; Ballets des Champs-Elysées
> —*sc.* orch. Respighi; *a.p.* N.Y., Apr. 9, 1951, MOH; BT

303

JEUX
> *bk.* Nijinsky; *mu.* Debussy; *ch.* Nijinsky; *s. & co.* Bakst; *w.p.* Paris, May 15, 1913, TCE; DBR
>> —*ch.* William Dollar; *s. & co.* David Ffolkes; *w.p.* N.Y., Apr. 13, 1950, CT; BT

JEUX D'ENFANTS
> *bk.* Boris Kochno; *mu.* Bizet; *ch.* Massine; *s. & co.* Joan Miro; *w.p.* Monte Carlo, Apr. 4, 1933, TMC; DB; *a.p.* N.Y., Dec. 6, 1933, SJT; DB
>> —*ch.* Balanchine; *s. & co.* Esteban Francés; *p.* N.Y., Nov. 22, 1955, NYCC; NYCB

JEUX D'ENFANTS
> see also *Children's Games*

JINX
> *bk.* Lew Christensen; *mu* Benjamin Britten; *sc. Variations on a Theme by Frank Bridge; ch.* Christensen; *s. & co.* George Bockman; *w.p.* Schenectady, N.Y., April 9, 1942, Erie Theatre; Dance Players; *p.* N.Y., Nov. 24, 1949, NYCC; NYCB

JONES BEACH
> *mu.* Juriaan Andriessen; *sc. Berkshire Symphonies; ch.* Balanchine and Robbins; *w.p.* N.Y., Mar. 9, 1950, NYCC; NYCB

THE JUDGMENT OF PARIS
> *bk.* Hugh Laing; *mu.* Kurt Weill; *sc.* excerpts from *Die Dreigroschenoper; ch.* Tudor; *co.* Lucinda Ballard; *w.p.* London, June 15, 1938, Westminster Theatre; Ballet Club; *a.p.* N.Y., Jan. 23, 1940, CT; BT

KALEIDOSCOPE
> *mu.* Kabalevsky; *ch.* Ruthanna Boris; *co.* Alvin Colt; *w.p.* N.Y., Dec. 18, 1952, NYCC; NYCB

LABYRINTH
> *bk.* Dali, based on the classic myth of Theseus and Ariadne; *mu.* Schubert; *sc.* Symphony No. 7; *ch.* Massine; *s. & co.* Dali; *w.p.* N.Y., Oct. 8, 1941, MOH; BRMC

LE LAC DES CYGNES
> *mu.* Tchaikovsky; *sc.* second act of *Swan Lake; ch.* after Petipa; *s.* Prince A. Schervachidze; *p.* N.Y., Mar. 9, 1934, SJT; DB

—*s.* Emile Bertin; *co.* Karinska; *p.* N.Y., Oct. 15, 1938, MOH; BRMC

LE LAC DES CYGNES
see also *Swan Lake*

LADY INTO FOX
bk. Andrée Howard, after a novel by David Garnett; *mu.* Honegger; *ch.* Howard; *s. & co.* designed by Raymond Sovey, after sketches by Nadia Benois; *w.p.* London, May 15, 1939, Mercury Theatre, Ballet Club; *a.p.* N.Y., Jan. 26, 1940, CT; BT

LADY OF THE CAMELLIAS
bk. after Alexandre Dumas, fils; *mu.* Verdi; *ch.* Tudor; *s. & co.* Cecil Beaton; *w.p.* N.Y., Feb. 28, 1951, NYCC; NYCB

THE LEAF AND THE WIND
mu. Paul Ramseier; *ch.* William Dollar; *w.p.* Dallas, Feb. 3, 1954, State Fair Auditorium; BT

LILAC GARDEN
bk. Tudor; *mu.* Chausson; *sc. Poème; ch.* Tudor; *s.* Horace Armistead; *co.* Karinska; *p.* N.Y., Nov. 30, 1951, NYCC; NYCB

LILAC GARDEN
see also *Jardin aux Lilas*

LOLA MONTEZ
bk. Dr. N. Wolf; *mu.* Fred Witt; *sc.* orch. by Ivan Boutnikov; *ch.* Edward Caton; *s.* Raoul Pène du Bois; *co.* du Bois and Paolo D'Anna; *w.p.* N.Y., Sept. 12, 1947, NYCC; BRMC

LOVE SONG
bk. Ruth Page. *mu.* Schubert; *sc.* orch. by Lucien Caillet; *ch.* Page; *co.* Nicolas Remisoff; *p.* N.Y., Mar. 1, 1949, NYCC; BRMC

LUTTE ETERNELLE
see *The Eternal Struggle*

MADROÑOS
mu. excerpts from Moszkowski, Yradier, etc.; *sc.* orch. by Ivan Boutnikov; *ch.* Antonia Cobos; *co.* Castillo of Elizabeth Arden; *w.p.* N.Y., Mar. 22, 1947, NYCC; BRMC

MAD TRISTAN

bk. Dali; *mu.* Wagner; *sc.* excerpts from *Tristan and Isolde,* orch. by Ivan Boutnikov; *ch.* Massine; *s. & co.* Dali; *w.p.* N.Y., Dec. 15, 1944, IT; BI

MAGIC SWAN

mu. Tchaikovsky; *sc.* third act of *Swan Lake; ch.* Alexandra Fedorova, after Petipa; *s. & co.* Eugene Dunkel; *a.p.* N.Y., Oct. 13, 1941, MOH; BRMC

MAM'ZELLE ANGOT

bk. Massine; *mu.* Charles Lecocq; *sc.* excerpts from *La Fille de Mme Angot,* orch. by Gordon Jacob; *ch.* Massine; *s. & co.* Mstislav Dobujinsky; *w.p.* N.Y., Oct. 10, 1943, MOH; BT

LE MARIAGE D'AURORE

see *Aurora's Wedding*

LES MATELOTS

bk. Boris Kochno; *mu.* Auric; *ch.* Massine; *s. & co.* Pedro Pruna; *w.p.* Paris, June 17, 1925, Theatre Gaîté-Lyrique; DBR; *a.p.* N.Y., Mar. 9, 1934, SJT; DB

MAZURKA FROM A LIFE FOR THE TSAR

mu. Glinka; *ch.* Balanchine; *w.p.* N.Y., Nov. 30, 1950, NYCC; NYCB

MECHANICAL BALLET

bk. Bolm; *mu.* Alexander Mossolov; *sc. The Iron Foundry; ch.* Bolm; *w.p.* Los Angeles, Aug. 12, 1932, Hollywood Bowl —*s. & co.* John Hambleton; *p.* N.Y., Jan. 18, 1940, CT; BT

MEMORIES

bk. based on a story by Winthrop Palmer; *mu.* Brahms; *sc.* Waltzes, orch. by Maurice Baron; *ch.* Simon Semenoff; *s. & co.* Raoul Pène du Bois; *w.p.* N.Y., Nov. 1, 1944, IT; BT

METAMORPHOSES

mu. Hindemith; *sc. Symphonic Metamorphoses on Themes of Carl Maria von Weber; ch.* Balanchine; *co.* Karinska; *w.p.* N.Y., Nov. 25, 1952, NYCC; NYCB

THE MIDNIGHT SUN
see *Soleil de Nuit*

THE MIKADO
bk. after Gilbert; *mu.* Sullivan; *sc.* orch. and adapted by Rieti;
ch. Antonio Cobos; *s. & co.* Bernard Lamotte; *w.p.* Baltimore,
Oct. 1, 1954, Lyric Theatre; BRMC

THE MIRACULOUS MANDARIN
bk. after Melchior Lengyel; *mu.* Bartók; *ch.* Todd Bolender;
s. & co. Alvin Colt; *w.p.* N.Y., Sept. 6, 1951, NYCC; NYCB

MOONLIGHT SONATA
mu. Beethoven; *sc.* Sonata in C sharp minor, Op. 27, No. 2, arr.
by Dorati; *ch.* Massine; *s. & co.* Sergei Soudeikine; *w.p.* Chicago,
Nov. 27, 1944, Chicago Civic Opera House; BT

LA MORT DU CYGNE
mu. Chopin; *ch.* Lifar, re-staged by Constantin Nepo; *a.p.* N.Y.,
Apr. 11, 1950, MOH; BRMC

MOTHER GOOSE SUITE
mu. Ravel; *ch.* Todd Bolender; *w.p.* N.Y., Nov. 14, 1943, Central High School of Needle Trades; American Concert Ballet;
p. N.Y., Nov. 1, 1948, NYCC; NYCB

MOZARTIANA
mu. Tchaikovsky; *sc.* Theme and Variations from Suite No. 4
in G; *ch.* Balanchine; *s. & co.* Bérard; *w.p.* Paris, 1933, TCE;
Les Ballets 1933; *a.p.* Hartford, Conn., Dec. 6, 1934, Avery
Memorial Theatre; Producing Company of the School of American Ballet; *p.* N.Y., Mar. 7, 1945, NYCC; BRMC

MUTE WIFE
bk. after Anatole France; *mu.* Paganini; *sc. Perpetual Motion,*
orch. by Rieti; *ch.* Antonio Cobos; *s. & co.* Rico Lebrun; *w.p.*
N.Y., Nov. 22, 1944, IT; BI; *p.* N.Y., Oct. 4, 1946, MOH; OBR
—*mu.* Domenico Scarlatti; *sc.* orch. and arr. by Soulima
Stravinsky; *co.* Castillo; *w.p.* N.Y., Sept. 16, 1949, MOH;
BRMC

NAUGHTY LISETTE
see *La Fille mal gardée*

The New Borzoi Book of Ballets

THE NEW YORKER

bk. Rea Irvin and Massine; *mu.* Gershwin; *sc.* orch. by David Raksin; *ch.* Massine; *s. & co.* Carl Kent, after Irvin; *w.p.* N.Y., Oct. 18, 1940, FFT; BRMC

NIGHT SHADOW (LA SOMNAMBULE)

bk. Rieti; *mu.* Rieti, after Bellini; *ch.* Balanchine; *s. & co.* Dorothea Tanning; *w.p.* N.Y., Feb. 27, 1946, NYCC; BRMC
—*s. & co.* André Delfau; *p.* London, Aug. 24, 1948, CG; MCGB; *p.* N.Y., Oct. 30, 1950, CYT; MCGB

NIMBUS

bk. Tudor; *mu.* Louis Gruenberg; *sc.* Concerto for Violin and Orchestra; *ch.* Tudor; *s.* Oliver Smith; *co.* Saul Bolasni; *w.p.* N.Y., May 3, 1950; CT; BT

LES NOCES

bk. Stravinsky; *mu.* Stravinsky; *ch.* Bronislava Nijinska; *s. & co.* Natalie Gontcharova; *w.p.* Paris, June 14, 1923, Theatre Gaîté-Lyrique; DBR; *a.p.* N.Y., Apr. 20, 1936, MOH; DB

LES NUAGES (THE CLOUDS)

mu. Debussy; *sc.* Nuages, from *Nocturnes; ch.* Nini Theilade; *s. & co.* Willem De Kooning; *w.p.* N.Y., Apr. 9, 1940, MOH; BRMC

NUTCRACKER (CASSE-NOISETTE)

bk. based on E.T.A. Hoffmann's *The Nutcracker and the Mouse King; mu.* Tchaikovsky; *ch.* Lev Ivanov; *s. & co.* M. I. Botcharov; *w.p.* St. Petersburg, Dec. 17, 1892, Maryinsky Theatre; Imperial Ballet
—*bk.* Alexandra Fedorova; *mu.* Tchaikovsky; *ch.* Petipa, revived by Alexandra Fedorova; Waltz in second scene with original choreography by Fedorova; *s. & co.* after Benois; *a.p.* N.Y., Oct. 17, 1940, FFT; BRMC
—*bk.* based on E.T.A. Hoffmann's *The Nutcracker and the Mouse King (1816); ch.* Balanchine; *s.* Horace Armistead; *co.* Karinska; *p.* N.Y., Feb. 2, 1954, NYCC; NYCB

ODE TO GLORY

bk. Yurek Shabelevsky; *mu.* Chopin; *sc.* Polonaise in A flat Major; *ch.* Shabelevsky; *s. & co.* Michel Baronov; *w.p.* N.Y., Jan. 25, 1940, CT; BT

308

L'OISEAU DE FEU

    bk. Fokine; *mu.* Stravinsky; *ch.* Fokine; *s. & co.* A. Golovin and Bakst; *w.p.* Paris, June 25, 1910; Opéra; DBR; *a.p.* N.Y., Jan. 17, 1916, CYT; DBR
        —*s. & co.* Natalie Gontcharova; *p.* N.Y., Mar. 20, 1935, M; DB

L'OISEAU DE FEU

    see also *The Firebird*

ONDINE

    mu. Vivaldi; *ch.* William Dollar; *s. & co.* Horace Armistead; *w.p.* N.Y., Dec. 9, 1949, NYCC; NYCB

ON STAGE

    bk. Mary and Michael Kidd; *mu.* Norman Dello Joio; *ch.* Kidd; *s.* Oliver Smith; *co.* Alvin Colt; *w.p.* Boston, Oct. 4, 1945, Boston Opera House; BT

OPUS 34

    mu. Schoenberg; *sc. Music to a Scene in a Moving Picture (1930)*; Suite for String Orchestra (1935); *ch.* Balanchine; *s.* Jean Rosenthal; *co.* Esteban Francés; *w.p.* N.Y., Jan. 19, 1954, NYCC; NYCB

ORPHEUS

    bk. after the Greek legend; *mu.* Stravinsky; *ch.* Balanchine; *s. & co.* Noguchi; *w.p.* N.Y., Apr. 28, 1948, NYCC; Ballet Society; *p.* Oct. 11, 1948, NYCC; NYCB

PAGANINI

    bk. Fokine; *mu.* Rachmaninoff; *sc. Rhapsody on a Theme by Paganini; ch.* Fokine; *s. & co.* Sergei Soudeikine; *w.p.* London, June 30, 1939, CG; OBR; *a.p.* Los Angeles, Oct. 12, 1940, Philharmonic Auditorium; OBR

LE PALAIS DE CRISTAL

    mu. Bizet; *sc.* Symphony in C; *ch.* Balanchine; *s. & co.* Léonor Fini; *w.p.* Paris, July 28, 1947, Opéra; Paris Opéra Ballet (presented in America as *Symphony in C,* which see).

PAS DE DEUX ROMANTIQUE

    mu. Weber; *sc.* Concertino for Clarinet; *ch.* Balanchine; *co.* Robert Stevenson; *w.p.* N.Y., Mar. 3, 1950, NYCC; NYCB

PAS DE DIX

    mu. Glazunov; *sc.* excerpts from *Raymonda;* *ch.* Balanchine; *w.p.* N.Y., Nov. 9, 1955, NYCC; NYCB

PAS DE QUATRE

    mu. Cesare Pugni; *sc.* transcribed by Leighton Lucas, orch. by Paul Bowles; *ch.* Anton Dolin; *co.* after A. E. Chalon; *p.* N.Y., Feb. 16, 1941, M; BT; *p.* N.Y., Sept. 18, 1948, MOH; BRMC; *p.* N.Y., Nov. 2, 1950, CYT; MCGB

    —*sc.* orch. and arr. by Leighton Lucas; *ch.* Keith Lester; *w.p.* London, Aug. 26, 1946, CG; BT; *a.p.* N.Y., Oct. 8, 1946, BYT; BT

PAS DE TROIS

    mu. Berlioz; *sc.* excerpts from *The Damnation of Faust;* *ch.* Robbins; *co.* John Pratt; *w.p.* N.Y., Mar. 26, 1947, MOH; OBR

PAS DE TROIS

    mu. Leon Minkus; *sc.* from *Don Quixote;* *ch.* Balanchine; *co.* Karinska; *w.p.* N.Y., Feb. 20, 1951, NYCC; NYCB

PAS DE TROIS (II)

    mu. Glinka; *ch.* Balanchine; *co.* Karinska; *w.p.* N.Y., Mar. 1, 1955, NYCC; NYCB

LES PATINEURS

    mu. Meyerbeer; *sc.* arr. and orchestrated by Contant Lambert; *ch.* Frederick Ashton; *s. & co.* William Chappell; *w.p.* London, Feb. 16, 1937, Sadler's Wells Theatre; Sadler's Wells Ballet.

    —*s. & c.* Cecil Beaton; *a.p.* N.Y., Oct. 2, 1946, BYT; BT

PAVANE

    mu. Fauré; *ch.* Lifar; *co.* José María Sert; *w.p.* N.Y., Nov. 25, 1940, FFT; OBR

LE PAVILLON

    bk. Boris Kochno; *mu.* Borodin; *sc.* orch. by Dorati; *ch.* Lichine; *s. & co.* Cecil Beaton; *a.p.* N.Y., Oct. 30, 1936, MOH; DB

PERSEPHONE

    bk. John Taras; *mu.* Schumann; *ch.* Taras; *s. & co.* Lila de Nobili; *w.p.* Monte Carlo, Apr. 11, 1950, TMC; MCGB; *a.p.* N.Y., Oct. 30, 1950, CYT; MCGB

PETER AND THE WOLF
>
> *bk.* Prokofiev; *mu.* Prokofiev; *ch.* Bolm; *s. & co.* Lucinda Ballard; *w.p.* N.Y., Jan. 13, 1940, CT; BT

PETROUCHKA
>
> *bk.* Stravinsky and Benois; *mu.* Stravinsky; *ch.* Fokine; *s. & co.* Benois; *w.p.* Paris, June 13, 1911, TDC; DBR; *a.p.* Jan. 24, 1916, CYT; DBR
>
> —*ch.* after Fokine; *p.* N.Y., Jan. 10, 1934, SJT; DB
>
> —*ch.* Fokine; N.Y., Nov. 21, 1940, FFT; OBR
>
> —*s. & co.* after Benois, courtesy of Avery Memorial Museum, Hartford, Conn.; *p.* Mexico City, Aug. 27, 1942, Palacio de Bellas Artes; BT; *p.* N.Y., Oct. 8, 1942, MOH; BT
>
> —*sc.* arr. by Maganini; *p.* Barcelona, Spain, May 24, 1950, Gran Teatro del Liceo; MCGB; *p.* N.Y., Nov. 7, 1950, CYT; MCGB

PICNIC AT TINTAGEL
>
> *mu.* Arnold Bax; *sc. The Garden of Fand; ch.* Frederick Ashton; *s. & co.* Cecil Beaton; *w.p.* N.Y., Feb. 28, 1952, NYCC; NYCB

PICTURES AT AN EXHIBITION
>
> *mu.* Mussorgsky; *sc.* orch. by Ivan Boutnikov; *ch.* Bronislava Nijinska; *s. & co.* Boris Aronson; *w.p.* N.Y., Nov. 3, 1944, IT; BI; *p.* N.Y., Mar. 25, 1947, MOH; OBR

THE PIED PIPER
>
> *mu.* Copland; *sc.* Concerto for Clarinet and String Orchestra; *ch.* Robbins; *w.p.* N.Y., Dec. 4, 1951, NYCC; NYCB

PILLAR OF FIRE
>
> *bk.* Tudor; *mu.* Schoenberg; *sc. Verklärte Nacht; ch.* Tudor; *s. & co.* Jo Mielziner; *w.p.* N.Y., Apr. 8, 1942, MOH; BT

POKER GAME
>
> *bk.* Stravinsky and M. Malaieff; *mu.* Stravinsky; *ch.* Balanchine; *p.* N.Y., Oct. 14, 1940, FFT; BRMC

POKER GAME
>
> see also *Card Party*

LES PRÉSAGES (DESTINY)
> *mu.* Tchaikovsky; *sc.* Symphony No. 5; *ch.* Massine; *s. & co.* André Masson; *w.p.* Monte Carlo, Apr. 13, 1933, TMC; DB; *a.p.* N.Y., Dec. 22, 1933, SJT; DB

LES PRÉSAGES
> see also *Destiny*

PRINCE GOUDAL'S FESTIVAL
> *mu.* Anton Rubinstein: *sc. The Demon* (excerpts; orch. by Maurice Baron); *ch.* Boris Romanoff; *s. & co.* Mstislav Dobujinsky; *w.p.* N.Y., Nov. 16, 1944, IT; BI

PRINCE IGOR
> *mu.* Borodin; *sc. Polovtsian Dances; ch.* Fokine; *s. & co.* Nicholas Roerich; *w.p.* Paris, May 18, 1909, TDC; DBR; *a.p.* N.Y., Jan. 18, 1916, CYT; DBR; *p.* N.Y., Jan. 10, 1934, SJT; DB; *p.* N.Y., Nov. 8, 1940, FFT; OBR

PRINCESS AURORA
> see *Aurora's Wedding*

THE PRODIGAL SON (LE FILS PRODIGUE)
> *bk.* Boris Kochno; *mu.* Prokofiev; *ch.* Balanchine; *s. & co.* Georges Rouault; *w.p.* Paris, May 21, 1929, Théâtre Sarah Bernhardt; DBR; *p.* N.Y., Feb. 23, 1950, NYCC; NYCB (without Rouault *décor*)
> > —*ch.* Lichine; *w.p.* Sydney, Australia, Dec. 1, 1939, Theatre Royal; OBR; *p.* N.Y., Nov. 26, 1940, FFT; OBR

PROTÉE
> *bk.* Lichine and Henry Clifford; *mu.* Debussy; *sc. Danse Sacrée et Danse Profane; ch.* Lichine; *s. & co.* Giorgio di Chirico; *w.p.* London, July 5, 1938, CG; OBR; *a.p.* Los Angeles, Oct. 12, 1940, Philharmonic Auditorium; OBR

PUNCH AND THE CHILD
> *mu.* Richard Arnell; *ch.* Fred Danieli; *s. & co.* Horace Armistead; *w.p.* N.Y., Nov. 12, 1947, NYCC; Ballet Society; *p.* N.Y., Oct. 18, 1948, NYCC; NYCB

QUARTET
> *mu.* Prokofiev; *sc.* String Quartet No. 2, Op. 92; *ch.* Robbins; *co.* Karinska; *w.p.* N.Y., Feb. 18, 1954, NYCC; NYCB

QUELQUES FLEURS

mu. Auber; *sc.* compiled by Harry G. Schumer; *ch.* Ruthanna Boris; *s. & co.* Robert Davison; *w.p.* N.Y., Sept. 30, 1948, MOH; BRMC

QUEST

mu. Johann Sebastian Bach; *sc.* orch. by Antal Dorati; *ch.* Nina Verchinina; *s. & co.* Carl Kent, after designs by Cristofanetti; *w.p.* N.Y., Jan. 11, 1941, FFT; OBR

QUINTET

mu. Raymond Scott; *ch.* Anton Dolin; *s. & co.* Lucinda Ballard; *w.p.* N.Y., Feb. 1, 1940, CT; BT

RAYMONDA

bk. Marius Petipa and Lydia Pashkova; *mu.* Glazunov; *ch.* Petipa; *s.* Allegri, Ivanov, and Lambini; *w.p.* St. Petersburg, Jan. 19, 1898, Maryinsky Theatre; Imperial Ballet
—*ch.* Balanchine and Alexandra Danilova, after Marius Petipa; *s. & co.* Benois; *p.* N.Y., Mar. 12, 1946, NYCC; BRMC

RED POPPY

bk. Igor Schwezoff; *mu.* Glière; *ch.* Schwezoff; *s. & co.* Boris Aronson; *w.p.* Cleveland, Oct. 9, 1943, Music Hall; BRMC

RODEO

bk. Agnes de Mille; *mu.* Copland; *ch.* de Mille; *s.* Oliver Smith; *co.* Kermit Love; *w.p.* N.Y., Oct. 16, 1942, MOH; BRMC
—*co.* Saul Bolasni; *p.* Wiesbaden, Germany, Aug. 14, 1950; BT; *p.* N.Y., Jan. 9, 1951, MOH; BT

ROMA

mu. Bizet; *ch.* Balanchine; *s. & co.* Eugene Berman; *w.p.* N.Y., Feb. 23, 1955, NYCC; NYCB

ROMANTIC AGE

mu. Bellini; *sc.* arr. by Dorati; *ch.* Anton Dolin; *s. & co.* Carlos Mérida; *w.p.* N.Y., Oct. 23, 1942, MOH; BT

ROMEO AND JULIET

bk. Shakespeare-Tudor; *mu.* Delius; *sc. Over the Hills and Far Away; The Walk to the Paradise Garden, Eventyr,* and *Brigg Fair; s. & co.* Eugene Berman; *w.p.* N.Y., Apr. 6, 1943, MOH; BT

ROMÉO ET JULIETTE

bk. based on Shakespeare; *mu.* Tchaikovsky; *ch.* staged by Constantin Nepo; *a.p.* N.Y., Apr. 18, 1950, MOH; BRMC

ROUGE ET NOIR

bk. Massine; *mu.* Shostakovich; *sc.* Symphony No. 1; *ch.* Massine; *s. & co.* Matisse; *w.p.* Monte Carlo, May 11, 1939, TMC; BRMC; *a.p.* N.Y., Oct. 28, 1939, MOH; BRMC

RUSSIAN SOLDIER

bk. Fokine; *mu.* Prokofiev; *sc. Lieutenant Kije; ch.* Fokine; *s. & co.* Mstislav Dobujinsky; *w.p.* Boston, Jan. 23, 1942, Boston Opera House; BT

ST. FRANCIS

bk. Hindemith and Massine; *mu.* Hindemith; *sc. Nobilissima Visione; ch.* Massine; *s. & co.* Tchelitchev; *w.p.* London, July 21, 1938, Drury Lane Theatre; BRMC; *a.p.* N.Y., Oct. 14, 1938, MOH; BRMC

SALOME

mu. Richard Strauss; *sc.* excerpts from *Salome; ch.* Rosella Hightower; *s.* Celia Hubbard; *co.* Jean Robier; *w.p.* Paris, Oct. 13, 1950, TCE; MCGB; *a.p.* N.Y., Nov. 9, 1950, CYT; MCGB

SARATOGA

bk. Jaromir Weinberger; *mu.* Weinberger; *ch.* Massine; *s.* Oliver Smith; *co.* Alvin Colt; *w.p.* N.Y., Oct. 19, 1941, MOH; BRMC

SCHÉHÉRAZADE

bk. Bakst and Fokine; *mu.* Rimsky-Korsakov; *ch.* Fokine; *s. & co.* Bakst; *w.p.* Paris, June 4, 1910, Opéra; DBR; *a.p.* N.Y., Jan. 17, 1916, CYT; DBR; *p.* N.Y., Nov. 14, 1940, FFT; OBR —*ch.* after Fokine; *p.* N.Y., Oct. 9, 1935, MOH; DB

SCHUMANN CONCERTO

bk. Bronislava Nijinska; *mu.* Schumann; *sc.* Concerto for Piano and Orchestra; *ch.* Nijinska; *s. & co.* Stewart Chaney; *w.p.* N.Y., Sept. 27, 1951, MOH; BT

SCOTCH SYMPHONY

mu. Mendelssohn; *sc.* Symphony No. 3 (2nd, 3rd and 4th movements); *ch.* Balanchine; *s.* Horace Armistead; *co.* girls' by

Karinska; boys' by David Ffolkes; *w.p.* N.Y., Nov. 11, 1952, NYCC; NYCB

SCUOLA DI BALLO (THE SCHOOL OF BALLET)
bk. Carlo Goldoni; *mu.* Boccherini; *sc.* orch. by Françaix; *ch.* Massine; *s. & co.* Count Étienne de Beaumont; *a.p.* N.Y., Jan. 2, 1934, SJT; DB

SCUOLA DI BALLO
see also *Ballet School*

SEBASTIAN
mu. Gian-Carlo Menotti; *ch.* Edward Caton; *s.* Oliver Smith; *co.* Milena; *w.p.* N.Y., Oct. 31, 1944, IT, BI; *p.* N.Y., Oct. 13, 1946, MOH; OBR

SENTIMENTAL COLLOQUY
mu. Paul Bowles; *ch.* André Eglevsky; *s. & co.* Dali; *w.p.* N.Y., Oct. 30, 1944, IT; BI

SERENADE
mu. Tchaikovsky; *sc.* Serenade for Strings; *ch.* Balanchine; *s.* Gaston Longchamp; *co.* Lurcat; *w.p.* N.Y., Mar. 1, 1935, Adelphi Theatre; American Ballet; *p.* N.Y., Oct. 17, 1940, FFT; BRMC
—*p.* N.Y., Oct. 18, 1948, NYCC; NYCB (production does not use scenery or costumes)

SEVENTH SYMPHONY
bk. Massine; *mu.* Beethoven; *ch.* Massine; *s. & co.* Bérard; *w.p.* Monte Carlo, May 5, 1938, TMC; *a.p.* N.Y., Oct. 15, 1938, MOH; BRMC

SHADOW OF THE WIND
bk. Tudor; *mu.* Mahler; *sc.* Das Lied von der Erde; *ch.* Tudor; *s. & co.* Jo Mielziner; *w.p.* N.Y., Apr. 14, 1948, MOH; BT

SLAVONIKA
bk. Vania Psota; *mu.* Dvořák; *ch.* Psota; *co.* Alvin Colt; *w.p.* Mexico City, Oct. 24, 1941, Palacio de Bellas Artes; BT; *a.p.* N.Y., Nov. 21, 1941, FF; BT

THE SNOW MAIDEN
bk. Sergei J. Denham; *mu.* Glazunov; *ch.* Bronislava Nijinska; *s. & co.* Boris Aronson; *w.p.* N.Y., Oct. 12, 1942, MOH; BRMC

SOLEIL DE NUIT (THE MIDNIGHT SUN)

mu. Rimsky-Korsakov; *ch.* Massine; *s. & co.* Michel Larionov; *w.p.* Geneva, Dec. 20, 1915, Grand Théâtre; DBR; *a.p.* N.Y., Jan. 17, 1916, CYT; DBR; *p.* N.Y., Oct. 16, 1935, MOH; DB

SOUVENIRS

mu. Samuel Barber; *ch.* Todd Bolender; *s. & co.* Rouben Ter-Arutunian; *w.p.* N.Y., Nov. 15, 1955, NYCC; NYCB

SPANISH DANCES

mu. Granados, Albéniz, and native folk tunes; *ch.* José Torres; *co.* Marcel Rigaud; *a.p.* N.Y., Oct. 8, 1948, MOH; BRMC

SPECTRE DE LA ROSE

bk. J. L. Vaudoyer, after the poem by Gautier; *mu.* Weber; *sc. Invitation to the Dance; ch.* Fokine; *s. & co.* Bakst; *w.p.* Monte Carlo, Apr. 19, 1911, TMC; DBR; *a.p.* N.Y., Apr. 3, 1916, MOH; DBR; *p.* N.Y., Oct. 20, 1935, MOH; DB; *p.* N.Y., Dec. 15, 1940, FFT; OBR; *p.* Mexico City, Oct. 31, 1941, Palacio de Bellas Artes; BT; *p.* N.Y., Nov. 4, 1941, FF; BT

THE SPHINX

bk. Boris Kochno; *mu.* Henri Sauguet; *ch.* Lichine; *s. & co.* Christian Bérard; *a.p.* N. Y., Apr. 21, 1955, MOH; BT

A STREETCAR NAMED DESIRE

bk. based on the Tennessee Williams play; *mu.* Alex North; *sc.* orch. by Rayburn Wright; *ch.* Valerie Bettis; *s.* Peter Larkin; *co.* Bolasni; *w.p.* Montreal, Oct. 9, 1952, Her Majesty's Theatre; Slavenska-Franklin Ballet; *p.* N.Y., Dec. 9, 1952, CYT; Slavenska-Franklin Ballet; *p.* Princeton, N.J., Oct. 26, 1954, McCarter Theatre; BT

SUMMER DAY

bk. Robbins; *mu.* Prokofiev; *sc. Music for Children,* Op. 65; *ch.* Robbins; *s. & co.* John Boyt; *p.* N.Y., Dec. 2, 1947, NYCC; BT

SWAN LAKE

bk. V. P. Begitchev and Vasily Geltzer; *mu.* Tchaikovsky; *ch.* Petipa and Ivanov; *s. & co.* Botcharov and Levogt; *w.p.* St. Petersburg, Jan. 27, 1895, Maryinsky Theatre; Imperial Ballet
 —*ch.* Michael Mordkin, after Petipa and Ivanov; *s.* James Fox; *a.p.* N.Y., Dec. 11, 1911, MOH

SWAN LAKE (*ACT II*)

mu. Tchaikovsky; *sc*. Act II of *Swan Lake; ch*. re-staged by Anton Dolin, after Petipa; *s*. Augustus Vincent Tack; *co*. Lucinda Ballard; *p*. N.Y., Jan. 16, 1940, CT; BT

—*ch*. after Petipa; *s. & co*. C. Korovine; *p*. N.Y., Nov. 23, 1940, FFT; OBR

—*bk*. V. P. Begitchev and Vasily Geltzer; *sc*. Act II of *Swan Lake;* specially orch. for B.T. by Rieti; *ch*. Petipa-Ivanov-Dolin; *s*. Lee Simonson; *co*. Lucinda Ballard; *p*. N.Y., Feb. 14, 1941, M; BT

—*sc*. orch. by Giuseppe Creatore; *ch*. after Petipa, supervised by Anatole Vilzak; *s*. Eugene Dunkel; *co*. Grace Houston (for the men); *p*. N.Y., Oct. 31, 1944, IT; IB

—*ch*. Balanchine; *s. & co*. Cecil Beaton; *p*. N.Y., Nov. 20, 1951, NYCC; NYCB

SWAN LAKE
see also *Le Lac des cygnes*

LES SYLPHIDES

bk. Fokine; *mu*. Chopin; *sc*. orch. by Glazunov and others; *ch*. Fokine; *s. & co*. Benois; *w.p*. Paris, June 2, 1909, TDC, DBR; *a.p*. N.Y., Jan. 20, 1916, CYT; DBR

—*sc*. orch. by Rieti; *ch*. after Fokine; *s*. Prince A. Schervachidze, after Corot; *p*. N.Y., Jan. 10, 1934, SJT; DB

—*ch*. Fokine; *s*. Augustus Vincent Tack; *co*. Lucinda Ballard; *p*. N.Y., Jan. 11, 1940, CT; BT

—*sc*. orch. Rieti; *ch*. Fokine; *s*. Prince A. Schervazhidze; *p*. N.Y., Nov. 20, 1940, FFT; OBR

—*sc*. orch. Maurice Baron; *ch*. Fokine, supervised by Vera Fokina; *s*. Eugene Dunkel; *co*. male costume by Grace Houston; *p*. N.Y., Oct. 30, 1944, IT; BI

SYLVIA PAS DE DEUX

mu. Delibes; *ch*. Balanchine; *co*. Karinska; *w.p*. N.Y., Dec. 1, 1950, NYCC; NYCB

SYMPHONIE CONCERTANTE

mu Mozart; *sc*. *Sinfonia Concertante* for Violin and Viola in E flat, K. 364; *ch*. Balanchine; *s. & co*. James Stewart Morcom; *w.p*., N.Y., Nov. 12, 1947, NYCC; Ballet Society; *p*. N.Y., Oct. 18, 1948, NYCC; NYCB

317

SYMPHONIE FANTASTIQUE
> *bk.* after Berlioz; *mu.* Berlioz; *ch.* Massine; *s. & co.* Bérard; *w.p.*
> London, July 24, 1936, CG; DB; *a.p.* N.Y., Oct. 29, 1936, MOH;
> DB; *p.* N.Y., Nov. 19, 1940, FFT; OBR

SYMPHONY IN C
> *mu.* Bizet; *ch.* Balanchine; *a.p.* N.Y., March 22, 1948, NYCC;
> Ballet Society; *p.* N.Y., Oct. 11, 1948, NYCC; NYCB

SYMPHONY IN C
> see also *Le Palais de cristal*

TALLY-HO
> *bk.* Agnes de Mille; *mu.* Gluck; *sc.* arr. by Paul Nordoff; *ch.*
> de Mille; *s. & co.* Motley; *w.p.* Los Angeles, Feb. 25, 1944, Phil-
> harmonic Auditorium; BT

THAMAR
> *bk.* Bakst; *mu.* Balakirev; *ch.* Fokine; *s. & co.* Bakst; *w.p.* Paris,
> May 20, 1912, TDC; DBR; *a.p.* N.Y., Apr. 12, 1916, MOH;
> DBR
> —*ch.* after Fokine; *p.* N.Y., Oct. 11, 1935, MOH; DB

THEME AND VARIATIONS
> *mu.* Tchaikovsky; *sc.* Theme and Variations from Suite No. 3;
> *ch.* Balanchine; *s. & co.* Woodman Thompson; *w.p.* N.Y., Nov.
> 26, 1947, NYCC; BT

THE THIEF WHO LOVED A GHOST
> *bk.* Herbert Ross and John Ward; *mu.* Weber; *sc.* arr. and orch.
> by Hershy Kay; *ch.* Ross; *s. & co.* Ward; *w.p.* N.Y., Apr. 11,
> 1951, MOH; BT

THE THREE-CORNERED HAT
> *bk.* Martínez Sierra, from a fable by Alarcón; *mu.* Falla; *ch.*
> Massine; *s. & co.* Picasso; *w.p.* London, July 22, 1919, Alhambra
> Theatre; DBR; *a.p.* N.Y., Mar. 9, 1934, SJT; DB; *p.* N.Y., Apr.
> 11, 1943, MOH; BT

THREE VIRGINS AND A DEVIL
> *bk.* Ramon Reed; *mu.* Respighi; *sc.* *Antiche Danze et Arie;* *ch.*
> Agnes de Mille; *s.* Arne Lundborg, after sketches by Miss Har-
> ris; *co.* Motley; *w.p.* N.Y., Feb. 12, 1941, M; BT

TIL EULENSPIEGEL'S MERRY PRANKS
  bk. Jean Babilée; *mu.* Richard Strauss; *ch.* Jean Babilée; *w.p.*
  Paris, Nov. 9, 1949, TCE; *a.p.* N.Y., Sept. 25, 1951, MOH; BT

TIL EULENSPIEGEL
  see *Tyl Ulenspiegel*

TIME TABLE
  mu. Copland; *sc. Music for the Theatre; ch.* Tudor; *s. & co.*
  James Morcom; *w.p.* N.Y., May 29, 1941, Hunter College auditorium; Ballet Caravan; *p.* N.Y., Jan. 13, 1949, NYCC; NYCB

A TRAGEDY IN VERONA
  bk. Skibine; *mu.* Tchaikovsky; *sc. Romeo and Juliet* Overture;
  ch. Skibine; *s. & co.* André Delfau; *w.p.* Monte Carlo, May 4,
  1950, TMC; MCGB; *a.p.* N.Y., Nov. 7, 1950, CYT; MCGB

TRIPTYCH
  mu. Brahms; *ch.* Edward Caton; *w.p.* N.Y., Oct. 2, 1952, MOH;
  BT

THE TRIUMPH OF BACCHUS AND ARIADNE
  mu. Rieti; *ch.* Balanchine; *s. & co.* Corrado Cagli; *w.p.* N.Y.,
  Feb. 9, 1948, NYCC; Ballet Society; *p.* N.Y., Nov. 1, 1948,
  NYCC; NYCB

TYL ULENSPIEGEL
  mu. Richard Strauss; *ch.* Balanchine; *s. & co.* Esteban Francés;
  w.p. N.Y., Nov. 14, 1951, NYCC; NYCB

UNDERTOW
  bk. Tudor; *mu.* William Schuman; *ch.* Tudor; *s. & co.* Raymond Breinin; *w.p.* N.Y., Apr. 10, 1945, MOH; BT

UNION PACIFIC
  bk. Archibald MacLeish; *mu.* Nicholas Nabokov; *ch.* Massine;
  s. Albert Johnson; *co.* Irene Sharaff; *w.p.* Philadelphia, Apr. 6,
  1934, Forrest Theatre; DB; *p.* N.Y., Jan. 9, 1941, FFT; OBR

LA VALSE
  mu. Ravel; *sc. Valses Nobles et sentimentales* and *Las Valse; ch.*
  Balanchine; *co.* Karinska; *w.p.* N.Y., Feb. 20, 1951, NYCC;
  NYCB

VALSE FANTASIE
> *mu.* Glinka; *ch.* Balanchine; *co.* Karinska; *w.p.* N.Y., Jan. 6, 1953, NYCC; NYCB

VIENNA—1814
> *bk.* Massine; *mu.* Weber; *s. Turandot* Overture and four-hand piano pieces; *sc.* orch. Robert Russell Bennett; *s. & co.* Stewart Chaney; *w.p.* N.Y., Oct. 14, 1940, FFT; BRMC

VIRGINIA SAMPLER
> *bk.* Valerie Bettis; *mu.* Leo Smit; *ch.* Bettis; *s. & co.* Charles Elson; *w.p.* N.Y., Mar. 4, 1947, NYCC; NYCB

VOICES OF SPRING
> *bk.* Michael Mordkin; *mu.* Johann Strauss; *sc.* arr. by Mois Zlatin; *ch.* Mordkin; *s. & co.* Lee Simonson; *w.p.* N.Y., Nov. 10, 1938, Alvin Theatre; Mordkin Ballet; *p.* N.Y., Jan. 11, 1940, CT; BT

WALTZ ACADEMY
> *mu.* Rieti; *ch.* Balanchine; *s.* Oliver Smith; *co.* Alvin Colt; *w.p.* Boston, Oct. 5, 1944, Boston Opera House; BT

THE WANDERER (ERRANTE)
> *bk.* Balanchine and Tchelitchev; *mu.* Schubert-Liszt; *sc.* "Wanderer" Fantasy; *ch.* Balanchine; *s. & co.* Tchelitchev; *w.p.* N.Y., May 21, 1943, MOH; BT

THE WAYWARD DAUGHTER
> see *La Fille mal gardée*

WESTERN SYMPHONY
> *mu.* Hershy Kay; *ch.* Balanchine; *s.* John Boyt; *co.* Karinska; *w.p.* N.Y., Sept. 7, 1954, NYCC; NYCB

WILL O' THE WISP
> *mu.* Virgil Thomson; *sc.* from *Louisiana Story*; *ch.* Ruthanna Boris; *s. & co.* Dorothea Tanning; *w.p.* N.Y., Jan. 13, 1953, NYCC; NYCB

YARA
> *bk.* based on story by Guicherme de Almeida; *mu.* Francisco Mignone; *ch.* Vania Psota; *s. & co.* Candido Portinari; *w.p.* São Paulo, Brazil, Aug. 5, 1946; *p.* N.Y., Oct. 8, 1946, MOH; OBR

320

Index

i

Index

ii

Bourrée fantasque (Chabrier-Balanchine), 52–4, 290
Boutique fantasque, La (Rossini-Respighi-Massine), 290
Boutnikov, Ivan, 262, 290, 302, 305, 306, 311
Bowles, Paul, 291, 310, 315
Bowman, Patricia, 107, 256
Boyt, John, 278, 316, 320
Bozacchi, Giuseppina, 74, 75
Bozzoni, Max, 267
Brae, June, 241
Brahms, Johannes, 12, 290, 292, 297, 306, 319
Brahms Variations (Brahms-Nijinska), 290
Brant, Henry, 301
Braun, Eric, 62, 108, 199
Breinin, Raymond, 319
Brianza, Carlotta, 234, 236
Brigg Fair (Delius), 219, 313
Britten, Benjamin, 152, 153, 164, 262, 264, 298, 302, 304
Broadway Theater (New York), 141
Brown, Vida, 274
Brozak, Edith, 111, 161, 246
Bruhn, Erik, 19, 87, 150, 176, 271
Buckle, Richard, 24
Buffoon, The (Prokofiev), 211
Bulgakov, Alexis, 116, 225
Burgin, Richard, 121
Burkhalter, Jane, 32
Burleske (R. Strauss), 12, 90, 296
Burr, Mary, 62
Burton, Robert, 120
Butsova, Hilda, 239
Buttignol, Val, 94
Byrns, Harold, 301

Caccialanza, Gisella, 36, 41, 111, 122
Cadmus, Paul, 111, 298
Cage, The (Stravinsky-Robbins), 55–7, 290
Cagli, Corrado, 319
Caillet, Lucien, 262, 305
Cain and Abel (Wagner-Lichine), 290
Cakewalk (Gottschalk-Kay-Boris), 14, 58–60, 277, 290
Camille (Schubert-Rieti-Taras), 290
Campbell, Anne, 111
Capital of the World (Antheil-Loring), 290
Capriccio Brillant (Mendelssohn-Balanchine), 291
Capriccio Espagnol (Rimsky-Korsakoff-Massine), 291
Capriccioso (Cimarosa-Malipiero-Rieti-Dolin), 291
Caprichos (Bartók-Ross), 61–3, 291
Caracole (Mozart-Balanchine), 291
Card Party (Stravinsky-Balanchine), 291. *See also Poker Game* and *Jeu de Cartes*
Carnaval (Schumann-Fokine), 291, 292
Carozzi, Felicita, 78
Casse-Noisette, see Nutcracker
Castellanos, Julio, 296
Castillo of Elizabeth Arden, 305, 307
Caton, Edward, 107, 305, 315, 319
Cave of Sleep, The, 121
Cecchetti, Enrico, 79, 116, 117, 194, 225, 234, 237
Cello Concerto (Thomson), 302
Cent Baisers, Les, see The Hundred Kisses
Center Theatre (New York), 62, 87, 107, 141, 167, 171, 256, 265
Central High School of Needle Trades (New York), 122, 178
Central Park in the Dark (Ives), 160, 303
Century Theater (New York), 117, 199, 225, 250, 257, 264

Cerito, Fanny, 73
Chabrier, Emmanuel, 52, 53, 290, 294
Chagall, Marc, 118, 213, 285, 299
Chailly, Jacques, 294
Chalon, A. E., 310
Chamie, Tatiana, 289
Chaney, Stewart, 32, 315, 320
Chaplin, Charlie, 198
Chase, Lucia, 51, 107, 141, 167, 199, 208, 241, 264
Chausson, Ernest, 12, 170, 173, 303, 305
Chevalier Noverre, The: Father of Modern Ballet (Lynham), 22
Chicago Civic Opera House, 44, 45, 256
Children's Games (Bizet-Massine), 292. *See also Jeux d' enfants*
Chirico, Giorgio di, 287
Chopin Concerto (Chopin-Nijinska), 292
Chopin, Frédéric, 30, 261, 262, 292, 293, 307, 308, 317
Chopiniana (Glazunov), 261
Chorearteum (Brahms-Massine), 124, 292
Choreographer's Workshop, 62
Chouquet, Gustave, 174, 175
Chout (Prokofiev), 211
Christensen, Harold, 111
Christensen, Lew, 13, 14, 31, 44, 58, 66, 68, 110, 111, 112, 122, 163, 267, 293, 298, 304
Christensen, William, 255
Chujoy, Anatole, 20, 21, 23, 111, 121, 122, 188
Cicéri, Pierre, 135, 136, 300
Cimarosa, Domenico, 291, 292, 303
Cimarosiana (Cimarosa-Massine), 292
Cinderella (Erlanger-Fokine), 292
Cinderella (Prokofiev-Ashton), 16
Circo de España (*Spanish Circus*) (Falla-Maracci), 292
Cirque de deux (Gounod-Boris), 64–5
City Center, *see* New York City Center of Music and Drama
Clarinet Concerto (Copland), 201, 202, 203
Clarke, Mary, 23, 85, 86, 176
Classical Symphony (Prokofiev), 129, 300
Classic Ballet, The: Technique and Terminology (Kirstein and Stuart), 21
Clifford, Henry, 299, 312
Cloëz, Gustave, 297
Cobos, Antonia, 305, 307
Cocteau, Jean, 286, 294, 303
Colman, John, 298
Colonel W. de Basil Ballet Russe, 199, 226, 240, 256, 281
Colonel W. de Basil's Original Ballet Russe, 15, 117
Colt, Alvin, 301, 304, 307, 309, 314, 315, 320
Colton, Ronald, 246
Combat, Le (Banfield-Dollar), 93
Combat, The (Banfield-Dollar), 94, 292
Combattimento di Tancredi e Clorinda, Il (Monteverdi), 93
Comedia Balletica (*Musical Chairs*) (Stravinsky-Bolender), 293
Complete Book of Ballets (Beaumont), 20
Complete Stories of the Great Ballets (Balanchine), 20, 21
Con Amore (Rossini-Christensen), 66–68, 293
Concertino (Françaix-Balanchine), 293
Concertino for Clarinet (Weber), 309
Concert Varieties, 158
Concerto barocco (Bach-Balanchine), 69–72, 293
Concerto in D Minor for Two Violins (Bach), 12, 69, 293

Index

Index

vi

Index

ix

Index

Index

A Note on the Type

The text of this book was set on the Linotype in a face called Baskerville, named for John Baskerville (1706–75), of Birmingham, England, who was a writing master with a special renown for cutting inscriptions in stone. About 1750 he began experimenting with punch-cutting and making typographical material, which led, in 1757, to the publication of his first work, a Virgil in royal quarto, with great primer letters, in which the types throughout had been designed by him. This was followed by his famous editions of Milton, the Bible, the Book of Common Prayer, and several Latin classic authors. His types foreshadowed what we know today as the "modern" group of type faces, and these and his printing became greatly admired. After his death Baskerville's widow sold all his punches and matrices to the SOCIÉTÉ PHILOSOPHIQUE, LITTÉRAIRE ET TYPOGRAPHIQUE (totally embodied in the person of Beaumarchais, author of THE MARRIAGE OF FIGARO and THE BARBER OF SEVILLE), which used some of the types to print the seventy volume edition, at Kehl, of Voltaire's works. After a checkered career on the Continent, where they dropped out of sight for some years, the punches and matrices finally came into the possession of the distinguished Paris type-founders, Deberney & Peignot, who, in singularly generous fashion, returned them to the Cambridge University Press in 1953.

Composed, printed, and bound by KINGSPORT PRESS, INC., Kingsport, Tennessee. Paper manufactured by S. D. WARREN COMPANY, Boston, Massachusetts. Designed by HARRY FORD.